THE ROYAL FLYING CORPS IN FRANCE

From Mons to the Somme

THE
ROYAL FLYING CORPS
IN FRANCE

From Mons to the Somme

RALPH BARKER

Constable · London

First published in Great Britain 1994
by Constable and Company Limited
3 The Lanchesters, 162 Fulham Palace Road
London W6 9ER
Copyright © 1994 by Ralph Barker
The right of Ralph Barker to be
identified as the author of this work
has been asserted by him in accordance
with the Copyright, Designs and Patents Act 1988
ISBN 0 09 468450 2
Set in Linotron Sabon 11 on 14 pt by
Rowland Phototypesetting Limited
Bury St Edmunds, Suffolk
Printed in Great Britain by
St Edmundsbury Press Limited
Bury St Edmunds, Suffolk

A CIP catalogue record for this book
is available from the British Library

CONTENTS

[v]

ILLUSTRATIONS

[vii]

Between pages 146 and 147

Lanoe Hawker (*Chaz Bowyer*)
Hawker's Bristol Scout (*Barry Gray*)
Jack Woodhouse with French agent
    (*Imperial War Museum*)
C.F.A. 'Peter' Portal (*RAF Museum*)
Hugh Dowding (*Imperial War Museum*)
Gwilym Lewis (*Chaz Bowyer*)
Lionel Rees (*Chaz Bowyer*)
W.R. 'Willie' Read (*Imperial War Museum*)
Read with Flight Commander Leslie Porter
    (*Imperial War Museum*)
A Sopwith 1½-strutter (*Jack Bruce and Stuart
    Leslie*)
Stanley Vincent (*RAF Museum*)
George McCubbin. (*RAF Museum*)
Harold Balfour (*Imperial War Museum*)
Roland Garros in his Morane (*Jack Bruce
    and Stuart Leslie*)
The Morane Type LA (*Jack Bruce and Stuart
    Leslie*)
The Morane Bullet (*Jack Bruce and Stuart
    Leslie*)
Sidney Attwater (*RAF Museum*)
Tom Mottershead (*Chaz Bowyer*)
An FE2d (*Jack Bruce and Stuart Leslie*)
Ball's Nieuport (*Chaz Bowyer*)
Albert Ball (*Alex Revell*)
JamesMcCudden (*Imperial War Museum*)
Ewart Garland (*RAF Museum*)
Arthur Gordon-Kidd (*RAF Museum*)
Harold Tambling (*Jean Tambling*)

ACKNOWLEDGEMENTS

In researching material for this book I have had generous and enthusiastic help from a great many people. These include veteran survivors, next of kin and copyright holders, museums, libraries and institutions, together with a number of distinguished air historians who have made their own work and researches available to me. In expressing my gratitude I must absolve them all for what appears in the finished work, which is my responsibility alone.

Material extracted from *Public Record Office* Files includes: Personal Memoirs and Recollections of individual RFC personnel from files in the Class Air 1 series, including 721, 2126, 2356, 2387, 2388, 2389, 2393, 2395 and 2413. Among those quoted from this series are D.L. Allen, J.O. Andrews, H.M. le Brock, L.E.O. Charlton, C.C. Darley, W.S. Douglas, R.M. Hill, A.C. Maund, T. Mulcahy-Morgan, G.W. Murless-Green, C.F.A. Portal, C.A. Ridley, J.C. Slessor and R. Smith-Barry.

Other files from Class Air 1 from which material has been extracted include Nos 5, RFC War Diary, August 1914; 675, The Air Dropping of Agents, 1915; 687, No. 3 Squadron; 710, An Investigation into the Phenomenon of Spin; 719, No. 3 Squadron Roll of Officers; 724, A History of Aerial Photography; 868, Parachutes for Kite Balloons; 1004, Casualties, Kite Balloons.

Air Board Meetings and Memoranda covering May–June, July–September, and October–December 1916 are in Class Air 6, Nos 1–3.

Extracts and condensations from material viewed at the *Department of Documents, Imperial War Museum* – Memoirs, Diaries, Letters etc. – are gratefully acknowledged, with thanks for staff help, to next-of-kin and copyright holders as follows: D.L. Allen, G.W. Armstrong, S. Attwater, H.A. Blundell, W. Sefton Brancker, A.W. Brown, C. Callender, F. Carr, J.G.H. Chrispin, W. Cobb, (R.W.

Cobb), E.J. Garland (Patrick Garland), M.S. Goodban, S.V. Gorringe (R.S. Gorringe), O. Greig, T.E. Guttery, (D.R. Guttery), P. Haarer, R.S.S. Ingram (Professor G.I.C. Ingram), Ronald Ivelaw-Chapman (John Ivelaw-Chapman), J.P.T. Jeyes (Anthony Jeyes), J.A. Liddell, N. Macmillan, E.R. Pennell (Rene Duperly), F.C. Penny (James and Joan Seakins), J.C. Quinnell (John Craig), F.C. Ransley, (Joanna Wrathall), W.R. Read (G.R.E. Brooke), E.J.D. Routh, H.B.R. Rowell (Elizabeth Rowell), H. Seymour, R.J.A. Sheraton (Barbara D. Sheraton), J.C. Slessor, H.G. Taylor, H.S. Ward (T.C. Le Grice), R.L. Wightman, J.W. Woodhouse, H. Wyllie (John Wyllie). Also A Short History of No. 6 Squadron (anon).

Similarly, at the *Department of Sound Records, Imperial War Museum*: E. Bolt, C.J. Chabot, J.V. Gascoyne, A.T. Harris, A.W.H. James, F.J. Powell, H.J. Sanders, J.C. Slessor.

At the *Royal Air Force Museum*, again with grateful thanks to next of kin, copyright holders, and Staff: F.P. Adams, E. Brewerton, G.I. Carmichael, T. Farquhar, M.A. Kay, W.R. Read, (G.R.E. Brooke), H.J. Sanders, J.G. Selby, R. Smith, J. Worstenholm. Also Tape and Video recordings: J.O. Andrews, E.D.G. Galley, M.M. Kaye, C.B. Lefroy, Mrs Morley (Remembering Albert Ball), J. Oliver, P.N. Shone.

At the *Museum of Army Flying*: Major J.R. Cross, and H.W. Foot, Archivist. Also Arthur Rosen.

The Royal Aeronautical Society, especially Arnold Nayler, Librarian, and Assistant Librarian Brian Riddell.

At the *Liddle Collection*, The Library, Leeds University, with grateful acknowledgements to Peter Liddle: J.C. Slessor, R. Smith-Barry, Thomas Traill, S.F. Vincent, Brian Sharwood-Smith.

The London Library and staff

For help with researches: Eton College Collections, through Mrs P. Hatfield, Archivist; Oundle School, through D.H. Ford, Archivist; Hertford College, Oxford, through Dr T.C. Barnard, Keeper of the Archives; and Roger Deayton, author of a History of the Old Caterhamians Association. Also the Ministry of Defence RAF Personnel Management Centre, Innsworth, Gloucester.

For help with finding and producing photographs I am especially grateful to: Chaz Bowyer, Jack Bruce, Norman Franks, Barry Gray, G.R.E. Brooke, William and Justin Harvey-Kelly, Peter Hearn, Stuart Leslie, Alex Revell, Jean Tambling; also Imperial War Museum, RAF Museum, and Royal Aeronautical Society Photographic Libraries.

Interviews with RFC veterans include Gerald Dixon, T.G. Mapplebeck, and Harold Tambling, the last two since deceased.

Among Air Historians and Researchers who have helped me I must especially thank David J. Barnes, who produced a wealth of biographical material for me on a wide range of RFC personnel. I am also indebted to Jack Bruce, Chaz Bowyer, Alan Cooper, Norman Franks, Kevin Kelly, Alex Revell, and many others from whose historical work I have benefited.

The printed sources I have used are listed on Pages 227–229. In all instances, whether of unpublished memoirs, diaries, letters, tapes cassettes and videos, or of published works, every effort has been made to trace copyright holders where any substantial extract is quoted. The author craves the indulgence of literary executors or copyright holders where these efforts have so far failed.

The Western Front 1914–1916

Movements of the Royal Flying Corps from 16 August to 12 October 1914

DATES OF RETREAT

Maubeuge	16-23 August	Senlis	30 August
Le Cateau	24 August	Juilly	31 August
St Quentin	25 August	Serris	2 September
La Fère	26 August	Touquin	3 September
Compiègne	28 August	Melun	4 September

0 10 20 30 miles 50

■■■■ Retreat
▨▨▨ Advance

Still as they run they look behind,
They hear a voice in every wind,
And snatch a fearful joy.

From *Ode on a Distant Prospect of Eton College*
by Thomas Gray (1716–1771)

1914

'A USELESS AND EXPENSIVE FAD'

F ROM Montrose on Tayside, from Netheravon on Salisbury
Plain, from Farnborough near Aldershot (home of the British
army), from Gosport on the Solent, and from Eastchurch on
the Isle of Sheppey, pilots and observers of the infant Royal Flying
Corps converged in their open-cockpit biplane two-seaters on their
final take-off point for France. This was on Swingate Downs, high
on the grassy cliffs above Dover, near the spot where Blériot had
landed from his cross-Channel flight five years earlier. From here
they would launch themselves on the greatest of all adventures in
the short-lived annals of flight, a massed Channel crossing of some
sixty machines to France and to war.

These men were the vanguard of a gallant and adventurous company, most of them in their early and mid-twenties, but destined to
give way, as time passed, to extreme youth. They would be among the
first to fight to the death for their country in the vast amphitheatre
of the sky. Preparing to lead these trail-blazers across the unforgiving
water was the commander of the senior unit of the new Corps (No. 2
Squadron), Charles James Burke, a major from the Royal Irish Regiment. Burke was a massive, broad-shouldered, barrel-chested giant,
known behind his equally broad back as 'Pregnant Percy'. A decorated Boer War veteran, and a hard taskmaster, he was notorious for
his rough landings. Respected for his courage, he had been one of

the first to learn to fly at Larkhill on Salisbury Plain and join the Air Battalion; his visionary zeal for service aviation was legendary. He had assigned to himself the role of 'first across'; yet his mechanics, keen students of the form book, were betting on a younger man from the same regiment, the brawny, free-spirited, fearless, irreverent, fair-skinned, baby-faced but highly competitive Lieutenant Hubert Harvey-Kelly. 'Mad as a hawk', according to J.C. 'Jack' Slessor, a future chief of the air staff, he was the popular favourite to win what the mechanics were pleased to see as a race. In their worm's-eye view, 'HK', as they knew him (behind his back again), was the man most likely to win.

Other names to conjure with, many of them acting as squadron or flight leaders of this precarious aerial armada, were: Wilfred Freeman, whom Slessor thought 'the greatest air force man there ever was'; Philip Bennet Joubert de la Ferté, whose memory was said to be as long as his name; Gilbert Mapplebeck, the tallest at 6'3" and the youngest at twenty-one; Gordon Shephard, author of 'Lessons Learnt on Divisional and Army Manoeuvres, 1913', derived from his experiences as both pilot and observer; and the Salmond brothers, Jack and Geoffrey, both future chiefs of the air staff. All but two of these were to survive the war. Equally distinguished in their way were the innovative Louis Strange, of 5 Squadron, and two contrasting Old Etonians whose careers were to be poignantly linked, the lean, aquiline Robert Smith-Barry (also of 5 Squadron) and the solid, soldierly, well-groomed Francis Waldron. 'Ferdy' Waldron, by far the senior of the three, was a flight commander on 2 Squadron.

Among the airmen mechanics, some of whom were filling the observers' front seats because of an order that no two pilots were to be risked together, there were also young men who would one day make their mark. One of them, crestfallen at having to travel by sea because his pilot, the dashing Lieutenant Eric Conran, had been switched from a lovingly tended two-seater to one of the few single-seaters, was destined to outshine peers and seniors alike and to achieve immortality. This was the nineteen-year-old former boy bugler James McCudden.

Following mobilisation on 4 August 1914, the four squadrons

earmarked to accompany the British Expeditionary Force (BEF), representing the entire operational strength of the RFC at that time, moved into prepared positions in the South of England, ready for the penultimate hop to the point of departure. The BE (Blériot Experimental) 2a two-seaters of Burke's squadron, formed two years earlier at Farnborough and subsequently based at Montrose, on the Scottish east coast, actually started their flight southwards on 3 August. Staging at Farnborough, they survived sundry minor accidents and incidents before reaching Dover comparatively unscathed. Before leaving Montrose their pilots secured everything 'not wanted on voyage' in lockers and dared anyone to touch them before their (expected) return. Meanwhile at Gosport, Lieutenant A.E. 'Biffy' Borton, of No. 5 Squadron, dapper, dashing and dare-devil, chuckling his way through life, sporting a monocle more for affectation than astigmatism, was pinning a warning notice to his door: 'No one is to enter this room until the end of the war.' Channel Islander Lieutenant Henry Le Marchant Brock was looking forward to the expedition as 'a great rag' that might last three months. All were confident of being home for Christmas.

The justification for Britain's declaration of war on 4 August was the German invasion of Belgium, whose frontiers Britain had guaranteed. After refusing permission for the Germans to enter their country, the Belgians were putting up a heroic resistance. But the pilots of No. 2 Squadron, in a mood of exuberant optimism, and impatient to get to the war zone, found themselves retained to fly coastal reconnaissances from Dover. Their immediate tasks were to search for hostile submarines that might interfere with the sea crossing of the BEF, and to patrol vulnerable target areas to deter attack by the much-feared German Zeppelins. At Farnborough, where wild rumours of spies and sabotage circulated, the pilots slept under their machines in anticipation of Zeppelin attacks on the airship sheds and on the aircraft factory. Against these bulbous dirigibles, credited with powers of destruction far in excess of their true capability, there was as yet no defence.

At Dover, 'Pregnant Percy' left his pilots in no doubt what was required of them. Unarmed apart from the revolvers, rifles and rifle grenades they were ordered to carry, they were not expected to shun any chance of mortal combat, whatever the odds. There was no special briefing: methods of attack were left to individual enterprise and resource. But lest imagination should fail, 'a certain gallant C.O.' as one of Burke's pilots put it, ruled that in the event of failure to achieve a positive result with their ludicrously inappropriate weapons, the inescapable alternative was to ram any marauding airship head-on.

Pilots seemed little daunted by this dire prospect, consoling themselves with the thought that even without the weight of an observer, who was to be left behind on the ground (for which the observers, feigning disappointment, secretly congratulated themselves), the ceiling of the BE2a was blessedly inadequate to reach the heights at which Zeppelins were known to fly.

The other squadrons bound for France experienced quite as many incidents in transit to Dover but were less fortunate in the outcome. No. 3 Squadron, flying tractor Blériots and Henri Farman pushers (engine behind the pilot, skeletal and transparent, more like kites than aeroplanes), lost one of its best pilots, Lieutenant Robert R. Skene, on 12 August soon after the squadron's dawn take-off from Netheravon for Dover. In a period when aerobatics were regarded as dangerous and unnecessary, Bob Skene, formerly company pilot for the firm of Martin-Handasyde, was both renowned and notorious as the first Englishman to loop the loop. He was not the only RFC pilot to practise this manoeuvre, Mapplebeck stunting spectacularly over Salisbury Cathedral and stimulating an order that no more attempts at looping were to be made: but Skene was certainly not looping that morning. Engine failure, combined with inexperience, was normally the bugbear, but not here. With two men on board whose combined weight varied from plane to plane, together with their kit, which included the mechanic's tools, plus a full load of fuel, it seems probable that Skene's plane was overloaded. McCudden was one of those who witnessed with alarm its bouncing, uncertain take-off run and faltering, taildown struggle to rise. Its disappearance behind the hangars was followed by a reverberating crash. McCudden's friend and colleague, Air Mechanic Ray Barlow, sitting in the vulnerable front seat, was killed instantly and Skene did not long survive him. They were the first RFC casualties of the war.

Lieutenant W.R. 'Willie' Read, of the 1st Dragoon Guards, dubbed a 'live wire' by his colleagues, hid a streak of self-willed obstinacy behind a façade of pipe-smoking maturity. A man of twenty-nine, he mixed easily with seniors and juniors alike, and knew how to look after himself and his men. Flying a Henri Farman of No. 3 Squadron and choosing to stage half-way at Shoreham for refuelling (inner man included), he reached Dover at 10 o'clock. Others of 3 Squadron who got away safely followed his example. One pilot wrecked his machine and injured his mechanic when he side-slipped on landing at Dover.

No. 4 Squadron had made the preliminary move from Netheravon to Eastchurch on 30 July, with no less a task than to protect Woolwich Arsenal – and London incidentally – from air attack. Their record was two machines smashed up on the way, one through engine failure, the other ostensibly through 'pilot error'. Already this phrase, apportioning the blame correctly enough in most instances, had its sceptics, especially amongst the colleagues of dead pilots. An inquest verdict on a pilot and observer of No. 4 Squadron particularly incensed the man who was flying alongside them at the time, Gibb Mapplebeck. He witnessed the structural failure as it happened and landed near the wreck to find both men dead. Of the inquest he wrote: 'I have never been present at such disgraceful proceedings in my life . . . the whole thing was a put-up job to screen the factory . . . the factory official who attended the inquest committed perjury, of which we have proof . . . we hope to carry the matter further but have no great hope of satisfaction.' Still less could exoneration of dead pilots through detailed scientific investigation be looked for in time of war.

'War preparations going on hard,' wrote Mapplebeck on 30 July. 'The worst is now expected.' The squadron's two flights of BE2a's (there was a third, of Henri Farmans) would be going abroad, he thought, at any moment. But at Eastchurch they learned they would be on defensive coastal patrols for at least a week. 'This is rotten,' complained Mapplebeck, who like his colleagues could not get to France quickly enough. Nearly all these men were professional soldiers turned airmen, and however undesirable war might be, it was what they were trained for, and the prospect of putting their skills to the test was an exciting as well as a daunting one. Peacetime soldiering had its rewards but its predictability could be stultifying. Their worst fear was that the war might be over before they got there.

Mapplebeck argued that hostile submarines and airships would still be around in a week's or a month's time: meanwhile the BEF, which began to embark on 9 August under Field Marshal Sir John French, would arrive in France without air support. Yet the squadrons could not leave before their motor transport and administrative tail were in place on the far side, and these were about to sail from various ports. In any case the squadrons were having enough difficulty assembling at Dover; so puny a force could not be in two places at once.

Theoretically the numbering of RFC Squadrons at this stage was consecutive; but No. 1 had been formed originally as an airship squadron under veteran airship and balloon pioneer Captain Edward Maitland (he was also a pioneer of the parachute, had made many jumps from balloons, and in 1913 made the first jump from an airship). Although airships had since been transferred to naval control, No. 1 had not yet been fully re-equipped with aeroplanes. Thus the fourth squadron converging on Dover was No. 5. Owing to a dearth of shipping to embark its administrative back-up, and to a nightmare of mechanical mishaps, 5 Squadron was still at Gosport when, at midnight on 12 August, Brigadier-General Sir David Henderson, the man appointed to command the Royal Flying Corps in the field, arrived at Dover with his second in command, Lt.-Col. Frederick H. Sykes, together with the man he was leaving behind to mind the shop at the War Office, Major W. Sefton Brancker; he promptly issued orders for all machines to be ready to start for France at 6 a.m.

*   *   *

In the years immediately preceding August 1914, Britain had lagged alarmingly behind the other European powers – and particularly France – in military aviation. Although the Wright Brothers had led the world with their flights at Kittyhawk in 1903, the real beginnings of practical aviation had to await the invention of a suitable power unit, and this came in 1909 with the introduction by French engineers of the rotary engine. Up to that time, the chief cause of engine failure had been overheating; but by fixing the crankshaft and rotating the radially-arranged cylinders about its axis, more efficient cooling was obtained. The revolving engine produced more even torque (tangential force) and ran more smoothly, and the power-weight ratio was reduced. French rotary engines were soon being produced elsewhere under licence, and British manufacturers became totally dependent on them, every single machine of the four squadrons bound for France being powered by French rotary engines.

The so-called Blériot Experimental range – the current example being the BE2a – was in other respects a genuinely British-built machine, designed for the government by Geoffrey de Havilland at Farnborough. So too was the Avro 504, less numerous (only four joined the armada), built by the pioneer A.V. Roe. But the Farman brothers, Henri and Maurice, although born in England, had resided in France all their lives, had established their factory near Paris, and were among the foremost French pioneers. A further inadequacy was a reliance on German magnetos.

In 1910 the Chief of the Imperial General Staff had decried the whole notion of military aviation as 'a useless and expensive fad', while the First Sea Lord had estimated that 'the naval requirement for aircraft was two'. Even the French general Ferdinand Foch, later to be appointed Allied Commander-in-Chief, pronounced aviation as 'worthless as an instrument of war'. Cavalrymen, jealous of their forward role as the eyes of the Army in battle, were contemptuous of the early box-kite contraptions, and they warned that their only positive contribution would be to frighten the horses. Connoisseurs of orthodox military and naval warfare saw the air as an element of startling inconvenience. Fortunately there were brass hats on both sides of the Channel who recognised the vital part air observation might play in a future war and foresaw that mastery of the enemy's air forces might be necessary to secure it.

At a lower level there were many enthusiasts. These were not merely the young, the dashing and the venturesome, although they would soon predominate. Among the first to have his imagination fired by Blériot's Channel flight of 1909, and to do something about it, was a 32-year-old mechanical engineer in the Royal Field Artillery named Captain J.D.B. Fulton. Finding his initial resolve to build himself a monoplane of the Blériot type a frustratingly slow process, John Fulton bought himself a Blériot machine and began experimenting with it on Salisbury Plain. But he was beaten to it as the first British officer to qualify as a pilot by a colleague from the same regiment, Captain Bertram Dickson, whose obsession with the dawn of aviation and all it portended for his country had taken him as a spectator to the Rheims Air Show of August 1909, one of the first great landmarks in aviation history. Dickson subsequently acquired a Henri Farman biplane and learned to fly it in France, gaining his certificate on 12 May 1910. Fulton followed in November of the same year.

Dickson flew reconnaissance sorties during the army manoeuvres that autumn with another pioneer, Lieutenant Lancelot Gibbs, but gusting winds impaired their effectiveness and with it their repute. Nevertheless Fulton's work at Larkhill, where he was joined under War Office agreement by the Bristol Company and their School of Aviation, bred a lively airmindedness in the surrounding army camps. Meanwhile the initiative of the Bristol Company in sending three of their boxkite biplanes to India to demonstrate their military value found an able if idiosyncratic disciple in a monocled, deceptively foppish Indian Army officer whose approachability, drive and enthusiasm belied his image. This was W. Sefton Brancker, and for the next 20 years, until his death in the R101 airship disaster in 1930, he was to prove one of the principal motive forces in British aviation. But first, in India, he flew as an observer in one of the boxkites during army manoeuvres and provided such accurate and unprecedented reports of troop movements that the Chief of the General Staff in India was favourably impressed. He was to prove,

in the not far distant future, a staunch and appreciative ally of the
embryonic air corps: his name was Douglas Haig. Haig was to have
another sharp reminder when, in pre-war army manoeuvres at home,
the side he commanded lost the 'battle' through inferior aerial
reconnaissance.

On 28 February 1911, under public pressure, an army order prepared
the way for the establishment of an Air Battalion of the Royal
Engineers, to take effect from 1 April. The 14 officers and 150 other
ranks of the original establishment formed a nucleus entrusted with
the task of creating a body of expert airmen. The training and instruction of men in handling kites, balloons, aeroplanes, and other forms
of aircraft would devolve upon this battalion. Officer recruits could
be selected from any regular arm or branch of the Service; other
ranks would be selected from the Corps of Royal Engineers. The
selection of pilots, however, was dependent upon their taking their
Royal Aero Club certificate independently at one of the many private
flying schools that were emerging. The standard charge at these
schools of £75 was reimbursed if and when the candidate passed.
High-handed and off-putting as this might seem, it ensured that every
aspirant was a genuine enthusiast, suited to the job in hand and not
easily deterred.

Belatedly, and some might think stingily, the War Office were
officially sponsoring British military aviation. What had previously
been known as the Balloon Factory at Farnborough was expanded
to become the Army Aircraft Factory, with a brief to build aeroplanes
and airships for the Air Battalion in addition to balloons. Airships
were originally assigned to No. 1 Company under Maitland, aeroplanes to No. 2 Company under Fulton. Yet in comparison with
other European nations the effort was puny. France already had over
200 aircraft in service compared to Britain's meagre dozen or so,
and British officers who visited the French army manoeuvres of 1911
noted that French aircraft were being employed not only for visual
reconnaissance but also for the control of artillery and for aerial
photography. Scepticism about the value of aeroplanes in war,

however, still lingered, the Germans tending to specialise in airships, attracted by their longer range and greater lifting capacity. But despite this apparent preference they set up corps of military and naval aviation and sought to train pilots and observers in reconnaissance work.

Further evidence of the potential of military aviation was provided in October 1911 when aerial reconnaissance and aerial bombardment were employed for the first time in war in the quarrel in Tripoli (Libya) between Italy and Turkey. But whereas the shelling of Turkish ground targets by artillery and warship attracted no comment, the use of aeroplanes for a similar purpose drew what some saw as illogical protest on moral grounds, initiating the first of countless controversies on the ethics of aerial bombardment.

Arising from this skirmish in Tripoli, governments were forced to review their attitudes, force being the operative word. Asked whether the British ought to seek command of the air as well as the sea in any future war, a naval spokesman replied: 'I do not say we *wish* to do so but I think we will be *forced* to do so.' Under Prime Minister Herbert Asquith, a reluctant Cabinet took the point and requested that a technical sub-committee be formed of the Committee of Imperial Defence to consider future policy and make recommendations. The key members of this committee were David Henderson, then Director of Military Training, and staff officer Frederick Sykes.

The most visionary comment came from one of those early army pioneers who had learnt to fly at their own expense and laid the first foundations – Bertram Dickson. 'In the case of a European war,' ventured Dickson, 'both sides would be equipped with large corps of aeroplanes, each trying to obtain information from the other, and to hide its own movements. The efforts which each would exert would lead to the inevitable result of a war in the air, for the supremacy of the air, by armed aeroplanes against each other. This fight for the supremacy of the air in future wars will be of the first and greatest importance . . .' Not even the great leaders who were to follow could have improved on this.

Thus pressurised from above and below, the appointed sub-committee recommended the formation of a new flying corps, divided into two wings, one naval, one military. A Central Flying School was to be established at Upavon on Salisbury Plain, and the army aircraft factory at Farnborough would become the Royal Aircraft Factory under the flamboyant Mervyn O'Gorman. An Air Committee of the CID, with representatives from both Services, would act as an advisory body. All this was duly approved by the Cabinet, and the Royal Flying Corps, intended to embrace all naval and military flying, was established under Royal Warrant on 13 April 1912. The motto chosen was '*Per Ardua ad Astra*'.

The apparent subservience of all forms of naval aviation to an army corps was much resented by the senior service, and the Admiralty, independently and without authority, having developed its own training centre at Eastchurch, established an autonomous existence for its flying branch by proclaiming the birth of the Royal Naval Air Service. Such was the political clout of the Admiralty at that time that this brazen act of unilateralism went unchallenged. It was not officially recognised as the Royal Naval Air Service until 1 July 1914.

One effect of this dichotomy was that two separate agencies were now competing for such meagre resources of aircraft design and construction as existed. War Office policy for both military and naval wings of the RFC, for reasons of economy, had been to build its own aeroplanes at the Aircraft Factory at Farnborough, where Geoffrey de Havilland was both chief designer and test pilot (a fortuitous insurance no doubt). But the policy of the Admiralty, consistent with cutting the RNAS off from War Office control, became to turn to private enterprise. By stimulating firms like A.V. Roe, Shorts, Sopwiths, Vickers and Handley Page to design new machines they overtook the RFC, though doing them a lasting service in the long run by encouraging the emergence of a civilian aeroplane and aeroplane engine industry.

2

'FLYING WILL CONTINUE AS USUAL'

A M O N G the first of the pioneer flyers later to become famous in the annals of the RFC (and later still of the RAF), one name was conspicuously absent, that of Hugh Trenchard. At the time of the formation of the Air Battalion in 1911, and of the RFC in 1912, Trenchard was serving as a major with the second battalion of his regiment in Londonderry. Having previously rebuilt and run the regiment as a temporary lieutenant-colonel during a long period of service in Nigeria, he understandably fretted now. All his efforts to secure a more promising outlet met with rebuttal, often without so much as acknowledgement, and he was now in his fortieth year. It would be many years before the War Office pensioned him off, and his despondency deepened. Several of his contemporaries understood the frustration of this brusque, tall (he was 6'3″), large-framed, physically arresting soldier with piercing eyes, distinctive visage and booming voice, but only one came up with any suggestion for alleviating it. This was a comrade who had served under him in Nigeria, Captain Eustace B. Loraine, scion of a distinguished naval family. Trenchard recalled the younger man's excitement two years earlier at Blériot's successful Channel crossing. 'I must find out more about this flying business,' Loraine had said. Since then he had learned to fly and joined the Air Battalion, and from there the RFC. Now he wrote from Larkhill urging Trenchard to transfer. 'You've no idea what you're missing. Come and see men like ants crawling!' It was this sense of God-like majesty and power, high above the pygmy affairs of earth, which most of the early flyers found so uplifting.

Nothing was more likely to infect Trenchard with his friend's enthusiasm than opposition, and this was available in plenty. He was too old. Forty was the limit for qualified pilots to join the RFC, and Trenchard was 39 and unqualified. It was a young man's game. He would probably kill himself. Anyway he was far too big and heavy. Had he seen the cramped cockpits of the flimsy flying machines of the day, where leg-room was at a premium? It would be a foolish venture, with no likely military bonus even if he avoided disaster. But no man was more stubborn than Trenchard; it was at once his strength and his weakness. He finally persuaded his commanding officer to endorse his application for three months leave of absence, which, if he succeeded in going solo and passing the requisite tests meanwhile, would just give him time to enrol as a pupil at the new Central Flying School – where he was pleased to learn that one of his instructors would be Eustace Loraine – and book his place on Course No. 1 before his fortieth birthday disqualified him.

As though some final acid test of resolve were called for, the news that confronted him from his newspaper on his return to London on leave provided it. It told of the RFC's first fatal crash, on Salisbury Plain, near Stonehenge, the previous day, 5 July 1912. A Nieuport monoplane of No. 3 Squadron which had set several records in other hands had apparently lost flying speed in the turn, side-slipped and nose-dived, and the pilot had been too low to recover. Both pilot and observer were dead. No doubt it was pilot error – but it was not the first black mark in that period against the monoplane form, leading to a War Office ban on monoplanes and a preference for the sturdier biplane. Staff-Sergeant R.H.V. Wilson, the squadron's senior technical NCO, had been in the front seat. The pilot, as Trenchard read with dismay, was Eustace Loraine.

An order promulgated that same day at Larkhill was to create an undying tradition. 'Flying will continue this evening as usual.' Trenchard's reaction was similar: his grief for his friend and exemplar, wrote his biographer, only steeled his determination. He took care to study the technique of tuition, rented a room within walking distance of the flying school he had selected – Tommy Sopwith's at Brooklands – and impressed his instructor, a man named E.W. Copeland Perry, with his dedication, if not with his skill. 'He would never have made a good pilot,' said Sopwith. Nevertheless he earned his ticket in one hour four minutes' flying time, spread over thirteen inclement days, and according to Sopwith he tackled the task in hand with wonderful spirit. 'He was out at dawn each morning . . . He helped to push the machine out . . . He was a model pupil . . .'

At the Central Flying School, which Trenchard reached in late August that same year, he was quickly co-opted on to the permanent staff as adjutant, where his personality and drive, coupled with an instinctive grasp of the likely function of air forces, handsomely rewarded the gesture. Although he remained an indifferent flyer, he was confirmed in office in October, his grading, poignantly, being as 'an instructor (Squadron Commander) vice Captain E.B. Loraine, deceased.' It was in this period that he conceived the need for the aggressive stance in operations which was to prove the hallmark of the RFC in war.

As it happened, Trenchard was far from being the senior soldier to qualify as a pilot and gain his wings. That honour belonged to RFC chief David Henderson, who learned to fly in 1911 at the age of 49. A man of unusual composure, tolerance and foresight, he was an acknowledged expert in the art of military reconnaissance, and he was quick to see the potential of aerial observation and the urgent need to develop it as a technique. The role of aviation in wartime, it was thought, would be mainly one of reconnaissance, and Henderson, having played a leading role on the CID technical sub-committee, was a natural choice as head of the newly-formed Directorate of Military Aeronautics. Subordinate command of the Military Wing alone (as opposed to the Naval Wing) went initially to Sykes: staff officer Sykes had attended the French Army manoeuvres of 1911 with Fulton and reported trenchantly on them, and he had qualified for his pilot's brevet in the same year.

When the four operational squadrons began their move to Dover on mobilisation, Trenchard confidently expected to go to France with them to join the Expeditionary Force, very possibly in command of the RFC in the field. But he was to be disappointed. The Army Council saw Henderson, the man who had nurtured and guided the force from the start, as the logical choice, and Henderson, equally logically, took the politically astute Sykes as his chief staff officer and deputy, leaving command of the RFC at home to Trenchard. Based at Farnborough, Trenchard's prime task, as delegated informally by Henderson, would be to build new squadrons for the rapid expansion that was now envisaged.

Sykes, who was no less of a thruster than Trenchard, now seemed to have been preferred as Henderson's likely successor. He saw Trenchard's role as the subordinate one of direct support of the squadrons leaving for France, and before handing over to him at Farnborough he took it upon himself to tell him so, leading to one of the acrimonious personal clashes which had already characterised their relationship. Sykes, lean and hungry-looking, was hampered by a personality which, it was said, 'strongly engendered mistrust', and the straightforward Trenchard, secure in Henderson's confidence, told him not to talk rubbish. He would get his reinforcements, but the top priority was to produce new squadrons. Trenchard, indeed, had an even more influential supporter in the newly-appointed Secretary of State for War, Lord Kitchener, who took the precaution, on 7 August, of promoting him to brevet lieutenant-colonel, a stratagem which preserved his seniority over Sykes. Nevertheless, with practically the entire reservoir of serviceable machines and experienced mechanics earmarked for France, and with the scheming Sykes having Henderson's ear on the spot as his right-hand man, Trenchard was in for an uneasy as well as an arduous few months.

There was one consolation. Another man who was being left behind, in sole charge of supply and equipment at the Military Aeronautics Directorate, was Brancker, who for all his idiosyncrasies was a man to be trusted. Brancker, like many others at the War Office, had almost despaired in late July and early August when it had seemed that the Government, anxious to avoid hostilities, were going to sit on the fence, an impression which rendered the French attitude towards its ally distinctly ugly. Then came the violation of Belgian

[17]

neutrality, and with it the declaration of War. Next day, crucially, came the recall to the War office of the 64-year-old Lord Kitchener, 'much to the joy and relief', as Brancker noted, 'of every soldier in the Army'. Yet, as Brancker sought to piece together the scattered remnants of the Military Wing of the RFC, with hardly any pilots or aeroplanes in prospect, Kitchener aggravated his problems by telling him, as a beginning, to raise five more aeroplane squadrons immediately.

At a second interview, Kitchener, one of the few who believed from the first that it would be a long war, ordered Brancker to prepare for a vast expansion, and when Brancker estimated in writing, with much trepidation, that the new armies Kitchener was planning would require as many as fifty squadrons in air support, Kitchener, with prophetic insight, penned a note in his own handwriting at the foot of the minute sheet which deserves to be as familiar to history as the famous 'Your Country Needs You' poster: 'Double this. K.'

Brancker laid down three main requirements, all of them urgent. First, the design and production of aeroplanes and aero engines. Secondly, the recruitment and training of pilots, of air mechanics, and of an administrative branch. Thirdly, the establishment of aerodromes and training facilities. For the supply of aeroplanes, the RFC were obliged by what proved to be a misguided pre-war policy to rely on the Royal Aircraft Factory. The urgent need was to standardise as far as possible on a single general purpose type, for ease of manufacture, training and servicing; and the operational requirement, as envisaged at that time, was for a stable reconnaissance two-seater, one that would virtually fly itself and allow pilot and observer to concentrate on their allotted tasks of observation and artillery support. The obvious choice – indeed there was no ready alternative – was Geoffrey de Havilland's latest development of his BE range, the BE2c. Modifications which gave increased stability, regarded as a bull point for reconnaissance work, and the installation of a 90hp engine of Factory design, the RAF1, improved its performance, but it remained slow and cumbrous and not by any stretch of the imagination a fighting machine. It carried no defensive armament and would

[18]

almost certainly be difficult to arm and fight effectively. Brancker himself objected to the choice on the grounds that until a satisfactory fighting plane could be evolved the Henri Farman pusher, even more primitive and sedate but with pilot and observer sitting forward of the engine, allowing an arc of fire forward, was preferable. Both the Henri and the Maurice Farman were being produced in Britain under licence from France. But with the need to fight for air space not generally accepted as yet, Brancker lost the argument – and later got the blame for the decision. When it was realised that the Factory was not and could not be geared to mass production, large orders for the BE2c were placed with civilian firms.

The folly of concentrating all aircraft design on a subsidised government factory, instead of encouraging civilian firms to compete, became retrospectively clear. Meanwhile, such firms as had shown interest in aircraft manufacture were now busy with orders for the Admiralty, where there was no keener advocate of private enterprise than the newly appointed First Lord, Winston Churchill. The only other machines the RFC had in more or less immediate prospect, for which limited orders were placed, were: two 'pusher' two-seaters (in which, as with the Farman, pilot and observer sat forward of the engine, allowing an arc of fire forward); the Bristol Scout; and a Factory machine similar to the BE but intended for bombing.

Of the two pusher types, one, the FE2 – Farman Experimental 2 – was a De Havilland design, the other, the Vickers FB5 fighter or Gunbus, owed its embryonic existence more to the enterprise of the Vickers firm, and to an order from the RNAS, than to the RFC.

One other Factory design worthy of mention was the SE2 – Scouting Experimental 2. The prototype was flown occasionally in France by selected pilots in the early months of the war, but it did not appear in its successful SE5 version until 1917.

The Government had shown more foresight early that year in offering a prize for a British aero engine, but the winning design proved far too heavy for practical use and this stimulated the Factory to produce the RAF1, designed for the modified BE2. Meanwhile the gap was filled by substantial new orders for French engines, placed just prior to the outbreak of war.

[19]

The recruitment of pilots and mechanics, fitters and riggers presented less difficulty. The favourable rates offered by Brancker enabled him to attract 1,100 of the best mechanics in Britain, and these formed the backbone of the new squadrons he was charged to establish. The only immediate sources of pilots were the civilian training schools, where the intention was to enlist the instructors as sergeant pilots, a breed already existing in the flying corps (one such was an older brother of Jimmy McCudden); but with the RNAS commissioning all pilots, the RFC, in enlisting experienced civilian pilots, had to commission them in order to compete.

The proclivity of established professional pilots for stunting – still strictly forbidden officially – was stifled by making them sign a declaration to the effect that they would not loop or perform any similar manoeuvre while serving in the RFC. But their expertise as instructors was invaluable. Facilities for training raw pilots, rather than recruitment, was the major problem, and the pre-war policy of making pilots pay for their initial training was abandoned, *ab initio* courses being started at CFS and at several requisitioned civilian schools.

When, five years earlier, youthful imaginations were fired by the exploits of Blériot and others, the attendance at aviation meetings had multiplied. Flying, although beyond the reach of the majority except for the occasional joy-ride, became a craze. Now one could learn to fly for nothing – and even get paid for it. The prospect appealed to emotions less immediate than patriotism, although that might have been part of it. Flying gave its practitioners a new conceit of themselves, an individuality, the opportunity to achieve tasks that the earthbound millions could only gaze at in awe. If, as many volunteers felt, they were in a rut, flying would lift them out of it. Self-doubt would be succeeded by self-belief. Subsequently, when the first solo flight was accomplished, a natural apprehension, and the sense of solitude, were submerged in an intense feeling of exhilaration. For the young men who now applied to join the new corps, or to transfer to it, the fact that one could kill oneself in the process of learning only magnified the fascination.

None of these emotions was likely to be stirred by the first question asked of many applicants: 'Why do you want to join the Flying Corps?' And this was only the beginning. Having got past that one, they were faced with what we would now call the 64,000-dollar question. To make a judgement, in a brief interview, on whether or not an applicant had what it took to fly the rickety wood, wire and fabric contraptions of the day was difficult enough, and the class system in which the interviewer operated must inevitably have loaded the dice in favour of the public schoolboy. Anyway, legend – and some reported experience – has it that the second question, intended as a measure of a likely aptitude for flying (it was a question that has been joyously ridiculed ever since), was: 'Do you ride?'

Was it, in fact, so ridiculous a question? A good 'seat', a natural equilibrium, and a sensitive pair of hands, would have been among the qualities the interviewer was looking for. Even more important, perhaps, would be the self-confidence necessary to control an animate object, and the ready acceptance of physical challenge. Many of these young aspirants would fly before they ever drove a fast car or rode a motor-bike as a means of channelling their aggression. And the question was not so élitist as it might appear: far more people were accustomed to horses as a means of transport than would be the case today. And a man who baulked at handling and controlling a horse might baulk at flying and fighting an aeroplane. No doubt the methods of selection were ill-conceived and arbitrary; but they seem to have worked. And the unsuitable pupil was soon weeded out – if he didn't kill himself first.

[21]

3

CHANNEL CROSSING:
THE FIRST RECONNAISSANCE

THE airmen alerted in their temporary encampment on Swing-ate Downs at midnight on 12 August, with a warning that they would be taking off at six o'clock next morning, had all won their places the hard way – through personal initiative, financial sacrifice, the civilian training schools, and the CFS. Now the testing time had come.

There was not much sleep that night for anyone, least of all for the pilots, bedded down beside their machines in the hangars, their rest interrupted by the prodigious snores of Pregnant Percy. They envied him his capacity to sleep soundly at such a time.

Drawn from over forty different regiments (only a handful, mostly from No. 5 Squadron, which had not yet reached Dover, were direct entrants into the RFC Special Reserve), and hailing from all parts of the United Kingdom (which then included the whole of Ireland, the Anglo-Irish being strongly represented), they had already developed fierce squadron loyalties and inter-squadron rivalries; but for the moment these emotions were subjugated by the infinitely stronger human ties of shared experience and danger. Already they had suffered losses. Now they faced a flight across a stretch of water which had already claimed the lives of distinguished pioneer flyers, in flimsy, ramshackle machines whose power units were continually faltering and failing. Yet many who encountered them that morning remarked on their optimism and exhilaration at the prospect before them. Without exception they had joined or been transferred to the RFC for adventure, and now more than ever before they stood on the threshold of it. 'Such exuberance of spirit I have never seen,' was the comment of a non-flying colleague.

Youthful naivety could not wholly account for this atmosphere of zestful panache. Most had attained the rank of lieutenant, all the flight commanders were captains, and the squadron commanders were majors. Nervous tension doubtless contributed, but the excitement was palpable. For many months they had endured the scepticism, even the ridicule, of their fellow soldiers – they were still professional soldiers first and professional airmen second – and now was their chance to prove themselves in battle. This romanticised their resolve to do or die.

Assembled at Dover were not only the aeroplanes of Nos 2, 3 and 4 Squadrons but also another 16 machines that had been allotted to form an Aircraft Park. These machines, together with 4 Sopwith Tabloids in packing cases which were to travel by sea, were the planned nucleus of what would be built up in the ensuing months into a vast system of supply and repair feeding the squadrons in France. They comprised 9 BE2a's, 1 BE2c, 3 BE8s, and 3 Henri Farmans. Half of these, however, had to be supplied to the squadrons at Dover to replace casualties and bring them up to strength before departure. The rump, crewed by spare pilots and mechanics, joined the expedition.

Briefing that morning was properly abbreviated; pilots and mechanics already knew what was expected of them. Maps of France and Belgium had been issued, sealed orders, giving their destination, were opened. Purchasing parties had scoured local suppliers in previous days for tyre inner-tubes, providing a lifebelt of sorts for each man, to be inflated by mouth on immersion. Other equipment to be taken included: for pilots, a revolver, field glasses, and a spare pair of goggles; and for mechanics, a roll of tools. Pilots were also ordered to carry, for sustenance in emergency, a water-bottle containing boiled water, a miniature stove, and a haversack containing biscuits, cold meat, a bar of chocolate, and a packet of soup concentrate. There was no sea rescue organisation, but pilots were not to set course before attaining 3,000 feet, sufficient, it was hoped, to glide across in the event of engine failure. After making landfall at Boulogne they were to coast-crawl south to the Somme estuary before following the Somme river south-east to the aerodrome at Amiens. Shipping bound for Boulogne had been alerted to look out for possible ditchings on the actual crossing.

Squadron ground personnel were sailing for Boulogne that day, mostly from Southampton, while personnel and equipment of the Aircraft Park were leaving from Avonmouth. First to sail, though, were the officers and men of the newly-established RFC Headquarters in France. Under Henderson and Sykes, they would have Major H.R.M. Brooke-Popham as DAQMG and Captain Geoffrey Salmond as GSO2. Others on the headquarters staff included medical and wireless specialists (there was a wireless flight attached rather speculatively to No. 4 Squadron), and the unmilitary and incongruous but urbane and highly literate Hon. Maurice Baring, personal staff officer to Henderson.

Also travelling by sea was a motley collection of motor transport that would have looked more at home amongst the roundabouts and roller-coasters of a fairground. From a pool of requisitioned commercial vehicles assembled in Regents Park in the first days of the war, the RFC, accorded the low priority to which they were becoming accustomed, had had to make do and mend with the remnants, which they proceeded to form into a tumbledown motorcade that towered above their own sombre, functional service conveyances in an orgy of colour. A high-sided roof rack for empty cubical biscuit tins disclosed a past life of delivery work for Peek Frean; and a giant blue-black splash on the side of another van boasted the superiority of Stephens Ink. More appropriate for removals, perhaps, were a white-on-green Maples pantechnicon and a black-on-green Carter Paterson juggernaut. There was a cosmopolitan neutrality in the presence of Sunbeam, Renault and Mercedes tourers and a Rolls-Royce donated by Smith-Barry, and a native touch of amateurism in the recruitment of a private two-seater coupé complete with its volunteer owner/driver, a Mr Weeding from Guildford. Bringing up the rear of this Lord Mayor's Show of vehicles, aptly enough, was a dust-cart.

Even this gaudy cavalcade paled in comparison with its principal exhibit, commandeered to serve as ammunition and bomb lorry for No. 5 Squadron. If other floats in the procession were loud in their praises of their peacetime wares, this one was deafening. Against a backcloth of brilliant scarlet it proclaimed in gold lettering the incomparable merits of HP (Houses of Parliament) Sauce, using the mouth-watering phrase 'The World's Appetiser'. To exchange, as a cargo, such a prompter of digestive juices for the stomach-turning horror of ammunition and bombs might seem Machiavellian; but this was no latter-day Trojan Horse. Neither deception nor camouflage was intended, and no one seems to have considered the vulnerability of these vehicles to observation and attack from the air. But virtue, however unwitting, was to have its reward in the landmark provided by the scarlet van for disorientated RFC pilots and observers during the chaotic retreat that was shortly to come.

First to take off, at 06.25 on what promised to be a perfect August morning, were the pilots of No. 2 Squadron. And first among these, as even the commanders of two of the other squadrons, Jack Salmond of No. 3 and J.F.A. 'Josh' Higgins of No. 5, had forecast, was Harvey-Kelly. He was followed soon afterwards by Burke. For the townsfolk of Dover, the choice of a rallying point so close to their homes created a sensation; and as, one by one, the fragile machines took off and battled giddily for height, the scene on Swingate Downs, overlooked by the Castle and watched by the populace, assumed an atmosphere of jamboree. Pilots and mechanics had too much to think about to be more than subconsciously aware of it, but the spectators were savouring the thrill of history being made.

All the machines of No. 2 Squadron were BE2a's, and all got safely across the Channel. But as Burke led them down the coast to the mouth of the Somme, one of his brood was seen to be missing. On reaching Boulogne, Harvey-Kelly, scorning to use the Somme as a guide, had elected to cut straight across country to Amiens. Just as Burke was gliding down to land at Amiens, he caught sight of another machine: it was Harvey-Kelly's. Landing at 08.20, the favourite beat Burke by two minutes. But with the other machines landing safely one by one, Burke's vexation rapidly gave way to euphoria. H-K, as usual, had got away with it.

No. 3 Squadron, led by its three flight commanders, Captains Philip Herbert, Lionel Charlton, and Philip Joubert (Jack Salmond, the squadron commander, travelled with the ground party), and with a briefed take-off time of 08.15, flew a mixture of BE2s; BE8s (a variant of the BE known somewhat derisively as 'Bloaters' because of their fish-like tail); and Henri Farmans. Lieutenant Willie Read, already mentioned, a man whose contentious individuality was apt to clash with obstacles on the ground as well as in the air, was aware from the start that his engine was not running well, but he managed to coax his BE2 up to 1,200 feet. Determined not to be left behind, he elected to risk it and carry on. One pilot had to abort with engine trouble (he followed five days later), but all the others got through, reaching Amiens at 11.05. Here they again found themselves the centre of attraction. The good people of Amiens, sickened by rumours that perfidious Albion was bent on betrayal, now had welcome evidence to the contrary, and they turned out in force to celebrate. With some thirty strange aeroplanes lined up on the aerodrome as though at a pageant, and the expectation of more to come, they gave the astonished airmen a truly Gallic greeting, showering them with all manner of flowers and goodies. For a brief honeymoon period, the *entente cordiale* flourished as never before.

Last to leave that day was No. 4 Squadron, which included the wireless flight attached to it. Here too it was the flight commanders – two of them in this case, Captains Gordon Shephard and F.J.L. Cogan – who led the way. Two flights of BEs made the crossing, the third flight, of Henri Farmans, being left behind for local patrol duties. Soon after the sea crossing was completed, Cogan's engine cut out, and although he cursed his luck he accepted it philosophically as an occupational hazard and looked for a likely field to force-land in. Unfortunately he had no means of communication with his flight except by hand signal, and his attempts to wave them on their way were misinterpreted; he could not stop them following him down. The field Cogan chose, uncorrugated in appearance, proved to have been recently ploughed, and most of his flight sustained minor damage. If this was not Fred Karno's Air Force it looked very much like it; but skill and resource in repair and improvisation, practised in innumerable forced and unauthorised landings away from base in peacetime, brought a measure of recovery, and after begging facilities for refuelling they got away again the same day and eventually joined the party at Amiens, though one pilot, Patrick Playfair (destined, as an air marshal, to lead another Advanced Air Striking Force to France 25 years later), was obliged to force-land a second time to ask an astonished pedestrian the way. Recording this many years later, he admitted to suppressing it at the time.

Forty-nine machines lay parked on Amiens aerodrome that night, with only two small sheds to accommodate them. Serviceability, in the days to come, would be proportionate to the state of the weather and would be much affected by high winds and rain, but for the moment they basked in perfect August sunshine. So far the expedition had been accomplished without casualty: but Amiens was only a staging post on the way to the selected forward base at Maubeuge, 70 miles to the west-north-west and 12 miles south of Mons. And No. 5 Squadron was still to come.

It was natural that 5 Squadron, the most recently formed of the expeditionary force, should have most of the direct entry special reserve pilots in its ranks, men who were not and never had been regular soldiers and who owed no regimental allegiance. They numbered no more than six, against a dozen regulars, but two of them, already mentioned, were to prove outstanding. The best-known, perhaps, and certainly the most eccentric, was the Etonian Bob Smith-Barry, known from an early stage as simply Smith-B. Sensitive, aesthetic features and a penchant for the unorthodox were rightly indicative of aristocratic descent, but the spare, angular physique scarcely hinted at the single-mindedness of the pedagogue. Nor did one of his early reports at Eton, which described him as '. . . *an awful little boy. He has no aptitude whatever*'.

Smith-B had been flying since 1911 and instructing at the Bristol School since 1912; and at CFS, where they found there was little they could teach him, they had employed him as an instructor. He had approached aviation with the same ardour he had once devoted to a career as a concert pianist, when for two years he had practised for eight hours a day. He believed that the emphasis in training on cautious, unadventurous flying was a danger in itself, leaving the pupil totally unprepared for emergencies, and in his own flying he practised what he preached. Reproached for handling a machine contrary to the rule book, and therefore dangerously, he met the criticism head-on. 'You know, Captain, I felt much safer flying that machine dangerously.' After that they left him alone.

Almost more colourful at first sight was the fearless, inventive, irrepressible Louis Strange. The son of a Dorsetshire farmer, his interests were mechanical rather than agricultural, and he was one of the first to apply his mind to the problems of air firing and air fighting. After taking his Royal Aero Club certificate at Hendon in August 1913 he applied for a commission in the RFC and was eventually posted to the sixth course of instruction at CFS. While he was waiting he offered his services to the Hendon School as an instructor, and he was soon teaching beginners to fly Bristol Boxkites. He flew passengers on joy-rides at week-ends, and he entered for the cross-country races that were gaining in popularity at the time with notable success. Here was a young man who was virtually a professional flyer when he arrived at CFS, perfectly at home in the air.

When war was clearly imminent, all pupils at CFS who were considered sufficiently advanced were posted to active service squadrons, and Strange joined No. 5 at Gosport. Of the three flights of four machines each, A was equipped with Avro 504s, B and C with Henri Farmans. Each flight was a self-contained unit capable of being detached with its own MT workshop and stores. The day after the departure of the other three squadrons for France, the pilots of No. 5 set out via Shoreham for Dover; but their passage was anything but smooth. One of the flight commanders, Captain George Carmichael, found himself without a mount when the interplane struts of his Farman collapsed as he was taxying out, so he set off for Dover by road, having been advised that he might pick up a spare machine from the Aircraft Park when he got there. Another pilot suffered concussion when he crashed near Shoreham, and a third force-landed on the South Downs between Brighton and Lewes with engine trouble, spelling a delay of several days in both cases.

None of these setbacks approached for incident the experience of Louis Strange. The squadron had been held back originally, it will be remembered, by a dearth of shipping. When the squadron transport eventually embarked at Southampton it proved to be short of a driver. Chosen to deputise, despite vigorous protest, was Strange's mechanic. When the missing driver eventually turned up, somewhat the worse for the celebrations that had delayed him, his reward was to be allotted to Strange as substitute mechanic. Since he had never flown before, it was an assignment that was well calculated to sober him up.

He was a big fellow, weighing, in Strange's estimate, about thirteen stone. His kit, too, looked bulky, having been packed to seaborne rather than airborne limits. From past experience Strange knew how to manage an overloaded Blériot, but a Farman, with a top speed of 59 miles an hour, against the Blériot's 72, was even more difficult to handle. To add to his weight problems, the inventive Strange had mounted a forward-firing Lewis gun in the front cockpit of his Farman. (The gun belonged to another 5 Squadron pilot, Lieutenant L. da C. Penn-Gaskell, a ballistics enthusiast who often flew with Strange.) Struggling against headwinds and at times nearly flattened on to the Downs, the Farman took 2½ hours to cover the 70 miles (a ground speed of 28 miles per hour) to Shoreham, where Strange had planned to refuel. He had another reason for alighting at Shoreham – a lady friend had promised to meet him there to say goodbye. The combination of delay at the start and slow-motion flight meant that she had gone when he got there.

At Dover, where the nucleus of a new squadron not yet operational, No. 6, had been given the task of setting up the facilities, red flags warned of obstructions, but an unmarked declivity, aggravated by the Farman's unusual load, caused a broken longeron (longitudinal strut). Into that same declivity, as Strange could not help but notice, his passenger discarded an empty whisky bottle; poor chap, it was Dutch courage he had been seeking this time, but the effect was similar. Strange put him under close arrest, as a kindness as

[29]

much as anything, and he was marched off to the guard tent.

The next task was to repair the Farman. Finding he could get no spares at Dover, and after having tea at the Castle, Strange set off in Smith-Barry's Rolls-Royce to collect a replacement longeron at Farnborough. It was two o'clock in the morning before he got back to Dover, but he worked through the night fitting the longeron – and was thankful to CFS for the training that had taught him the knack. Then it was breakfast at the Castle and a return to the aerodrome to release his passenger, only to find that he had somehow escaped from the guard tent during the night.

When apprehended, the driver would face a serious charge, perhaps of desertion. But Strange, feeling that the guard must be equally at fault, acted with compassion. Police assistance was sought and the escaped prisoner, still the worse for wear, was run to earth in the town. At last Strange was ready to go.

Meanwhile Carmichael, having picked up the only spare aeroplane available at Dover, a BE8 two-seat tractor biplane from the Aircraft Park, had got away with the rump of the squadron the previous day, 15 August. Carmichael later described the BE8 as 'a nasty contraption with insufficient fin surface, one of the least successful products of the Royal Aircraft Factory', and he was not keen to fly it. But he wasn't going to be left behind, and he coaxed it to Amiens in 2 hours 10 minutes. Others who crossed that day included Smith-Barry. The atmosphere at Amiens remained one of frenzied acclaim, and first General Henderson and then Field Marshal Sir John French visited the camp and congratulated pilots and crews. Henderson told them he hadn't heard so far of any air fighting by the French and added that he 'didn't think there would be any', thinking perhaps to reassure men who, apart from Louis Strange, carried only revolvers and rifles. He was soon to revise this opinion.

Next day, 16 August, a Sunday, the weather broke, but Strange finally got away from Dover at midday. At once he was faced by a strong north-east wind, and it took him an agonising forty-five minutes to cross the water by the shortest route to Cap Gris Nez, with a rough, inhospitable sea swirling beneath him to remind him of the caprices of aero engines and the frailty of tyre inner-tubes.

His grudging sympathy with the predicament of his abducted, half-inebriated front-seat passenger was enhanced. But despite deteriorating visibility he identified his pinpoint, and he was amazed, when he circled the aerodrome at Amiens, to see crowds of people milling around the perimeter, undaunted by the drizzle, and a phalanx of more than fifty aeroplanes lined up in rows as though on display. Landing and taxiing up to align his Farman with the other machines, he had scarcely come to a halt when his passenger sprang to life, stood up in the front cockpit, and waved another empty bottle to acknowledge the cheers of the throng.

For Strange there was the satisfaction of catching up with his squadron colleagues after the lone flight across. For his passenger, somewhat unkindly perhaps, there was a reckoning with his commanding officer, the monocled Josh Higgins, who had crossed by sea with the ground party. Fidgeting as was his habit with eye-glass and swagger stick when obliged to deliver a reprimand (his jutting backside had earned him the sobriquet of 'all bum and eye-glass', sometimes shortened to 'arsy-glassy'), and a man generally popular because he flew whenever he could and also looked after his men, he nevertheless awarded the unfortunate MT driver 56 days' field punishment. It could, of course, have been much worse for the man but for Strange.

All four squadrons had been ordered that morning to fly to their forward base at Maubeuge, ten miles behind the section of the line to be guarded by the BEF. But low cloud had delayed them, only No. 2 Squadron getting off before Strange's arrival. No. 4 Squadron followed, and then No. 3. All went well until the last aircraft but one took to the air. The pilot, Second Lieutenant Evelyn Copeland Perry, was one of the most experienced flyers in the Corps (he was the man who had taught Trenchard to fly). But he was piloting one of the dreaded BE8s. He was climbing over the aerodrome when the plane stalled and appeared to catch fire. Last to take off was Copeland Perry's flight commander, Lionel Charlton, and as he circled before heading east he saw below him on the ground the machine which had preceded him, crumpled and burning. Both Perry and his air mechanic, a lad named Herbert Parfitt, were killed.

Carmichael, having himself flown a BE8 to Amiens for 3 Squadron, was given the task of collecting one of three new Henri Farmans from the French base at Buc. Another pilot, Lieutenant R.M. Vaughan, forced down with engine trouble in a machine which bore no national markings, was arrested as a spy by the gendarmes and dumped in the local jail, where he languished for three days until he was released into the hands of the local mayor and his two lovely daughters.

Carmichael's good fortune was compounded when Smith-Barry, the pilot selected to fly his BE8 on to Maubeuge, suffered a control failure near Peronne and sustained multiple injuries in the subsequent crash. His mechanic, Corporal Frederick Geard, in the front seat, was killed.

Languishing in hospital at St Quentin with two broken legs and a smashed knee-cap, Smith-B was heartened by a letter he received from his squadron commander, Josh Higgins. 'Don't worry about the smash. I am quite sure it was not your fault.' This uncritical verdict, written before the causes of the crash were known, was a tremendous compliment to the known skill and natural ability of Smith-Barry. In Higgins's experience – and few knew better, since he flew all machines delivered to the squadron himself and learned their tricks before allowing others to fly them – no one in the Corps handled and manoeuvred aeroplanes with the confidence and indeed the mastery of Smith-B, and he guessed that somehow he would get back to flying.

The third of the replacement BE8s provided by the Aircraft Park was written off soon afterwards, happily without serious injury to the crew.

On the approach to Maubeuge – in stark contrast to their reception at Amiens – several machines were fired on by the French. Fortunately their marksmanship was poor, only Waldron's plane being much damaged.

They were now near the Belgian frontier, billeted in a fortified town no more than forty miles from the invading German Army. But they were reassured, on 18 August, by their first glimpse of the BEF, marching boldly through the town on their way north to Mons to the stirring accompaniment of regimental bands. However, as Joubert noted, the arrival of the British only meant, for the RFC, an impartial peppering from the ground by ally and compatriot alike, both armies having sensibly resolved to shoot first and face questions afterwards. As soon as anyone took off and crossed the Maubeuge –Mons road he was welcomed by a roar of musketry. To counter this the crews worked all night painting Union Jacks on the underside of lower wings and on fuselages, only for these emblems, in the days that followed, to be mistaken for the German cross and riddled accordingly. It wasn't only the British who suffered. In the middle of a Zeppelin scare, the French shot down one of their own airships.

Read was told to hold himself in readiness to take off as soon as any Zeppelin was sighted. He and his observer were armed with three bombs to drop on the Zeppelin from above, supposing they could outclimb it, and a revolver each to deter interference from hostile aeroplanes. 'There was no sign of the gasbag,' wrote Read sardonically.

For the ground party, steering a triumphant, flower-bedecked course by road and rail from Boulogne through Amiens to Maubeuge, fêted at every stopping place and showered with gifts, the euphoria lasted a little longer. Even at Maubeuge, where they bedded down on the aerodrome, the French did their best to make them comfortable. But for the flying men, the sequence of accidents and crashes, the loss of comrades, and the novel experience of being fired at, especially by their own side, led to some unspoken but gloomy forecasts. What would happen when the fighting started, Read asked himself – as it was surely about to do? 'Estimates are that not more than 5% of those who have come out with the Corps will go back,' he noted. Proud of being in the vanguard, and as high-spirited as ever, pilots began to accept that they might not be home for Christmas after all.

The German invasion plan, prepared some years earlier by Count von Schlieffen when he was Chief of the German General Staff, was a daring scheme aimed at knocking France out of the war at the outset. Inherent in the plan was the blatant infringement of Belgian neutrality, the German armies sweeping round through Belgium and Northern France to encircle Paris and cut off the major portion of the French army from reinforcement, compelling the French Government to surrender. The plan had since been modified by von Schlieffen's successor, von Moltke, to take account of an expected French counter-offensive in Alsace and Lorraine, Moltke strengthening the left wing at the expense of the strong right wing which von Schlieffen had seen as the decisive element. Despite the delay imposed on the advance by the heroic resistance of the Belgians, the anticipated French counter-offensive was stillborn by setbacks and losses, and General Joseph Joffre, the French Commander in Chief, ordered a retreat on the whole front. The British contingent had barely taken up its positions to make a stand at Mons on a 25-mile sector when the French on their right were forced to pull back, leaving the British right flank exposed. This was on 22 August. News of the French retreat was not immediately passed to the British, though the Germans soon found the gap and started pushing through.

The distinction of flying the first RFC reconnaissance of the war – they took off at 09.30 on 19 August – had meanwhile fallen to Philip Joubert of No. 3 Squadron and Gibb Mapplebeck of No. 4. Each had a designated task. For the first part of their reconnaissance they were to keep together, so that if one were forced down through mechanical trouble – a perpetual anxiety – the other could report where he was. To save weight and improve performance they flew without observers, but this proved a false economy, both pilots losing their way – and each other – in poor visibility and low cloud. Mapplebeck somehow completed his task, reporting only a small cavalry force at Gembloux instead of the concentration suspected; but Joubert, despite landing several times to fix his position, lost his way repeatedly and spent an abortive eight hours before returning to Maubeuge. It was not a very convincing performance.

Reconnaissances flown on 20 and 21 August disclosed no enemy troops immediately in front of the BEF; but on Saturday the 22nd the twelve reconnaissances that were flown built up a picture of a substantial enemy force moving towards the British front. GHQ had previously been wary of Intelligence based purely on air observation, but it was afterwards admitted that the RFC's efforts that day, led by Gordon Shephard, 'did much to dissipate the fog of war'. Trust in and reliance on the RFC, although still far from complete, was at least embryonic. But there was a price to be paid. Several machines came under accurate rifle and machine-gun fire and Sergeant-Major D.S. Jillings, an observer with No. 2 Squadron, was hit in the leg by a rifle bullet, the first British soldier to be wounded in an aeroplane. Worse was to follow when one of 5 Squadron's Avros failed to return; it had been shot down by ground fire while the crew were noting the progress, from 2,000 feet, of a German infantry column. After the chastening experience of Joubert and Mapplebeck the rule that two pilots must not fly in the same plane had inevitably been relaxed in order that qualified observers could be carried, and Lieutenants V. Waterfall and C.G.G. Bayly were missing.

Gordon Bayly's half-completed reconnaissance report, picked up near the crash site, survived in the hands of Belgian peasants, who secreted it, and it eventually found its way to the War Office – too late for practical use. Stranger still, the arrival of the Avro in enemy-held territory seems to have given the Germans their first sure knowledge of the presence in France of British forces.

On the same day the first German airborne intruder, alerted perhaps by Waterfall's crash, appeared over Maubeuge airfield at 5,000 feet, and two BE2 crews went after it with hand grenades and bombs. Meanwhile Strange took off in his Farman, with Penn-Gaskell to work the gun. Struggling for altitude, he had got no higher than 3,500 feet when the German, having had plenty of time to complete his reconnaissance, bade them a disdainful farewell. Frustrating as this was for Strange and Penn-Gaskell, it was nothing to their disappointment when Higgins, blaming the weight of the gun for their ponderous ascent, ordered them to dispense with it. In vain did they argue that the Blériots had done no better. 'You'll have to manage with a rifle in future,' ruled Higgins.

[4]

THE RETREAT FROM MONS:
THE MIRACLE OF THE MARNE

T HE BEF under Sir John French consisted of two army corps, a cavalry division, and a cavalry brigade, comprising a total, at most, of 80,000 men and 250 guns, a contemptible enough little army in all conscience by comparison with France's 72 divisions, and even on this 25-mile front it was heavily outnumbered and out-gunned by the First German Army under von Kluck. Horace Smith-Dorrien's Second Corps were to hold the line westwards from Mons, Douglas Haig's First Corps eastwards to Binche. For these men, the cream of the British Army, war was their job, and they expected to stem the tide of the German advance before mounting an offensive that would drive the invaders back on their tracks. But with the battle of the frontiers impending, and liaison with the Fifth French Army on the British right not yet established, GHQ gave the RFC — even more contemptible in its way — a new task. In addition to locating enemy forces and reporting on their strength and progress, they were asked to find out what they could about the movements of their Allies.

Philip Joubert and Dermott Allen of 3 Squadron, as pilot and observer, were among those detailed, their machine — a rarity — being a Blériot two-seater monoplane. The Anglo-Irish Allen, a slim, upright figure with piercing blue eyes, had already proved himself an above-average interpreter of what he saw from the air, his verbal

amplifications, despite a marked stammer, always being worth waiting for. From heights varying between 1,500 and 2,000 feet, in good
weather, they found they could detect practically all ground movement; and as they flew over the battle area in and around Charleroi
they saw quite clearly that the French were being driven back. Yet
despite the reputation they had earned, their report, when they
landed back at Maubeuge, was coolly received, no reference to a
withdrawal having yet been made by the French. It was not long,
however, before the report was confirmed and Joubert and Allen
were vindicated. The BEF had barely reached their decreed positions
when they were seen to be untenable. From the start it was a case
of retreat or be annihilated.

That evening, 22 August, Sir John French held a conference at Le
Cateau with Haig and Smith-Dorrien at which the request of the
commander of the Fifth French Army that the British, to relieve
pressure on the French, undertake a local offensive action at Mons
before joining them in a strategic retreat had already been pre-empted
by events. Yet they could not disengage without making a stand and
fighting their way out, thus providing the requested cover for the
French left wing. Next day, 23 August, the British infantry, supported
by artillery, fought the Battle of Mons. By inflicting losses on the
enemy almost comparable with their own they delayed the German
advance, and despite almost intolerable pressure they somehow
covered their own retreat from daybreak on the 24th. Men snatched
what sleep they could where they fought, and the withdrawal did
not develop into a rout; but to the RFC the sight of their comrades
returning to Maubeuge in war-torn disarray, so soon after their
triumphant passage north, was agonising.

Some of the RFC contingent had already abandoned Maubeuge
for Le Cateau, to the south-west, while the Aircraft Park had begun
withdrawing from Amiens to St Omer, 30 miles inland from Boulogne. Among those who witnessed distressing scenes of chaos near
Maubeuge was Read. 'Roads everywhere were crowded with troops
retiring,' he noted, 'not a good sight.' The atmosphere was one of
dejection and even despair. 'Poor fellows, they've had no sleep and
little food for three nights and days, being driven back and pressed

always by the advancing enemy. The Germans have us on the run, fighting a rearguard action against big odds.' It was easy to see they were in a tight corner, with men, guns and transport blocking the roads, and he was reminded of campaign histories he had studied describing disorderly retreats. Some of the casualties were riding on the limbers of guns, and walking-wounded were throwing away their haversacks, even their rifles. He made one of these men pick his rifle up, but others were carrying their wounded pals, and he turned away in embarrassment.

The notion of making a stand before the fortress of Maubeuge was collapsing as fears of envelopment grew. When shells began falling close to the aerodrome, Brooke-Popham sent Read to take up a position on a low hill which gave a commanding view of the surrounding countryside. He took two orderlies with him to act as couriers for the warning messages he expected to initiate. Suspecting and then confirming that German cavalry were using a wood in the middle distance as cover, he sent first one orderly then the other back to report. He was already aware of increasing activity behind him on the aerodrome, but no message came for him to abandon his post, and when he finally returned, without orders, practically everyone had gone. One defective Henri Farman had been set on fire lest the Germans capture it, but his own Farman was still there, his mechanic, bless him, was standing by to swing the prop, and they took off for Le Cateau as German cavalry approached.

Le Cateau was a pleasant enough town, but accommodation was lacking. 'We slept', wrote Maurice Baring, 'and when I say we I mean dozens of pilots, fully dressed in a barn, on the top of, and underneath, an enormous load of straw ... Everybody was quite cheerful, especially the pilots.' Baring's phrase, of course, included observers, who were spending their days directing pilots over and behind the battlefield, looking for enemy movements and locating enemy batteries, and learning fast. German uniforms were appearing with increasing frequency where once there had been British, and the threat was evidently aimed at Le Cateau. On the afternoon of the 25th, while the BEF prepared to make a stand at Le Cateau, the RFC retreated south-west to St Quentin.

[38]

That afternoon Lieutenants C.W. Wilson and C.E.C. Rabagliati of No. 5 Squadron, having just filed a reconnaissance report, were refuelling their Avro, No. 398, when an intruder was seen approaching the aerodrome from the south. 'There you are,' shouted Josh Higgins, adjusting his monocle, 'go and take his number!' Already the swept-back wing-tips of the intruder had identified it as an Etrich Taube. Heading north and climbing steeply, Wilson and Rabagliati were tacitly agreed on putting into practice the tactics they had often discussed, namely, getting ahead of and below the 'hostile' (enemy aircraft) so that Rabagliati, in the forward seat (but aft of the tractor engine), could fire upwards and rearwards over Wilson's head. Wilson was forced to duck below his cockpit coaming when the firing started, to avoid the ejected 'empties', but when it ceased he followed Rabagliati's pointing finger earthwards. The Taube pilot appeared to have surrendered: he continued to descend, and he finally force-landed in a field. They would have liked to land beside him and claim their prize, but they could see troops nearby and could not identify them, so they decided to return to Le Cateau. In fact the action had taken place so close to Le Cateau that they were applauded on landing, a dubious pleasure as it exposed their poor navigation, and they now wished they had landed beside their victim.

They were to wish this even more fervently when they caught up some time later with Harvey-Kelly, who had also tangled with the Taube and was posing as the victor. He had landed beside it and he and his observer had chased the pilot into a wood. They had removed a small plaque from the wreckage, which they were now displaying as booty. 'Stopped him in full career,' wrote Wilson in his diary, 'and claimed first Hun for 398. H-K handed the plaque gracefully to me. "Your bird I think."' Wilson and Rabagliati passed the trophy on to Higgins laconically. '"Number you asked for, Sir."'

The contrasts between luxury and discomfort experienced by the crews from day to day as the retreat accelerated were extreme. Sometimes they slept on billowing feather beds surrounded by lace curtains, with all the comforts of a provincial hotel, sometimes they were billeted in private houses; but more often they dossed down in the open, under hedges or the wings of their machines, sheltering in their greatcoats from thunderstorms that muddied and water-logged the fields and drenched the flimsy contraptions they must fly again next day. Yet several pilots managed to nurse their original steeds throughout the retreat.

Their routine, as recorded by Carmichael, although mainly reconnaissance, included patrolling the rear of von Kluck's army, searching for targets for their makeshift bombs, and attacking enemy machines with rifle fire whenever opportunity offered. They were even called upon, when units of Haig's Corps lost contact with Smith-Dorrien's, to help in locating them. Towards the end of each day they would be looking for their next landing ground, often at dusk and sometimes after dark, homing as often as not on their motley column of transport. Yet rations and fuel, even letters and parcels, continued to reach them, striking proof of the efficiency of Brooke-Popham and his supply services, while the mechanics often laboured all night to repair damage and wear and tear to the machines. No wonder they found that whenever and wherever they could get their heads down they slept. Yet, as Carmichael wrote, 'it was a picnic' compared with the nightmare horrors and privations from which, for the infantry, there was no escape and no respite. This bred in them an anxiety and determination never to let their earthbound comrades down, accounting, in the days ahead, for sacrifices that in retrospect sometimes seemed obstinately wasteful. RFC leaders were imbued – even perhaps obsessed – with this same anxiety.

Meanwhile the retreat continued. Stragglers who had lost touch with their comrades were often visible from the air, some with their rifles and equipment but 'too many without either', noted Charlton, while the Corps staff, whenever he reported to them, looked increasingly haggard. As a former fighting soldier and Staff College graduate his sympathies were engaged, and he developed a guilt complex about his own comparative immunity. Meanwhile the military retreat was hampered by multitudes of civilian refugees and their animals and impedimenta, jamming the roads in a panic attempt to escape the consequences of enemy occupation. Their own vulnerability, too, increased as they harassed advancing enemy troops and transport columns with grenades, *flechettes* (steel arrows), and improvised petrol bombs. Yet they often felt safer in the air than on the ground.

'Our Second Corps was unable to disengage without fighting,' noted Dermott Allen, 'and was being heavily attacked by four German Corps on the line Cambrai–Le Cateau.' Anxious to know how the battle was going, GHQ called that afternoon for further air reconnaissance, and 2nd Lieutenant Vivian Wadham, with Allen as observer, was sent to search and report. For more than an hour they flew over the battle, the pattern of which Allen found clearly discernible. He watched the withdrawal of some British guns, the crews of which had all apparently been killed or wounded, and saw salvoes of enemy shrapnel bursting continually amongst the relief teams of cavalry as they galloped up. It was a sickening sight, when the smoke cleared, to see groups of wounded horses struggling panic-stricken on the ground. 'The general retirement along our whole line could be seen,' continued Allen, 'with officers rallying and reforming the infantrymen as they streamed back over the fields.' His urgent message pinpointing the German concentrations did not immediately reach GHQ, which was in the process of evacuating St Quentin, but on landing he was taken to report personally to Sir John French and his Head of Intelligence, a welcome sign of the enhancement of RFC prestige. He returned to the aerodrome to see aircraft hurriedly pre-paring to fly off to the south-west, directly into an approaching thunderstorm.

Such was the speed and pressure of the German advance that they were driven out of St Quentin after a single night, falling back on La Fère, fifteen miles to the south. Short of fuel and sustenance, forced down to 300 feet by the rain, and with all pinpoints blotted out by the mist, they had their digestive juices activated by a glimpse, through the murk, of the old sauce lorry, in the middle of the circus-like convoy heading for La Fère.

Left behind in hospital in St Quentin was the unfortunate Smith-Barry. 'What's going to happen to me?' he demanded of the hospital staff. The evacuation of the town, he was told, meant that immobile patients would be left behind. The idea of being exposed to the mercies of the advancing German Army did not appeal to Smith-B, and he shouted to one of the hospital orderlies, 'Get me a cab.'

Despite his broken legs he got himself out of bed, down the stairs, and into the horse-drawn four-wheeler that was somehow procured for him, placed his splinted legs on the front seat and, still in hospital pyjamas, was driven out of the west side of the town as the Germans entered the east. For the rest of his life he would limp and walk with a stick, but his escape was to prove infinitely more significant than anyone could have foreseen at the time.

The move south to a makeshift aerodrome at La Fère was accomplished without casualties despite the thunderstorm, pilots landing almost anywhere on the outskirts of the town. Two days later, on the 28th, with the noise of battle creeping ever nearer, those about to head north on reconnaissance or bombing were told to fly approximately 30 miles south-west from La Fère after completing their tasks and to look out for machines on the ground near Compiègne. Again the sauce lorry proved the best pinpoint. Here they were billeted in a school. The move was undertaken under continual threat of encirclement and capture, with no semblance of aerodrome defence, yet, according to Baring, spirits were high.

An appeal for high calibre replacement observers to improve interpretation of what was seen from the air brought two temporary attachments, Captains H.C. Jackson and E.W. Furse, both former students of the Staff College at Camberley. Jackson soon established a reputation as the best observer with the RFC, and his reports were given special credence at Smith-Dorrien's headquarters, exerting a notable influence on orders for each day's retreat. Jackson sometimes flew with Read, who found him an aggressive partner. 'Jackson spotted a German Taube machine,' wrote Read. 'I'd also seen him, but we'd done our job and I didn't want a fight.' According to Read, this was the conversation that ensued:

> Jackson, excitedly: 'Look, old boy!'
> Read, dismissively: 'Yes, I know.'
> 'I think we ought to go for him, old boy.'
> 'Better get home with your report.'

Jackson, more urgently: 'I think we ought to go for him, old boy.'

Resignedly: 'All right.'

Read altered course, and, as they passed the Taube, Jackson got in two shots with his rifle, which the German returned. This happened several times as the pilots manoeuvred, until ammunition on both sides was exhausted.

'Have you got a revolver, old boy?'

'Yes, but no ammo.'

'Give it to me then, old boy. And this time, fly past him as close as you can.'

Humouring Jackson, and assuming he carried some ammunition of his own, Read did as he was asked. To his amazement, as they got opposite the Taube, Jackson flung the revolver at the German's propeller. 'Of course it missed,' said Read. Honour being satisfied, they flew home. How Read explained the loss of his revolver, a court martial offence, is not recorded. Soon afterwards Jackson returned to his regiment, though this must surely have been coincidental: he went with one of the RFC's first individual mentions in despatches.

After two days at Compiègne under the protection of a military guard, with the enemy in the vicinity of the aerodrome, they moved again, eventually escaping across the Marne. The French retreat, too, continued, while understanding and confidence between the Allied commanders, so far from improving, deteriorated. Bombed at each new aerodrome, the squadrons only just got away as the enemy closed in. The Germans, having crossed the Marne a day after the BEF on 4 September, were now approaching to within 30 miles of the capital city, and pilots strove hourly to keep Headquarters informed.

'In spite of the great efforts of the First Army,' wrote von Kluck later, 'the British had escaped the repeated attempts to envelop them. They continued their retreat southwards.' He made one final attempt to settle with the British, but again they eluded him, finishing up

[43]

south of Paris at Melun. Eventually he abandoned the encirclement of Paris from the west and changed tack, turning to cut inside Paris to exploit the successes of the German Second Army on his left against the French: by executing a wheeling movement to the southeast he would develop a threat to the French flank. The switch was soon suspected by the RFC, Captain Furse, with 'Biffy' Borton as pilot, being among the first to interpret the signs and warn GHQ.

It seemed to the British, regrouping south of Paris, that the apparently endless retreat had been halted. Yet the High Command remained uneasy. Although pressure from their pursuers seemed to have relaxed, the enemy cavalry corps was unaccounted for; it had not been seen for two days. Misgivings multiplied as widespread air reconnaissance failed to locate it.

Joubert, with Allen as observer, was sent out in the late evening in an attempt to solve the mystery. They located groups of German infantry of about company strength on the BEF's right, presumably acting as advanced guard, but they seemed unusually thin for the numerous divisions supposed to be lurking behind them. Where, Allen asked himself, studying his map, were the serried ranks of marching men, the long columns of horse-drawn artillery, the endless supply trains they were accustomed to seeing? It was not until darkness was falling, when hundreds of bivouac fires suddenly twinkled, that the picture became clear. As Allen finished marking the main concentration of fires on his map, he and Joubert simultaneously made the same discovery. Around a haphazard formation of streams and backwaters which had been selected as watering-places, groups of horses were so crowded together that only one interpretation was possible: the missing German cavalry corps had been found.

Flying low in the gathering dusk, almost unseen from the ground, Joubert and Allen could easily discern the horses drinking at their waterholes, with horse lines concentrated round every farmhouse. They flew back at once to report.

It was clear beyond a doubt that von Kluck, ignoring the BEF to the south, had turned east of Paris to assist the German armies on his left, aiming at a final showdown with the French. Moving, undiscovered until now, across the British front, the cavalry corps had taken up their orthodox position in the van of von Kluck's wheeling movement.

The Germans believed that the Allies were virtually beaten and that victory was within their grasp. What they failed to appreciate was that the French retreat had been genuinely strategic, and that the French Army, although suffering severe casualties and forced to give ground, remained a cohesive force. Trusting to the strength of their eastern fortifications, the French High Command had even withdrawn troops from that area and formed a new army of 150,000 men to operate north of Paris.

When further air reconnaissance revealed that von Kluck's change of plan had left his right flank exposed, an opportunity presented itself for counter-attack, and General Joffre, exhorted and cajoled by General Galliéni, the military governor of beleaguered Paris, seized his chance. On 5 September he told Sir John French that he intended to take offensive action forthwith: next day he did so. For three days, from 6 to 8 September, on a 100-mile front from Compiègne east to Verdun, the course of the battle fluctuated. At one point the newly-formed French Sixth Army was under such pressure that 600 taxis were requisitioned to ferry vital reinforcements from Paris. But the line was held, and with the British now moving forward purposefully and recrossing the Marne, the Germans feared a breakthrough. On 9 September the German attack was called off and the entire invading forces, monitored hourly by the RFC, began a 40-mile fighting retreat to the River Aisne.

The 'Miracle of the Marne', recognised as one of the decisive military engagements of history, had been wrought, frustrating the German plan for a lightning victory. With the 'contemptible' British Army, according to the plan, cut off and rendered impotent, a brief but victorious campaign against Russia had been scheduled to follow. Instead, despite heavy casualties on both sides, the Allies had won a strategic victory.

Withdrawing northwards until they had crossed the River Aisne, the Germans halted on 13 September on high ground above the river. On the same day the Allies began to cross in pursuit, in torrential rain and under heavy fire. The RFC had moved forward in support the previous day, but that night the wind rose to gale force. The spotting and ranging of hostile batteries now became the primary task – but the RFC could not discharge it. Blinded by mist and rain, pilots returned to their bases empty-handed only to see their machines wiped out on the ground as the storm raged. One Farman of 3 Squadron, hurled 30 feet into the air, crashed on top of another in a lethal coupling. BEs of 2 Squadron, caught by a sudden shift in the wind before they could be pegged down, were blown across the aerodrome in fragments, presenting an appalling spectacle next morning. Screw pickets were used from this point on, undercarriage wheels were sunk so that wing skids rested on the ground, and vehicles were parked to windward as a screen. But it was a chilling reminder of the dependence of pilots and observers and their flimsy machines on the weather.

Even the hasty first-aid administered by the ground crews could not put more than ten or a dozen soggy machines in the air next day, and the reports rendered by pilots and observers, braving appalling weather in patched up machines, were inevitably sketchy. Unhappily, the best use was not made of such information as was gathered, at great personal risk, and heavy casualties were sustained in the Battle of the Aisne.

Frontal assault by infantry alone had been shown to be unavailing, and outflanking movements, attempted by both sides, were successfully countered. As Joffre moved his forces north-west, the BEF were switched to coastal defence, and the RFC, following them northwards, established themselves at St Omer. The enemy now concentrated on seizing the Channel ports, and the subsequent race to the sea developed into the First Battle of Ypres. Although often grounded by bad weather, the squadrons gave warning of German build-ups and reported accurately on troop movements. When the Germans did finally break through, a counter-attack by an improvised force achieved such success that Ypres, which thereafter stood as a symbol of Allied resistance, was saved.

A defended front line had meanwhile been established on a roughly north–south axis from Dunkirk to Compiègne before swinging east for Verdun and south again for the Swiss border. Within a few weeks the war of movement had thus given way to the beginnings of the static and attritional trench warfare which, punctuated by costly and abortive offensives, was to characterise ground operations for three and a half slaughterous years. In such a war, it was confidently expected, the Allies, with their greater resources of manpower, must prevail.

How the RFC would adapt to this change to static warfare remained to be shown. The story so far was not one of unqualified success, far from it, but the tiny nucleus of what was to grow into a massive force of nearly 300,000 officers and men and over 22,000 aeroplanes had justified its existence under enormous pressures. Their earlier reconnaissances had detected the enemy's attempt to encircle the BEF at Mons. As the BEF sought to escape they had hedgehopped to pinpoint their pursuers and even to harass them with makeshift bombs. Above all, with their French allies, they had spotted the wheeling movement executed by von Kluck's army and the dispositions of his forces which opened the way to victorious counter-attack.

'I wish particularly to bring to your Lordship's notice', wrote Field Marshal Sir John French in his despatch on the retreat, 'the admirable work done by the Royal Flying Corps under Sir David Henderson. Their skill, energy and perseverance have been beyond all praise. They have furnished me with the most complete and accurate information which has been of incalculable value in the conduct of operations. Fired at constantly both by friend and foe, and not hesitating to fly in every kind of weather, they have remained undaunted throughout.'

5

THE BEGINNINGS OF BATTLE FATIGUE: 'BOMB THE KAISER!'

AFTER the nomadic, precarious but eventful life of their first weeks in France, pilots and observers of the four RFC squadrons began to complain of boredom as the front line stabilised and they found themselves scouring much the same ground every day. Yet they accumulated a variety of fresh experience that winter.

It was not long, either, before the enemy co-operated in relieving their boredom. This co-operation, far from fraternal, lay in the proliferation and improved accuracy of their anti-aircraft weapons in and behind the front line. In the early days the German system of ranging was so rudimentary it was derided, and by skidding sideways on an even keel after each salvo it was generally possible to avoid the next one. 'Biffy' Borton was one of the first to demonstrate this. Each time the ploy succeeded he gave one of his typical chuckles and sang out, in triumph, a phrase from a George Robey music-hall monologue charged with that comedian's infamous innuendo: 'Archibald, certainly not!' Abbreviated to 'Archie', it became the standard RFC vernacular for all anti-aircraft fire.

As the shell-fire intensified, pilots sought to fly at safer heights. But it was difficult to get most machines above 5,000 feet, and below that they were vulnerable. Rifle fire frequently caused minor damage and casualties, but only a lucky hit was likely to be serious; indeed, to come back without boasting a few bullet-holes suggested over-caution. Flesh wounds, so long as they were minor, could be a source of envy, resulting in a few days' leave, perhaps in Paris. But sympathy sometimes gave way to hilarity, as when Mapplebeck, although seriously hurt in the groin, sustained a real 'flesh' wound by losing the tip of his penis.

Mapplebeck had set off with the idea of destroying a German observation balloon by dropping petrol bombs on it, taking no observer or firearms to save weight. At the mercy of an intercepting enemy aeroplane, he had been wounded while manoeuvring to bomb that instead. Losing consciousness, he had recovered in time to land without damaging his machine. This exploit, coming on top of another in which he blew up an ammunition train, brought him a DSO to soothe his wounded feelings.

There was less laughter over the prospect of a direct hit from Archie, though even here familiarity bred fatalism, though hardly contempt. 'Very glad to get out of the heaviest fire I have been under so far,' noted Strange on 4 October. 'At one time shells were simply bursting all round; in addition to the deafening roar of their guns we could easily hear the whistle and shriek of bullets.' Yet he added: 'I am getting used to being shelled now, almost indifferent to it in fact; it is marvellous that we don't get hit more often.'

Read, too, out spotting for the artillery, was heavily Archied. 'The air was thick with shell-bursts from anti-aircraft guns,' he noted. He kept turning, diving, and climbing, but in doing so he lost height. Finally at 3,000 feet a shell exploded near enough to put a splinter through his propeller, but he managed to limp home. The fair-minded Read could not help but admire the zeal of the German gunners: they had brought nothing down by shell-fire as yet but it was not for want of trying, and it was only a question of time. 'Archibald can reach you at 10,000 feet, it belches forth dirty yellow and black smoke and chain shot, and the noise of the shell bursting is almost enough to make one stall the machine with fright.' This battering, in an ever more concentrated form, was what the crews were to face for the next four years.

'It was normal for each crew to do two operational flights a day,' wrote Carmichael. 'Owing to low cloud, close reconnaissance and artillery observation were frequently carried out below 1,000 feet, and one Henri Farman was hit twelve times in three days.' Read wondered how his nerves would stand this daily bombardment. 'I notice several people's nerves are not as strong as they used to be. I'm sure Archie is responsible for a good deal. I would not mind quite so much if I was in a machine that was fast, and would climb a little more willingly.' Pilots were already conscious of the inadequacy of their machines.

Read was up four times on 23 October, totalling four and a half hours, mainly observing for the artillery. 'A good dressing-down from Archibald,' he wrote, 'and the Germans shelled the airfield after we got down and we were very lucky to escape. Some of the shells burst much too near and I could hear the pieces of shell whistling past. Well, I suppose the end will be pretty quick if one of Archie's physic-balls catches one. I think I would rather it caught *me* than crumple up Henri, because one would have too long to think when falling from 4,000 feet.' The helpless, falling-leaf plunge to destruction, more and more protracted as greater heights became commonplace, was to be a recurring nightmare. At least there was no resentment at the absence of parachutes, which had barely been tested yet in practical form for heavier than air machines.

After two months in France, pilots were beginning to feel, if not to show, the symptoms of battle fatigue. '27th October: arrived back at camp at 5pm,' wrote Read, 'nearly dark, feeling dog tired and absolutely fed up, having done 14½ hours' flying in the last five days, 4½ again today, and tonight I do not feel as if I shall be able to go on for long at this rate without an easy. It isn't that my nerve is going but I feel stale.' Archie was not the only threat. Every flight was a gamble, either through engine fallibility or structural decay caused by weeks of exposure to storm winds and torrential rain. One Henri Farman climbed so ponderously that it was opened up, disclosing a rear spar so saturated that it was sprouting fungus.

One of the most abiding handicaps was the meteorological phenomenon of the prevailing westerly wind, which drove them deeper into enemy territory than they sometimes intended and then treacherously delayed their return. For Farman pilots it was especially

Hugh Trenchard. 'He gave the RFC determined leadership and a clear sense of direction.'

W. Sefton Brancker. 'Deceptively foppish' – but a man to be trusted.

J.F.A. 'Josh' Higgins. 'All bum and eyeglass.' Seen here with the squadron mascot.

Frederick H. Sykes. 'Hampered by a personality which strongly engendered mistrust.'

Charles James Burke (centre) with pilots of No. 2 Squadron, the first across the Channel. On Burke's left is 'Ferdy' Waldron. Top left (standing) is Hubert Harvey-Kelly.

Hubert Harvey-Kelly refuelling his Maurice Farman Longhorn on a pre-war flight. 'He kept one in roars of laughter the whole time.'

Philip Bennet Joubert de la Ferté, said to have a memory as long as his name.

John D.B. Fulton. Bought himself Bleriot monoplane and began experimenting with it on Salisbur Plain.

(Left): Bob Smith-Barry. 'An awful little boy' – but he revolutionised air training world wide.

(Right): Louis Strange. Handsome, fearless, innovative, irrepressible, he flew right through the war and again in World War II.

Dermott Allen. His verbal dilations, despite a stammer, were worth waiting for.

'Bron' James. 'Much the best artillery officer out here.'

W. Sholto Douglas fought Boelcke and Immelmann. 'I was thoroughly frightened.'

Matinée idol Bobbie Loraine. 'Actor and airman, hero and lunatic.'

Will Rhodes-Moorhouse VC. 'If I must die, give me a drink.'

Aidan Liddell, VC, MC, in the uniform of the Argyll and Sutherland Highlanders. He gave 'an astounding display of fortitude'.

Fokker fodder. BE2c's of No. 13 Squadron about to take off for France, October 1915.

The Fokker *Eindecker*.
This is an EIII.

A Vickers FB5 Gunbus in
enemy hands after being
forced down intact.

The cockpit of a DH2, the
RFC's first single-seat fighter.
'Spinning incinerator?' Not
so, said Lanoe Hawker.

Oswald Boelcke. 'Our brave and chivalrous foe.'

Max Immelmann. Anima
magnetism – and the inve
the Immelmann turn.

Manfred von Richthofe
called Lanoe Hawker 'T
English Immelmann.'

A captured Albatros DI. With the DII and the
Halberstadt it turned the tables on the RFC in the
autumn of 1916.

burdensome; an optimum speed of under 60 m.p.h. could sometimes leave them hovering motionless over the lines, the target of every gun within range. Lieutenants Abercromby and Small, of 5 Squadron, elected to abort a reconnaissance when, turning into wind on the outward flight to test its strength, they found they were actually going backwards.

The greatest toll still came from crashes on take-off and landing, not always from pilot error. Read himself, given a new Henri Farman, smashed it when the engine failed at a critical moment near the ground. It was his third crash in a week. He tried to pancake, the wheels touched prematurely, and the machine did a somersault. Everyone thought he and his observer must have been killed, but miraculous escapes from apparently fatal crashes through structures breaking up at slow speed were among life's compensations. Read was knocked out, but he got away with a broken nose. His sympathies were all for the man in the front seat, Major L.B. Boyd-Moss, the squadron's senior observer, incapacitated with back injuries.

As if the inherent dangers in handling these obsolescent machines, coupled with the broadsides of the enemy, were not enough, the shoot-first-and-face-questions-afterwards mentality of the troops, however understandable, was bound to cause tragedy sooner or later. When disaster came, the victims had descended to 1,000 feet in order to locate the batteries whose fire they were briefed to observe, only to be mistaken by the infantry for an enemy reconnaissance machine. German small arms fire had been generally wayward, but the British gunners, mistaking the Union Jack painted under the fuselage for the Maltese Cross, were right on target. Lieutenant Cyril Hoskins and his observer Captain Theodore Crean were the unfortunate crew, the plane caught fire and came down in flames. It was the first of the many 'flamers' that were to become the obsessive dread of some of the most famous 'aces' of later years.

The French, whose infantry never seemed able to distinguish British aircraft from German, and who fired impartially at either, were taken to task on one occasion with impeccable courtesy by the stuttering Dermott Allen. 'Do you m-mind t-telling your m-men not to f-f-fire on us,' he asked a French infantry commander. 'It p-p-puts us off.' To this masterpiece of understatement the commander pleaded, in justification, that the red cross on the Union Jack was all that was clearly visible from below and that it was sometimes mistaken for the German marking. Typically, it took the loss of Hoskins – one of the pilots who had helped to identify von Kluck's wheeling movement – and his observer to induce a change. Wouldn't it avoid confusion, suggested the French commander, to adopt the same circular marking as the French? National pride could not quite stomach this, but a compromise was reached in which the French roundel replaced the Union Jack but with the blue and red circles in reverse order (red centre and blue on the circumference, with white between).

Although a sharp reminder to British troops ordered them not to fire on any machine unless they were absolutely certain of its identity, pilots and observers, with their military background, understood without bitterness that ground troops were bound to be trigger-happy when there were aeroplanes about. It was just another hazard to be faced. Here too it was a wonder so few aircraft were hit. However, special detachments of flights and squadrons briefed to work direct with chosen formations in forward areas were already operating, and as this closer association between soldier and airman developed, errors became less frequent.

Valour, fear, aggression, apprehension were often a matter of mood. A good night's sleep could work wonders. Forty-eight hours after committing his self-doubt to his diary, and twenty-four hours after his flight commander Philip Herbert, noticing his nervous tension, had offered him a week's leave in England to recharge his batteries, Read noted: '. . . feel awfully fit today, after my long lie-in this morning.' He appreciated Herbert's thoughtfulness, but 'I do not want a rest. Feel as fit as when I came out.' Nevertheless it was a welcome treat next day when he and fellow pilot Alexander Shekleton had a day off to go into St Omer. He noted that the methodical Shekleton, whom he greatly admired, had not broken a single machine since coming out with the squadron in August. Yet on a recent 'show' (every trip was a 'show', not a sortie, or a mission, or an operation), he had had to turn back through feeling unwell.

'A few days rest at St Omer would do him good,' diagnosed Read.

The strain got to everyone sooner or later. 'After a long day's flying you feel you have had enough and don't ever want to go up again,' wrote Strange, 'but after a day's rest you are as keen as ever.' His reactions varied. 'One day you come down absolutely sick and tired of it all, while on another you just feel you have enjoyed a fine flight.' Rifle fire still caused more casualties than Archie, but 'it is the continual shelling that puts such a strain on you.' It would have been horribly monotonous, thought Strange, but for the opportunity to drop a few bombs on their tormentors. These home-made bombs, released haphazardly over the side, with no bomb sight devised as yet, could be little more than an irritant, but 'you feel you can get a bit of your own back.'

Squadron commanders, many of whom did little or no flying themselves, had already concluded that every man's stamina was exhaustible. Flight commanders, too, seeing their charges' reactions in the air, soon knew, when men turned back, whose excuses were genuine and whose were not. For all Read's independence of mind, there was never any question of his reliability, but he soon had further evidence of an intention to rest him. 'It was my turn for recce today and he [Herbert] went instead. Never felt less like wanting a rest in my life.' This may well have been a false bravado, the onset of a compensating aggression that could lead to recklessness. Anyway, when a major strike of a dozen machines was mounted next day, 1 November, Read was again omitted.

The target, openly and unashamedly, was none other than Kaiser Wilhelm himself. 'Hang the Kaiser' was to come later; it was 'Bomb the Kaiser' now, perhaps the first modern attempt to assassinate a war leader. The order came at the crisis of the first battle of Ypres: the Kaiser was reported by Intelligence to be inspecting forward troops at Gheluvelt, six miles east of Ypres. His approximate programme was known, and each pilot was given a place and time to bomb. 'Everyone went off bristling with bombs,' recorded Read. Observers had been left behind to increase the bomb-load. Critical of the exaggerated expectations of the effects of aerial bombing, Read added, with conscious irony: 'No official information so far

[53]

that the Kaiser is dead.' Carmichael provided an excuse: 'He had left before we arrived.'

Nerve and luck were apt to run out simultaneously; it happened too often to be purely coincidental. 'The next day,' wrote Read, 'I stopped one with my leg at 5,000 feet over Courtrai and was invalided to England.' The day he got his 'Blighty' wound, as he put it, his observer was the famous actor and pre-war flyer Robert Loraine.

Matinée idol Bobbie Loraine had earned his pilot's certificate on 21 June 1910 at the age of 35. A complex and contradictory character, he could be charming and infuriating in turn, and as an actor his undoubted talent was rarely taken seriously because of his physical beauty. As a pilot, as in life, he was erratic and accident-prone, but his courage was undoubted, and he enjoyed great success as a pioneer aviator before the theatre reclaimed him. His French air mechanic, asked whether his boss was lunatic or hero, answered that he was both in turn – and often both at once. Volunteering his services on the outbreak of war, Loraine was accepted by the RFC – but rejected as a pilot when he crashed several machines. He still pleaded to go to France, and Brancker sent him there as an observer on probation. He was attached to No. 3 Squadron and was soon flying his first reconnaissance.

A fortnight after Read's departure, Loraine himself was wounded, so seriously that 'for a week it was touch and go'. But he recovered, and his acceptance of the supporting role of observer, despite a reputation for megalomania, compensated for his record at Farnborough. In September 1915 he was back in France as a flight commander with 5 Squadron, where his popularity with the mechanics contrasted sharply with the resentment of his pilots at being ordered about by 'this old man', who was not a brilliant pilot, was an erratic disciplinarian, and worst of all, was an *actor*. An attempt to force him out failed, and he was awarded the MC for shooting down an Albatros (after which he dropped a sympathetic message over the lines). 'We had to admit,' said his 19-year-old senior lieutenant, 'that there was something in Loraine.'

Read, too, got back into action in France that year, but it was not intended that he should stay long. The experience of some of those first across was needed to form new squadrons at home and help with training. Gordon Shephard, Biffy Borton, George Carmichael, Lionel Charlton and many others had either gone or were earmarked, and Read was booked for a spell of instructing. 'A great loss' was the squadron's verdict on Read's departure: but he would be back.

Gibb Mapplebeck, after hospitalisation in Paris, refused home leave. He had been befriended by an attractive nurse who made him an equally attractive offer: she would drive him to a villa in Nice to recuperate – in the bosom of the Mumm family, to which she was related. There he was introduced, among other luxuries, to vintage champagne. The medicine worked, and early in 1915 he was back on the squadron, fully operational in all respects, according to his brother Tom (the nurse was not consulted).

6

HUGH DOWDING: LANOE HAWKER: LEWIS AND JAMES AND THE 'CLOCK CODE': AERIAL PHOTOGRAPHY: TRENCHARD LANDS IN FRANCE

ARLY attempts at air fighting were often more farcical than frightening, though the first sight of an unidentified aeroplane never failed to somersault the stomach. Willie Read's experience, apart from the Jackson incident, had not been untypical. 'Had an awful fright today. Saw a strange-looking machine coming along at the same height, 5,000 feet. We got rifles and revolvers ready — and then we saw, to my great relief, that it was a French Voisin.' They passed each other peaceably at 20 yards' range. Not so the Taube which, unarmed but carrying bombs, Read had tried to chase off while observing for the artillery. 'He was about 300 feet higher than we were,' which Read reckoned was quite a handy position in a Henri, giving his observer a good field of fire. While Read closed the range, his observer opened up with the rifle. 'The German turned twice, trying to get us immediately below him so as to drop a bomb on us, but I kept clear.' Bombing a stationary ground target without a bombsight was speculative enough: hitting a moving target with a bomb in mid-air reduced air combat to the level of Mack Sennett comedy. Yet Read took it seriously. Two machines flying one above the other on the same course at the same speed might conceivably narrow deflection to something like point-blank level.

Armament in RFC machines remained crude and ineffectual: the Bristol Scout, for instance, a single-seater tractor of pre-war racing design, was fast and manoeuvrable by contemporary standards, but its potential was cramped for this reason. It was also delicate and unforgiving, which meant that any examples available tended to be appropriated by squadron commanders, not always the best shots. The armament improvised initially was a rifle with a sawn-off stock clamped to shoot diagonally forward, missing the propeller but leaving the pilot aiming round corners. Josh Higgins loved it, but unlike Borton he did not wear a monocle merely for show, and Carmichael wrote that 'unfortunately his sight was not equal to his enthusiasm'. He could never get close enough to his quarry to shoot.

After being ordered to abandon the mounting he had improvised for Penn-Gaskell's machine-gun, Strange introduced an alternative modification in his Farman which moved the pilot forward to the front cockpit. This allowed the observer to stand up in the rear cockpit, secured by a safety strap, and fire in almost any direction. It was the best arrangement so far devised, though Strange recorded a rueful comment. 'The noise the observer made when shooting over my head was something terrific.'

Strange's Farman was the last survivor of the original machines of No. 5 Squadron that had left Gosport two months earlier; every other Avro or Farman had been crashed or otherwise lost. Finally, on 15 October, Strange was allotted a brand new Avro 504, all-British apart from the 80 h.p. Gnome engine. It was a development of this type, the 504K, that was later to become the standard trainer in the RFC. Any sentimental attachment to the old Farman was minimised for Strange by the much improved performance of the Avro. This improvement, however, did not extend to the armament, which was much the same as that generally adopted as standard in the Blériot with the observer in the front seat firing a rifle upwards and rearwards over the pilot's head. When a German reconnaissance machine overflew the aerodrome at St Omer, Strange and his observer, eager to test the Avro in combat, ran to their machine and climbed in without helmets, coats, or maps. It took them an hour to get within range of their quarry, and then the observer fired 70 rounds at about 100 yards' range before the German pilot escaped unscathed into cloud.

Angered at their impotence, they unwisely chased after the German – and with their primitive instruments, and without maps, they got lost. Running out of fuel over the North Sea, they managed to glide in and land on the beach near Le Touquet. It was a chastening experience, teaching Strange that it was folly to put themselves at risk in combat with such feeble armament. Against orders, he fitted a cross-bar between the centre section struts over which a rope was slung, so that a Lewis machine-gun, mounted on top of the fuselage decking, could be hauled up on a pulley in mid-air, free to fire in all directions. A chance to use it came on the morning of 22 November when, on reconnaissance with observer Lieutenant Freddy Small, they spotted a German reconnaissance machine heading for St Omer at about 7,000 feet. Recognising it as an Aviatik, Strange climbed and turned in front of it, manoeuvring for position. When he gave the signal, Small fired two long bursts, after which Strange closed the range to 50 feet only to see the German observer taking pot shots at them with a Mauser pistol. Small was in the act of changing a drum, standing up immediately in front of Strange, when his face suddenly contorted and Strange saw blood oozing from his gloved hand. Nevertheless Small completed the drum-change, and after another long burst the Aviatik pulled up, stalled, and side-slipped before flattening out and coming down near some reserve trenches on what appeared to be the British side of the line.

Landing at an aerodrome nearby, Strange delivered Small for first aid before cadging a motor-cycle to see what had happened to the Aviatik, convinced that Freddy Small had shot it down. He found it just where he expected, with twenty bullet holes in it but apparently capable at the very least of having continued into friendly territory. Presumably the pilot thought he had already crossed the lines. His observer and superior officer, of the Prussian Guard, was furious at being captured, and when he discovered his NCO pilot was uninjured he broke away from his captors, knocked him down, and began kicking him viciously before he was overpowered and dragged away.

There were differences of opinion between pilot and observer in the RFC – as with Read and the impulsive Captain Jackson – but there is no record that they ever came to blows. The status of observers fluctuated with the tasks they were expected to perform, and a practice that crept in of taking almost any volunteer was disapproved of and corrected; but it was soon established in the RFC that the man at the controls was in charge.

The rage of the German observer, although perhaps understandable, was a poor advertisement for discipline and comradeship in the German Air Force. But it seems – unfortunately for the RFC – to have been untypical. A shortage of trained observers probably accounted, in this instance, for the selection of an unsuitable man. The choice in the RFC, too, was limited, and a call went out for men with artillery experience to volunteer for transfer. One who answered the call was a young man named W.S. Douglas, Sholto Douglas. Training for these volunteers was 'extraordinarily little', wrote Douglas, 'nearly all at the front'. He told the story of a flight with Harvey-Kelly when, because they were both big men, they had discarded rifles to save weight. The confrontation that followed with an unarmed 'hostile' produced frustration on both sides but ended with a smile and a comradely wave. A bond quickly developed between opposing airmen, a bond of shared experience in an exciting new element, which sometimes brought reactions approaching chivalry.

Recruits from the artillery brought with them an experience of battle conditions which was invaluable; but they did not all prove eagle-eyed. 'We have a lot of new observers,' Mapplebeck learned from his CO on his return to duty. 'The pilots have to do all the observing nowadays.' Many pilots felt that they were better placed anyway for accurate observation, while observers found themselves concentrating increasingly on gunnery, and this eventually became the pattern.

The first squadron to reinforce Nos 2 to 5 in France was No. 6, the squadron which, when in embryo, had prepared the ground at Dover for the August departure. Under Major John H.W. Becke, with a mixture of BE2a's, BE8s, and Farmans, they flew to Bruges on 7 October, to support a ground force that was to attempt the relief of Antwerp. This plan was soon overtaken by events, and they joined their fellow squadrons at St Omer. One of the flight commanders was Cyril Newall, who, 25 years later, when World War II began, was to hold the highest post in the Royal Air Force. And a man of even greater subsequent achievement actually flew with the squadron as an observer; this was Captain H.C.T. Dowding.

Hugh Dowding had shown his peculiar brand of stubborn independence by negotiating a unique no fly no pay contract with the Sopwith school. He had refused to put down a penny of his own money: they were to teach him to fly on credit, and he would pay up when he got his ticket and could claim a refund from the army. Sopwith must have been impressed by the man's implicit assumption of superiority, because he agreed.

On mobilisation, Dowding had been retained by Trenchard to run the despatch camp at Dover, and he chafed at being kept in England, just as Trenchard did, pestering Trenchard for a posting to France. The more extrovert, self-assertive Trenchard was up against a man of quiet reticence who proved as stubborn as himself: it was a case of the irresistible force and the immovable object. When the exasperated Trenchard finally relented, however, it was with characteristic abruptness, and with a sting in the tail. 'You want to go to France, do you? Very well, you shall go tomorrow – with No. 6 Squadron, as an observer.' Dowding was undismayed. Once in France, the right opening would come.

Dowding's facility for seeing things as they were and not as others, especially his seniors, wanted to see them, was soon demonstrated. The day before Antwerp fell he was sent to observe the roads west of the city. He spotted Belgian troops but no Germans, and after filing his report he was called, with his squadron commander, to the headquarters of Sir Henry Rawlinson, the general responsible for that section of the front. 'You say you saw no Germans?' queried Rawlinson. 'But they're there, we know that they're there.' Dowding stood his ground. 'Well, sir, you wouldn't wish me to say I'd seen them if I hadn't. It was a very clear day, and if there had been any Germans I must have seen them.' This direct contradiction of a general marked Dowding as a man not easily shaken from his convictions.

Of more immediate significance, perhaps, was the arrival with 6 Squadron of a 23-year-old former sapper of varied experience named Lanoe Hawker. Hawker had given up a naval cadetship through ill-health before studying at the RMA at Woolwich, meanwhile learning to fly at Hendon, and in March 1913 he transferred to the RFC. A man of moods, sensitive and introspective, with an exceptional capacity for friendship, he was deeply upset by the loss of a contemporary in Gordon Bayly, who, with Waterfall, had been the first RFC crew to be reported missing. Hawker, who had become a friend of the family and was in love with Bayly's sister Beatrice, still hoped to hear that his friend had survived as a prisoner, as indeed Waterfall had.

Whether the loss contributed to Hawker's belligerence is uncertain: he seems from the first to have set an exceptional standard of tenacity and aggression, foraging deep into enemy territory to seek antagonists. His pugnacity, especially when facing superior numbers in inferior machines, did much to inspire that eagerness for combat which was to characterise the operations of the RFC. No one was more skilful at handling and fighting the BE2c than Hawker, and he became the first of the RFC's great fighter pilots, many months before the emergence of Albert Ball. This, though, was in a period when Trenchard, deploring the publicity given to French and German 'aces', as against the anonymity of the tenacious and vulnerable men on artillery co-operation, succeeded for a time in keeping the Press at bay.

Opportunities for aerial combat that winter, though, were rare, and the RFC, like its adversary, was frequently grounded by the weather. There was no thought as yet of forming specialist homogeneous scout squadrons; each squadron held one or perhaps two scout-type machines on strength. When conditions allowed, pilots demonstrated the aggressive spirit that was to become a byword by bombing approved targets and ground-strafing enemy troops. But with the front now static, the dominant factor was the artillery, and far and away the main priority lay in co-operating with the gunners to seek out and pinpoint enemy batteries and correct the fire of our own batteries on these and other targets.

As with air fighting, so with artillery co-operation, early attempts had been crude, cumbersome and chancy, such vague phrases as 'south of the final e in Compiègne', or 'above the d in Gueudecourt', to give an enemy battery's position on the map, being both wordy and imprecise. A simple and accurate method was urgently needed. Even more pressing was the need to pass the required information rapidly and efficiently from air to ground. Klaxon horns blasting messages in morse code from the heavens were at the mercy of wind and weather. Signalling lamps and flags were too easily misread, and coloured flares, fired by Very pistol, were limited in scope. The ideal method of communicating information to battery commanders was by wireless telegraphy, and attached to No. 4 Squadron, it will be remembered, was a wireless flight. It was during the opposed crossing of the Aisne that the spotting of hostile batteries became of prime importance, and when the war of movement was succeeded by static trench warfare, the artillery settled into prepared positions and the pilots of the wireless flight came into their own. Co-operation extended to taking up gunnery officers to help with aerial survey work, while the sites of enemy batteries were confirmed and noted on maps. Positions were continually revised and copies of amended maps circulated. Soon the wireless flight was expanded into No. 9 Squadron, with Hugh Dowding to command. He had found a niche.

Much of the flying was done by two pioneers whose enthusiasm and perseverance had overcome the usual peacetime inertia and eventually convinced their masters of the potential of wireless telegraphy in aerial reconnaissance. Both men were lieutenants in the Royal Engineers, both had learned to fly in the summer of 1912, and both were signals specialists in their middle to late twenties who knew precisely what they were about. Their names were Donald Lewis and Baron (usually contracted to Bron) James. Lewis proved a natural organiser and leader, James had been head of his house at Harrow. Recognition of their expertise brought demands for their services exceeding all possibility of supply. Because of their bulky wireless equipment – it weighed 75 lbs and filled the front cockpit of their BE machines – they were obliged to fly solo, controlling their machines with one hand, frequently under fire, and operating the wireless 'buzzer' with the other. How much the Harrow-educated James enjoyed these lone forays is not recorded, but Lewis was said to revel in them. 'Lewis came in from spotting with his machine full of holes,' was one comment. 'I believe he likes it!' These two machines, easily recognisable from the way they were flown, seemed ubiquitous to the troops on both sides that winter.

Both men were professionals who worked tirelessly to improve their effectiveness and for whom soldiering was a career. Like most of their kind, they had no personal quarrel with the enemy and respected his professionalism in turn. 'Why,' demanded Lewis of a visiting 'personality' (it was Hilaire Belloc), 'do the newspapers abuse the Germans in so foolish a manner?'

Running commentaries on the fall of fire, which would be acknowledged by the laying out of ground strips by the battery (there was no reverse communication by wireless, just a transmitter in the aeroplane and a receiver on the ground), followed a familiar pattern. After contact was established and the firing started it might continue: 'A very little short ... Fire ... Fire ... Fire again.' Each time a correction was transmitted, two or three minutes might elapse as the gun-crew adjusted their aim and resumed firing. Then might come: 'Over ... Over and a little to the left ...' Another short wait, and then, of the next salvo: 'You were just between two batteries ... Search two hundred yards either side of your last shot ...' The same terse, staccato, dispassionate morse later announced that success was imminent. 'You have them!' (The exclamation mark was understood.) Four minutes later would come: 'Hit ... hit ... hit!'

Another twenty minutes might be spent over the target, refining directions and reporting results. Finally, after an hour or more of intense concentration, half-smothered at times by Archie, it was time to leave after a job well done. Unemotional as it appeared, the pilot's understandable relief was implicit in his final message: 'I am going home now.'

The use of such approximations as 'left', 'right', 'short', or 'over', to indicate the correction required, still lacked precision, and eventually Lewis and James devised between them what they called the 'clock code'. Having already learned to 'square' his maps and those of the battery commander with whom he was working, Lewis fashioned a transparent celluloid disc, with a centre spot which he placed at the chosen point on the map. Eight concentric circles on the disc signified varying distances from the target, from 10 yards to 500, each circle being identified by a letter. A set of radial lines on the disc numbered by the hours on the clock face, one to twelve, indicated direction. Thus by means of a brief coded message containing a single letter and a single number the target was located with some accuracy, time was saved, and the chances of error reduced if not eliminated. As each shell landed the pilot or observer signalled to the gun battery the ring within which it had fallen and the hour on the clock face. The squared map and the 'clock code' became standard on the western front throughout the war.

The greater sophistication of air-to-ground wireless communication conferred no immunity on its practitioners, and it is surprising, in view of their persistence, that the two pioneers lasted as long as they did. James, who had been promoted to flight commander on 6 Squadron, was ranging a battery alone as usual in July 1915 when his BE was hit by a shell and plunged to destruction. There is no doubt that the Germans recognised the specially adapted plane and knew of the pilot, and fears that James's last moments must have been anguished were dispelled when they dropped a note to say he was dead when he fell.

Gordon Shephard, by this time commanding 6 Squadron, had believed that in Strange, Hawker and James he had the three best flight commanders in France. Of James's death he wrote: 'He is a great loss to me: much the best artillery officer out here. He also started wireless in the RFC and has never been properly recognised by the authorities.' He and Lewis had shown, from the earliest days, the momentous contribution to artillery shoots that wireless communication could make, and as more compact equipment became available it was widely introduced.

At about the time of James's death, Lewis was appointed to succeed Jack Salmond in command of No. 3 Squadron, by then equipped with the French-built Morane Parasol (a monoplane two-seater); but this did not stop him flying, nor did a subsequent promotion to command what had become the RFC Second Wing, with the rank of lieutenant-colonel. But on 10 April 1916, with an artillery officer to whom he had been showing the results of his own battery's trench mortar fire, he was shot down and killed by a direct hit from the guns he was pinpointing.

The loss of such men could be ill-afforded, stimulating Trenchard to order that squadron commanders must no longer be risked over the lines. Many were to chafe under this ruling, though there were some who ignored it.

Although there were pre-war pioneers of aerial photography in the RFC as well as of wireless telegraphy, mainly in No. 3 Squadron under Salmond, most of them were little more than dabblers, pilots who modified their own personal cameras and took photographs mostly for the fun of it. But on one pre-war exercise they undertook a genuinely useful experiment by producing a photographic mosaic of Britain's south-coast defences, to show what might be done. Outstanding was Lieutenant Charles Darley who, with Lieutenant George Pretyman and others as pilot, began taking photographs experimentally once the front stabilised.

'I don't think anyone else in the squadron did any photography at this time,' wrote Darley later. 'I had to buy my own chemicals in Bethune, develop the slides in an emergency dark room in the stables of the château in which we were billeted, and send them out. I personally took the results each evening to Corps HQ (Fourth Corps) and explained them, often to Henderson himself.' But Darley found non-flying topographers slow in comprehending aerial pictures, each of which, from medium altitudes, covered only a small area. Often in a Blériot he could get no higher than 4,000 feet, but he began to do better when the squadron got a few Morane Parasols in the New Year.

The potential value of Darley's work went unrecognised at first, still less was much thought given to the science of photographic

[65]

interpretation. As an instance, Sholto Douglas, when he became an observer on 2 Squadron, was appointed air photographer to the unit 'because I had had a box camera as a boy'. But towards the end of January 1915, a map of the trenches that Darley had produced largely for his own use so impressed Jack Salmond that he took it to Headquarters. Sykes, who had seen something of French efforts in this field, sent Salmond's brother Geoffrey to study their methods, and it was immediately apparent to the younger Salmond that he was among experts. A four-man Wing Photographic Section was formed under Lieutenant J.T.C. Moore-Brabazon, holder of the Royal Aero Club's Aviator Certificate No. 1, with Sergeant Victor Laws, who had been taking photographs from airships and man-carrying kites since 1912, as his technical chief. (In time Sergeant Laws was to become Wing Commander Laws, chief photographic officer with the Air Component of a later British Expeditionary Force.) These men set about designing a camera specifically for air use.

After the departure of the four operational squadrons to France in August 1914, only two RFC stations remained in action at home: the Central Flying School at Upavon and the Royal Aircraft Factory at Farnborough. Thus the task given to Trenchard by Henderson, under Brancker's patronage, to recruit and train men to form new squadrons for France, demanded pertinacity and drive. None of the machines being built by a variety of firms under Government contract – the BE2c, the Avro, the Henri Farman, even the Vickers Gunbus – possessed the armament or fighting qualities that were going to be needed when the Fokker *Eindecker*, with a synchronised machine-gun firing through the propeller arc, was introduced in the second half of 1915. Meanwhile the bulk production of the BE2c that was in progress at selected factories would ensure that the majority of pilots and observers would be condemned to battling for their lives in this sedate and comparatively toothless biplane ('Stability Jane' was one of its nicknames), against infinitely superior opposition for many months to come. Yet it is hard to see how it could have been otherwise. Most of the new designs ordered were little beyond the development stage, and if there was a lack of urgency in conceiving and building more advanced types, and in improving their fire-power, the requirement was barely apparent as yet. Certainly Brancker and Trenchard, left with a seemingly impossible task, rose to the challenge, acting expeditiously and often precipitately to speed the progress demanded by Kitchener. New RFC stations were opened, pilots, riggers, mechanics and fitters were recruited and trained, and the nucleus of new squadrons was formed. Expansion was the watchword, and if it was largely expansion for its own sake, that was inevitable. To expect Brancker and Trenchard to have hastened slowly in the circumstances would surely be unrealistic. But for the airmen they were taking such trouble to recruit and to train, quantity without quality was to prove lethal.

For three months Trenchard channelled his frustration at being denied what he deemed his rightful place at the front into sowing the seeds of abundant growth. But in November, at last, came the call to France. Ironically it emanated from a decentralisation of the RFC in France masterminded by Sykes. As the line stabilised, and the work of the crews became more and more localised, squadrons worked increasingly in direct contact with corps commanders, and in November these attachments were regularised by the creation of Wings. The First Wing, consisting of Nos 2 and 3 Squadrons, was to operate with the Indian Corps and the Fourth Army Corps, the Second Wing – Nos 5 and 6 Squadrons – with the Third Army Corps. Command of the Second Wing fell, on promotion, to Lieutenant-Colonel C.J. Burke (Pregnant Percy). Command of the First Wing went, again on promotion, and at Henderson's insistence, to Trenchard. No. 4 Squadron and the wireless unit (soon to become No. 9 Squadron) were retained under the direct control of RFC Headquarters. A Third Wing was formed in March 1915 under Brooke-Popham.

At home, the Military Wing at Farnborough, formerly under Trenchard, was split into two central commands, an Administrative Wing, with headquarters at Farnborough, commanded by Lieutenant-Colonel E.B. Ashmore, and a Fourth Wing, a training wing, with headquarters at Netheravon, commanded by Josh Higgins, repatriated after picking up a thigh wound in his Bristol Scout. This wing embraced squadrons preparing for France.

1915

[7]

THE BATTLE OF NEUVE CHAPELLE

'If you can't fly because of the weather,
I shall probably put off the attack.'

DOUGLAS HAIG

TAKING aerial photographs with the new box camera, the 'A' Type, manufactured by a civilian firm to the photographic wing's specifications, required the observer to hold the camera by its straps or handles, while he leant over the side of the cockpit and performed eleven distinct operations for the first exposure and ten for each subsequent one. During this laborious process, he was usually being well quartered by Archie. Yet by early February the whole German trench system facing the British First Army had been photographed, building up a detailed mosaic of the area.

It was with the help of this mosaic, and the registering by the RFC of enemy batteries, strong points, and possible transport bottlenecks, that Sir John French based his plans for a spring offensive. Weakened though he was by his losses so far, and unable to deliver a heavy or prolonged assault, he had nevertheless been able to expand the two corps of the original BEF into armies, and he was anxious to keep them active and to exploit any enemy tactical weakness that air reconnaissance might reveal. It soon became clear that the Germans in the village of Neuve Chapelle were holding a salient in no great strength, open to assault on two sides.

The immediate objective of the British plan, devised in detail by Sir Douglas Haig and agreed by French on 19 February, was to

[71]

capture the village. If this went well, the Aubers Ridge, further to the north-east, might come within their grasp, threatening Lille. This was a capture that might prove of lasting significance. 'For the first time,' records the official RFC history, 'the British army went into action with a picture of the hidden intricacies of the enemy defences.'

Against this, Intelligence reports suggested that the Germans would be capable of rushing in substantial reinforcements within a day or so. Here, too, in addition to their primary tasks of reconnaissance, photography, and artillery co-operation, the RFC was asked to play a vital role. They were to bomb railway facilities in the enemy's lines of communication so as to harass and hamper the drafting in of reinforcements.

The bombing of enemy targets had hitherto been of a whimsical, free-lance nature, carried out with makeshift bombs that were man-handled over the side, aimed at targets of opportunity. Pilots and observers engaged on other duties got a wry satisfaction from hitting back at their tormentors, but the influence of their bombs on the campaign was nil. Now they were to be detailed for the first serious attempt at disrupting enemy communications by bombing. Indeed, a bombing mission aimed at a specific target was to spearhead the assault.

Early in March Haig sent for Trenchard and revealed something of his plans. What could the RFC contribute? It was the first time the two men had met. Strangely incoherent at the best of times, Trenchard was the worst possible advocate when arguing a case verbally, and he began badly, his explanations sounding faltering and inadequate even to him. But Haig didn't want to be bothered with detail: he was judging the man. Trenchard scored through avoiding exaggeration and not promising more than he was confident he could deliver. He indicated the positioning of the reconnaissance and artillery co-operation squadrons of his wing in relation to the First Army and described the tasks of which he believed them capable, subject always to the weather. This, he warned, could quite conceivably ground the whole force, Second and Third Wings – the wings that were to bomb the lines of communication – as well as the First.

Haig's reaction gave tremendous encouragement to Trenchard. 'I shall expect you to tell me before the attack whether you can fly, because on your being able to observe for the artillery, and carry out reconnaissance, the battle will partly depend. If you can't fly because of the weather, I shall probably put off the attack.'

Trenchard could hardly believe his ears: here was a brass-hat who properly appreciated the contribution the RFC could make. Even if Haig's reaction was no more than a psychological ploy, aimed at inspiring the RFC to redouble its efforts by emphasising, even exaggerating, its importance to him, it was a welcome change from the cynicism of the past. Indeed, it was the start of a rapport between soldier and airman that had its foundations in the pre-war Brancker reconnaissances in India.

Soon after six o'clock on the morning of 10 March, three machines of No. 3 Squadron set out to bomb what was believed to be an enemy defence headquarters at Fournes, six miles east of Neuve Chapelle. The raid was led by Eric Conran (now promoted to captain and flight commander), with whom McCudden still flew occasionally; but on this day the man in the front cockpit was squadron commander Jack Salmond. The other two pilots flew solo in order to increase their bomb-load. Attacking at three-minute intervals, they reported direct hits which set fire to the target; Conran and Salmond made doubly sure by dropping their bombs from a hundred feet in three separate runs. Whether the enemy's battle control was seriously hampered by this raid was not known.

The main tactical bombing programme for the first day of the battle was timed for mid-afternoon, to coincide with a lull in the infantry attack. Considering the hopes of violent disorder that were vested in it, it is instructive that it consisted of no more than a single aircraft on each of two targets. Such were the illusions, in 1915, of the effects of aerial bombardment, curiously naive from men who would have given a much more realistic estimate of the weight of shell-fire required to eliminate a similar target.

Confidence in the men who were to discharge the duty was similarly blithe, though perhaps with better reason. Both the men selected had served with the BEF from the beginning. Strange was the natural selection on 6 Squadron: following reports that German reinforcements were already passing through Courtrai station by the trainload, that was to be his target. He would be flying a BE2c. Stripped of all armament and with an empty front cockpit to compensate for the weight of the bombs, it had crude bomb-racks fitted under wings and fuselage for carrying and jettisoning three French-made bombs. With these weapons, each weighing less than 25 lb, Strange was expected to devastate a target whose destruction, he was led to believe, was a matter of life or death to the soldiers of Haig's First Army. Imagining the reception he was likely to get, he did not rate his chances highly.

The second target chosen was a railway junction north of Menin station, some ten miles short of Courtrai. Here the choice of pilot, although limited, was less clear-cut. The task was allocated to Strange's old squadron, No. 5, where the squadron commander decided that the most suitable bomb-carrier was the new single-seater Martin-and-Handasyde S1, a small sporting tractor biplane which had been adapted for military purposes and fitted with a Lewis gun above the centre section, firing outside the radius of the propeller blades. It had a maximum speed of 87 m.p.h. and was capable of carrying a 100 lb bomb. Competition for the privilege of ferrying this monster was limited to the only three men on the squadron who had mastered the Martinsyde – Carmichael, Rabagliati, and Wilson. All three were among the original contemptibles, 'Daddy' Wilson, at 37, being much the eldest. But it was bulk rather than age that disqualified him, and Carmichael and Rabagliati tossed up for the honour. Carmichael won.

The two attacks were roughly synchronised. First to take off, at 15.23, was Strange in the BE2c, with Carmichael following seven minutes later. The weather, which had promised well enough for Haig to open his attack, was beginning to break; the cloud-base had lowered to 3,000 feet, and visibility was poor. To keep track of his position Strange stayed below cloud, but as he neared the lines the flashes of the German guns, piercing the afternoon gloom, and the dark puffs that hung with menacing proximity around him, forced him to seek the cloud's sanctuary. He aimed to the north of Courtrai, easing gently down to the level of the cloud base before sighting the clustered roofs of the town. A diving left-hand turn and there below him, through straggly low cloud, he saw the railway, running in a straight line towards his target.

Flattening out below two hundred feet, he followed the track and almost immediately sighted the station. It was time to descend even lower. A train was standing at the platform, several coaches long, probably a troop train. Perhaps after all he could do something positive for his comrades in the infantry. A solitary German sentry was aiming a rifle at him from the platform, and he remembered the hand grenade he had thrust into his flying jacket before take-off. Gripping the control stick with one hand, he withdrew the grenade with the other and extracted the pin with his teeth. Then he pitched it overboard. It fell at the sentry's feet as the plane careered on.

Small-arms fire was now converging on him from all angles, and suddenly the platform roof was rushing towards him. He yanked back on the stick and pulled the bomb-release lever before skimming the roof. After twisting his neck round to see where his bombs had fallen, he straightened up to find his escape route blocked by a stockade of telegraph poles. Another yank on the stick and a climbing turn and he was shooting a final, kaleidoscopic glimpse at the mayhem he had evidently caused.

Three dozen bullet holes in the BE2c testified that once again Strange's luck had held. He was lucky, too, in getting first-hand evidence, through an Allied agent in Courtrai, of the results of his attack. It had indeed been a troop train standing at the platform, about to unload. Seventy-five men had been killed or wounded and rail traffic had been delayed for three days.

Carmichael's brief was no less compelling: his task, too, was directly related to the ground battle. And whereas Strange had carried a stick of bombs any one of which might score, success for Carmichael depended on a single shot. Aware how chancy this must be, he had a hole cut in the cockpit floor between his feet so that he could look vertically down at the railway line, the better to judge his approach.

With its unaccustomed load the Martinsyde climbed ponderously, and even before he crossed the lines at 4,000 feet a shell fragment pierced the fuselage inches behind his back. Picking out the railway line leading to Menin, he switched off his engine with the idea of making a stealthy approach, but as he descended to 800 feet a solitary machine-gunner dissuaded him and he restarted the engine, dived for the track and clung to it, descending from 300 feet to 100. The sleepers raced by under his feet, but he still had to judge the right moment of release. This he had worked out beforehand, and five seconds after Menin station passed beneath him he pulled the toggle. Nothing happened. He had expected the aeroplane, freed of its load, to soar involuntarily; the release mechanism must have failed. But then the blast seized the Martinsyde and thrust it forwards and upwards on a billowing cushion of air. Half-concussed himself, but collecting his senses, he looked back to see a column of black smoke rising 200 feet or more above him, the point of impact, so far as he could judge, being just about right, a few yards short of the junction.

Turning east to confuse the German gunners, he found himself over a parade ground, with troops rushing to and fro, taking pot shots at him. He threw a rifle grenade at them to put them off their aim, but his machine was badly hit, one engine cylinder was put out of action, and his only remaining lateral control was his rudder. Nevertheless by low flying and jinking he crossed the lines without further damage and landed safely after what he afterwards called 'two hours 10 minutes of a somewhat exhilarating afternoon'.

On that first day the German positions were overrun and the village was captured, but next day, 11 March, the weather clamped. Little could be seen from the air, and artillery co-operation ceased. The Germans were rushing in reinforcements and preparing to counter-attack, and the British were unable to exploit their advantage. However, early that morning three pilots of No. 4 Squadron took off in darkness from Bailleul, using electric torches to monitor their instruments, their objective another rail junction, this time at Lille. They had moved up to Bailleul to be near their target, their course was indicated by lamps on the ground, and they were to arrive over the target at daybreak. Apart from a short practice flight at St Omer on the previous evening, none of them had flown at night before.

Sending three aircraft against a single target might seem more realistic, but the weather was such that Major Charles Longcroft, the squadron commander, sought a cancellation. Someone at GHQ, surely with his tongue in his cheek, said that if the raid was successful it might end the war: therefore the pilots must go. The order, described as ridiculous by the forthright Longcroft, brought disaster. One pilot crashed soon after take-off and the other two failed to return. One of these was shot down and died from his injuries, the other, also shot down, but enjoying better luck, was Mapplebeck. He had just set fire to his BE2a when he glimpsed three figures approaching out of the mist. Hiding in a convenient ditch, and subsisting on chocolate, he somehow avoided discovery from a massive search before being kitted out by the Belgian he eventually approached. But the garb only accentuated his height, and he was grateful to another Belgian for hiding him for a week in a garret in Lille. He did not know that he was being personally protected by the Mayor. When the hunt got too hot he moved on, tramping across Belgium, always at night and always in fear of compromising the good people who helped him. After another night in a ditch near the Dutch frontier he crossed while the sentry was lighting his pipe, and the shots that were fired at him missed. Next he crossed Holland, took passage on a fishing smack, and presented himself at the War Office, where they feigned surprise: they had known of his escape but dare not reveal it for security reasons. Among the mementoes he brought with him was a poster offering a reward for information leading to his capture and threatening death to anyone who helped him, signed by the German military governor of Lille. Sadly the Mayor of Lille, M. Emile Jaquet, and three other Belgians, were later apprehended and shot by the Germans. Mapplebeck was back with his squadron five weeks later.

The third day of the battle was marked by storms and enemy counter-attacks, and the British took no more ground. RFC tasks included locating the line of battle and reporting its fluctuations. The bombing of tactical targets, too, was resumed. This time the raiders included No. 1 Squadron, recently arrived from England under Geoffrey Salmond and comprising eight Avros and four of the hitherto unlucky BE8s.

Further bombing raids were made, notably by Pretyman of 3 Squadron on the railway station at Don, where he blew up the centre carriages of a train; but an accident to a Morane of the same squadron while it was being loaded with French bombs resulted in an explosion in which twelve men, including the pilot, were killed and four more seriously wounded.

Later that day it was discovered that some of the bombs had not gone off, and Jack Salmond, commanding 3 Squadron, put the wreckage out of bounds until further notice. 'Next morning,' wrote Pretyman afterwards, 'we found some of the wreckage had been cleared and the remaining bombs removed and buried. Major Salmond had done this himself at daybreak.' Fifteen years later Jack Salmond was to succeed Trenchard as chief of the air staff, to be succeeded in turn by his brother Geoffrey.

The influence of the RFC on events at Neuve Chapelle lessened as the weather worsened, and the very limited success of the First Army – a dent in the German line little more than a mile wide and 1,000 yards deep – scarcely justified the gamble or the casualties. For many it was their first experience of battle, and one young infantryman who later transferred to the RFC described it in detail, from the initial bombardment, when his rifle 'steamed like a boiling kettle and became so hot I could scarcely hold it', to the taking of about 300 prisoners, many of them wounded, and the occupation of their forward trenches. The reporter was Private Goodban, Monty Goodban, of Clapham High Street, where his father ran a domestic store. 'We have to wade through trenches waist deep in water, which is like soup and as cold as ice, not much worried by our personal discomfort, the excitement is too great. This is our first glimpse of real warfare. What a sight. I cannot describe it.'

Hungry, wet, and smothered in mud, they were ordered to make a bayonet charge, across fields which were believed to contain the original German trenches. 'What a gruesome sight. Dead and wounded strewn everywhere, the latter groaning and moaning in the most heartrending manner. There are British and Germans all mixed up lying side by side.' An attempt to take the new German positions after dark failed disastrously. 'As soon as the Huns discovered us they opened a terrific fire of machine-guns, rifles and artillery, cries of chaps getting hit go up on all sides.'

Goodban and three of his pals lost touch with their battalion and tramped back to their base. 'Arrive there at 5.30 a.m. absolutely done up. All day chaps kept turning up who had got lost in a similar manner to ourselves.'

That summer Goodban 'stopped about 20 pieces of a rifle grenade with his leg' and was evacuated home. Commissioned in January 1916, he volunteered for the RFC later that year, one of a great many who felt, with some justification, that they had had enough of the trenches and would like to try something else. On 7 May 1917, after 22 hours 50 minutes' solo flying, he was posted back to France to fly two-seaters on 22 Squadron. It was a period of catastrophic inferiority in the air, especially for newcomers, and twelve days later he was shot down and killed.

Insulated as they were from the horrors of the trenches, it was through transfusions like this that the men of the RFC were continually reminded, even in the midst of appalling losses, how lucky they were.

8

THE RFC's *RAISON D'ETRE*:
ITS FIRST VC:
THE BALLOONATICS

'No call from the army must ever find the RFC wanting'

HUGH TRENCHARD

P REPARATIONS for a combined Allied offensive, intended to dwarf the limited objectives of Neuve Chapelle, were begun in mid-April with an assault on an eminence dominating the Ypres area – Hill 60 – to test the enemy's strength. But the plan was pre-empted by a surprise German assault. A recently captured German prisoner had been boasting of a lethal gas which he claimed was about to be used against the Allies to eliminate the Ypres salient and force a major breakthrough. Special reconnaissances were flown to see what could be detected, but it was not until 22 April that Louis Strange, cruising to and fro over the salient at dusk, noting the flashes from the German 17-inch howitzers which had begun the bombardment that morning, watched aghast as the evil secret unfolded: borne on a breeze that for once was blowing off the German trenches, a stream of bilious, yellow-green smoke was being wafted westwards towards the Allied lines. The captured German infantryman had been right: this could only be poison gas. Strange landed and reported at once to Headquarters.

The eruption was indeed a cloud of toxic chlorine gas, and its effect was immediate, the bewildered Allied troops, after a moment's asphyxiation, fleeing in terror. The gap was eventually closed, and

minor counter-attacks restored the position, but ground was conceded. Subsequent air reconnaissance prepared the Allies for a
German attack north of the salient, and this was beaten off, but a
second gas attack forced further withdrawals.

When agents reported strong reinforcements moving towards the
salient, the two newly-formed RFC squadrons attached to Brooke-
Popham's Third Wing at St Omer, Nos 7 and 8, were ordered to
attack trains and rail centres in the feeder line, armed with 20 lb
bombs. When these attacks proved futile (some of the crews lost
their way, some of the bombs failed to release), First Wing were
called in to attack vital targets. Four machines were despatched, each
carrying a 112 lb bomb, but even of these, only two reached their
objectives.

One pilot, from 2 Squadron, was briefed to bomb the railway
junction and marshalling yards outside Courtrai station, 35 miles
behind the lines: Intelligence reports indicated that as many as 40,000
troops were being rushed through Courtrai to the salient, making
this a priority target. The pilot chosen was a man whose background
was unique. Because his grandparents, cattle-farming in New Zea-
land, were childless, a liberal Maori chief had sent one of his daughters to co-operate in bearing them a child. She duly obliged, and
father and stepmother adopted the girl that resulted as their own.
When the girl grew up she married her step-mother's brother; soon
afterwards they moved to England. Their second child, Will Rhodes-
Moorhouse, now twenty-five, was the pilot briefed to bomb the vital
rail junction at Courtrai.

Small and slight, he exuded vitality, and he was well known pre-
war on both sides of the Atlantic as a fearless and even recklessly
competitive car racer and aviator. Marriage did not change him, and
as soon as the war started he joined the RFC.

The vortex of fire that was known to surround Courtrai seemed
likely to be almost impenetrable, and Rhodes-Moorhouse was
warned not to come down too low. But he knew well enough that
the only chance of creating havoc with a 112 lb bomb, with no
proper bomb-sight, was to attack from low level.

Air interception was extremely unlikely, and there were no

navigation problems, so observers were left behind. The man spared in Rhodes-Moorhouse's machine was Sholto Douglas.

The expectation that a single aircraft with a single bomb could eliminate a sprawling and complex target emphasized the misconceptions of the Allied commanders. Pilots knew better, but they wouldn't admit it; for them, optimism was everything. Rhodes-Moorhouse took off in his BE from the aerodrome at Merville at five minutes past three that afternoon, 24 April 1915, and set course in good heart. Crossing the lines at 1,000 feet, he got through safely to Courtrai and easily located the junction. He dived on the target, dropped his bomb from 300 feet, and felt the blast as it exploded.

At once he was the focus of a nest of guns ringing the junction, backed up by hundreds of rifles and machine-guns fired by the assembling troops he had come to delay. A direct hit from a gun being fired at him point blank from the belfry of a church rocked the biplane to its roots and a bullet pierced his thigh, but somehow he pulled away. Bleeding profusely, with his plane crippled, his best chance of survival was an immediate forced landing; but half the value of the destruction he had caused lay in making it known, and he headed back to the lines. Wounded again, this time in the abdomen, he could still have crash-landed with honour and sought medical help, but surrender was not in his lexicon. He must file his report.

Among those who helped him from his machine back at Merville was Sholto Douglas. 'We were amazed,' he wrote afterwards, 'that he ever managed to get back.' A cluster of bullet holes in the observer's seat told him what his own fate would have been.

Rhodes-Moorhouse still shunned medical help until he had made his report; he made it verbally, in Trenchard's hearing. Mortally wounded, he disclaimed any tag of heroism. 'If I must die,' he told the padre, 'give me a drink.'

A last request that his body be sent back to England, to be buried on the family estate in Dorset where he had planned to build a cottage for his wife and infant son, was granted by Sir John French. Three weeks later he was posthumously awarded the Victoria Cross, the first RFC man to be so decorated. He had set an example that many would follow.

This was not quite the end of the Rhodes-Moorhouse story. In 1937 his son joined 601 (Auxiliary) Squadron, fought as his father had done in France, from the same airfield at Merville, won the DFC in the Battle of Britain, and was killed in his Hurricane at the height of the Battle, on 6 September 1940.

We know what the son achieved. What of the father? Confirmation came that he had indeed blasted the junction, delaying enemy reinforcements, and an official despatch rated his 112-pounder 'the most important bomb dropped in this war so far'. Yet his contribution stood out more for its rarity than for its influence on the battle – the Second Battle of Ypres, as it came to be known. Of 141 bombing raids launched between 1 March and 20 June 1915 only three could be regarded as successful, and the cost in men and machines was prohibitive.

What was needed was a complete reappraisal of the effectiveness of aerial bombardment, together with a more sophisticated bomb-sight than the crude contrivance, consisting of little more than a few nails and some lengths of wire, improvised by Louis Strange with the help of an Intelligence Corps officer, Second Lieutenant Robert Bourdillon, whose fascination with the subject led to his transfer, late in 1914, to the experimental flight at the Central Flying School. A graduate of Balliol and St Mary's Hospital, London, Bourdillon had returned to Balliol as a Lecturer in Chemistry. He had enlisted in August 1914 and was now 25.

At CFS, by mid-1915, Bourdillon had combined with others to evolve a less primitive instrument. Speed over the ground was measured, with the aid of a stop-watch, by two sights taken on one object, the same principle being employed to give the correct angle for release of the bomb. The new CFS bombsight was adopted by both the RFC and the RNAS, gave much improved results in the offensive that autumn, and remained in use on the western front until the end of 1916.

A review of bombing policy was also attempted, one conclusion being that bombs were most effective when dropped on railways, especially in cuttings, where the blast was contained, diversion diffi-cult, and the line might be blocked for days. A more realistic estimate of the weight of bombs required to destroy a given target was also attempted, with the resolve that British and French air units should co-ordinate their attacks in future in strict conjunction with ground operations.

The British had clung to Ypres as a symbol of their obligation to Belgium, and the salient, although diminished in size, was held. The RFC kept GHQ in touch with enemy movements as they occurred and even in one instance gave a résumé of the battle as it unfolded, penetrating the veil for army commanders otherwise 'blinded by the fog of action'. Meanwhile many hundreds of hours were flown spotting for and directing the artillery, achieving a fair degree of mutual understanding. Much could be seen from the air, photographed, and even sketched by war artists, that was otherwise hidden – but against this, mist and low cloud could frustrate even the persistence of a Bron James or a Don Lewis, blanketing the battleground just when enlightenment was most wanted. Some commanders were still sceptical of the reliability of air reconnaissance, leaving crews to risk their lives to get information that was mistrusted and even ignored. 'Where,' asked one corps pilot bitterly, 'would the artillery be without us?'

Another VC, in circumstances similar to those of Rhodes-Moorhouse – severely wounded twenty miles beyond the lines but concerned only to get back with his report, together with machine and observer – was recommended in June by Pregnant Percy, then commanding the Second Wing: the presumptive pilot was none other than Biffy Borton, a man who in other respects so looked after his comforts that he sent home for all manner of luxuries. But there was one circumstance that told against him: he had survived. His chuckle when he realised he'd missed a posthumous VC may be imagined. Curiously enough his brother 'Bosky' (they were family nicknames) *did* win a VC – in the army.

For the armies of the BEF, support that summer for continued Allied aggression in the Neuve Chapelle region was attenuated and then suspended through heavy losses and a shortage of ammunition, so that reorganisation and the replenishing of supplies in preparation for the major offensive planned for the autumn became the rule. It was a time of consolidation, too, for the RFC. But there was no diminution in the work of reconnaissance and artillery co-operation during the build-up. Sorties began with a telephone call from the observer to the battery with which he would be working to learn or confirm the objectives, check map co-ordinates on the large-scale squared map, and agree the time the shoot was to start. Over the target the observer, having let out his trailing aerial, called up the battery in morse code. The ground operator put out his coded strips, and when all was ready the observer called upon the battery to fire. After he had reported on the fall of shot, the battery corrected its sights and fired again. Eventually, when the range was found, the observer signalled the OK. Throughout this sequence, as always, he would be under fire.

A weakness became apparent in the lack of standardisation of procedures for air/ground communication. Squadrons and flights were allocated to work with particular batteries, they exchanged visits, mixed socially and developed a mutual respect and understanding; but there was a loss of efficiency when they were called upon to work with unfamiliar units. There was also a conspicuous void, frustratingly revealed during the fighting for Hill 60 in April, when splendid opportunity targets, which a number of guns were in a position to have engaged, escaped unscathed because no appropriate signals procedure existed. Only in No. 1 Squadron (one flight of Avro 504s, two of Morane Parasols), was a method evolved, the observer sending an agreed signal and a map reference, the code letters meaning 'I see a good target. All guns please engage it.' Pressed by Geoffrey Salmond, Henderson called a conference in June, and a pamphlet was issued laying down a basis for future army/air co-operation.

Following his posting to No. 6 Squadron as an observer, Hugh Dowding, having drawn attention to himself by his confrontation with Rawlinson, had soon found an appointment more to his liking by being placed in charge first of the wireless flight attached to 4 Squadron and then of the two wireless flights that formed 9

Squadron. When it was decided, in February 1915, that wireless should play a part in the routine work of every squadron, 9 Squadron was disbanded, to become the first home wireless school, and Dowding was appointed to take over No. 16 Squadron, with the warning that its pilots had been driven too hard by his predecessor, and that it was not a happy squadron.

To seventeen-year-old Second Lieutenant Herbert Ward, who had learned to fly as an Eton schoolboy and was now reporting to 16 Squadron at an aerodrome near Merville, the rather squalid farmhouse that served as Dowding's office accentuated Dowding's dry, scholarly appearance and general air of detachment: he seemed decidedly off-putting. 'Pernickety, interfering, querulous, and impossible to work with', was the summary of Dowding by a contemporary, Archibald James, who later gained distinction in Parliamentary and diplomatic circles.[1] But when Dowding quoted to Ward something from Hilaire Belloc's *Cautionary Tales* and Ward was able to volunteer the next couplet, a working relationship seemed possible. Dowding then announced his intention of accompanying Ward on a test flight to see if he was ready to go over the lines, which Ward interpreted as a brave and avuncular gesture. He evidently passed the test, because afterwards he was presented with a BE2c for his personal use. Yet it was soon apparent to him that Dowding lacked that outward show of geniality that makes for popularity, and he must have seemed a perverse choice for the task of revitalising a tired and disaffected squadron. Ward could not help but notice that two of the flight commanders cordially disliked each other, and he felt that Dowding could have been more forthcoming in knocking their heads together – a curious parallel with his failure to intervene nearly a quarter of a century later in the Keith Park/Leigh-Mallory Big Wing controversy. 'He seldom allowed his dry style of humour to emerge from behind a barrier of terseness,' wrote Ward later. 'Thus he acquired a reputation for unfriendliness. We were an oddly assorted group.'

1. Wing Commander Sir Archibald James, MC, educated at Eton and Trinity College, Cambridge, retired from the RAF in 1926 and was MP for the Wellingborough Division of Northants, 1931–1945.

Ward's great friend on the squadron was Duncan Grinnell-Milne, who described the atmosphere under Dowding as one of 'chilliness and gloom'. But whereas Ward, a more gentle creature, bore the Germans no personal ill-will, Grinnell-Milne detested them. Ward liked the BE2c for its ability to extricate itself from the most provocative handling, and he enjoyed photographic missions because of the concentration demanded. Having manoeuvred his machine over precisely the right map square, he then had to insert each fresh photographic plate into the externally mounted camera, at an angle which would prevent it from being snatched out of his hand by the force of the airstream. Most of his reconnaissances were relatively uneventful until October, when he had cause to appreciate the superiority of the Fokker *Eindecker*. He was eventually shot down on 30 November, a few days before his eighteenth birthday; but he survived as a prisoner, and later made a successful escape.

At home, the need for an officer of more senior rank than Brancker to argue the RFC's corner in the battles for men and material led to Henderson's return to the War Office. Replacing him, on 19 August, in command of the RFC in France, was Hugh Trenchard. He had arrived where he had always expected to be.

Trenchard's guiding principles were simple and clear-cut. First and foremost, the RFC was part of the British Army, and no call from that army must ever find the RFC wanting. This was the RFC's *raison d'être*, never to be forgotten. Second, air superiority must be fought for, gained, and retained at any cost, necessitating an aggressive posture even in adversity. Third, war could not be conducted effectively without casualties. It was in this spirit that he sent countless men to face the enemy against fearful odds – in plain words, to their deaths. There were times when he was forced by events to temper all-out aggression with defensive measures, but he relied throughout on the morale of his crews, visiting them frequently and encouraging them personally. Many spoke of the inspiration his presence provided. Yet they were well aware of his ruthlessness. He

[87]

accepted, as Haig did, that it was a war of attrition, in the air as on the ground: of keeping it up longer than the Hun.

Archibald James, the man who had been so dismissive of Dowding, thought Trenchard the greatest man he had ever met, calling him 'a totally inarticulate genius'. His opinion was later supported by historian Arthur Bryant.

The man in France who proved of the greatest value to Trenchard was Maurice Baring, who had been Henderson's ADC. Yet, as opposites, the brusque, dominating military personality and the urbane, highly literate civilian, they viewed each other with mutual suspicion. 'I'm prepared to let you stay on a month's trial,' said Trenchard in his abrupt manner. 'If you're no good to me you'll have to go.' Then, softening, he added: 'I'd also like you to give me a trial. Whatever you've heard to the contrary, I think you'll find I'm not such a bad person to work for.' It is revealing that even the orderlies employed by Trenchard supported this. After returning to England to consult Henderson (an act of loyalty to his old boss and friend of which Trenchard did not disapprove), and finding nothing there to excite or distract him, Baring agreed to the trial month with Trenchard. Shortly came the famous incident with the Oxford marmalade, a jar appearing on the breakfast table soon after Trenchard had expressed a wistful longing for it. 'I see you've got a memory, Baring. I shall use it.'

Baring was to accompany Trenchard wherever he went, and the command 'Take a note, Baring,' was to become a catchphrase. It proved the happiest of partnerships, linking Trenchard's single-mindedness, mastery of detail, and flair for getting things done with the interpretive powers of Baring, who translated Trenchard's apparent incoherences into lucid and convincing prose. Trenchard's reputation for following things through, never letting them rest until they were accomplished, owed much to Baring and his note-taking.

Henderson's return released Brancker to take over the Third Wing. Ashmore, formerly commanding the Administrative Wing in the UK, took over the First Wing from Trenchard, and Jack Salmond replaced Burke (sent to Canada to discuss an air training scheme) in the Second. Of the twelve squadrons then in France, Ashmore and

Salmond controlled four each and Brancker three: the twelfth was attached to GHQ. A squadron still consisted of three flights of four aircraft with one or two spare machines. Not all squadrons were homogeneous, but the ubiquitous BE remained the most numerous. Other types were Morane Parasols, Maurice Farmans, and the Vickers FB Gunbus. All squadrons carried one or two so-called scout machines in addition, on the principle, later reversed, that each should have a leavening of offensive aircraft, rather than grouping such aircraft together in special squadrons. The Germans, initially, made the same mistake.

Useful aids to artillery co-operation, hitherto neglected by the RFC, were kite balloons. Prompting came from Douglas Haig, who had learned of the successful spotting and direction of artillery fire by the French using hydrogen-filled balloons. Before the summer ended, four kite balloon sections, lent by the RNAS and comprising fourteen balloons in all, were in position opposite their German counterparts, responsibility for them being gradually taken over by the RFC. The advantage of the balloon was that, unlike the aeroplane, it could stay up all day, only needing to be hauled down for a change of observer, or to escape air attack. A deterrent to such attack could be provided by anti-aircraft batteries located nearby; but there was no defence against long-distance shelling. Although captive, the balloon came complete with its own transport and engine-operated winch and could be moved to a different site as required, giving a degree of mobility.

Working generally in pairs, the observers climbed into the basket suspended from the balloon and were released to a height of anything from 1,000 to 5,000 feet. They carried with them the call-sign of the relevant battery and the co-ordinates of the target which the battery was to engage. A telephone line gave them direct communication with the battery. Having located the target, the method of correcting the fall of shot was exactly similar to the code established by Lewis and James for the corps squadrons.

So useful was the information gleaned by the 'balloonatics', as they were known, that within a few months there were more than 40 kite balloons dotted along the British front, roughly parallel but a mile or more behind it. Their enemy opposite numbers were equally numerous. 'In good, cloudless weather,' wrote balloonatic G.D. Machin, 'visibility was superb.' But being so near the front they had 'no cosy safe billets as the aeroplane flyers had', recalled another balloonatic, Sergeant Bernard Oliver. Instead they found themselves 'camping in dug-outs in the mud . . . often blasted out by shell fire.'

Whereas batteries could remain silent when aircraft were spotting, and thus remain virtually invisible, opening up again for business when the air was clear, they could hardly hold their fire all day, while balloon observers, relieved at intervals, could remain aloft indefinitely. 'In theory,' wrote 18-year-old balloonatic Leonard Field (who later, appropriately enough, rose to the heights of brigadier), 'nothing could be simpler.' But he cited one factor which made life 'less than idyllic', and a second 'which tended to shorten it'. As with heavier-than-air machines of the period, the wind was a natural enemy. It acted on the balloon capriciously, spinning it round on itself 'like a polo pony', always choosing the most inconvenient moment. Worse still was the bending of the cable in a gusting wind, which might yank the balloon down by a hundred feet or so. Then, when it eased, the balloon shot up again. All these disturbances could happen suddenly and speedily, with disastrous effects on the balloonatic's stomach.

One who was not so fortunate as Field was West-End actor and entertainer Basil Hallam, whose balloon broke free in a high wind – an occurrence not totally unknown – and, in the prevailing westerly, headed for the trenches. Hallam and his companion, after jettisoning their maps and instruments, took to the parachutes provided, but Hallam's failed to open.

The third particular unpleasantness was enemy action. Just as the British disliked being overlooked by prying eyes, so did the Germans, and like the British they took active steps to prevent it. 'One of the more interesting sights on a fine clear day,' reminisced Field, 'was that of an enemy fighter suddenly appearing out of nowhere and shooting up a row of balloons like a child popping toy ones at a

Fair.' Field was grimly aware that his compatriots in the front line found this as diverting as did the Germans. 'Life in the trenches was monotonous,' he said, 'and this gave them something to look at.' There were also the German heavy guns, some of which could be elevated sufficiently for target practice on kite balloons.

'It was a matter for nice judgement when to get to hell out of there,' said Field. Sometimes, if the winch crew thought things were getting too hot, they pre-empted the decision, hauling the balloon down. But if a balloon was set on fire, the occupants jumped.

The extreme vulnerability of balloon observers was recognised from the start by the provision of parachutes. 'You'll have to jump out of one of these things sooner or later,' Field was told on arrival, 'so you may as well learn how to do it now.' The learning process was minimal. 'When you go up, just jump out. Oh – and try to keep your feet together when you land.'

Parachutes, of the C.G. Spencer Static-Line (Automatic) type, were attached to the outside of the basket, packed into an elongated wicker container shaped like a candle-snuffer. When the observer jumped, his weight pulled the canopy open. 'You hoped, first,' said Field, 'that the parachute would come out of the container without tearing itself, and second, that it would open.' For Field it always did, but only after he had fallen several hundred feet, when 'it opened with a bang which shook you in the tenderer parts.' Bernard Oliver recalled that, because of the discomforts of the Spencer-type harness, 'we made our own harness with webbing and string.'

'These flyers were the pioneers of the parachute,' wrote Oliver, and the claim is well-founded. The types of parachute and packing, however, would have been too bulky for the confined cockpits of the time, and for use in heavier-than-air machines a miniaturisation was needed, also a means of clearing obstacles, interior and exterior. The problem should not have been insurmountable, but there were other obstacles to be cleared. For instance, it was argued that air crews, unlike balloon observers, were in a position to defend themselves, removing, it was suggested, the moral imperative.

Because of the intense protective fire that was assembled on the ground by both sides, balloon-busting became a specialised and

[91]

highly dangerous sport. Jimmy McCudden, after a particularly fraught attempt, wrote: 'I was very glad to get down, and since then I have never liked balloons.' Albert Ball, at a second attempt, got his balloon and set it on fire, but his engine was hit. 'Oh, it was rotten, for I only just got back.'

At first, pilots were content to shoot down the balloon: they recoiled from shooting the balloonatics when they were down – or half-way down. But they came to realise that the balloon was more easily replaced than the trained balloonatic, and the man in the basket was at the mercy of the man in the cockpit.

An incident that occurred on a September evening was not untypical. An ascent to 3,000 feet was made at 6 p.m. by a balloon with a crew of two, a Lieutenant Walls and a Flight Sergeant Moncreiff. Reports that hostile aircraft were approaching caused the winchmen to start hauling down at 6.27. At 6.31 the hostile was sighted – it was an Albatros single-seater – and the ground gunners opened fire. The balloon was still on the way down. At about 200 yards range the pilot opened fire, aiming at the men in the basket. The tracer was clearly seen.

Next the pilot went for the balloon, attacking from the stern. Finally he banked round and attacked from the bow before making off over the lines, pursued by artillery and machine-gun fire.

The basket crew were unhurt, but the balloon itself was aflame and descending, and at 6.32 Moncreiff jumped, followed almost immediately by Walls. Prior to jumping they had thrown out all their maps and papers, but these were sucked in by the furnace of the burning balloon. Somehow the two observers managed to avoid the flames and land safely.

Thirty-three balloons had to be replaced that month, which was about average for the period. Destruction by shelling (eight, with two unserviceable) was double the destruction by enemy aircraft (four, with one unserviceable), which was an emerging trend. Half the replacements were simply due to wear and tear, mostly through porosity.

The balloonatic, then, like the men of the corps squadrons, faced protracted and sometimes concentrated exposure to enemy fire.

Many wartime hazards were reduced as experience was accumulated, but the law of averages decreed that, with some hazards, the longer the exposure the greater the risk. Enemy guns were no respecters of persons, and the Spencer parachute, as we have seen, sometimes snagged or suffered damage from enemy fire and failed to open.

In most other respects, experience remained the key to survival. G.D. Machin, shot down in flames on his second ascent but surviving, saved his balloon on two other occasions by electing to stay aloft rather than be winched down once an attack had started. 'The German machines took the "easy ones" at low level.' On yet another occasion a chapter of accidents, including a broken winch and a collapsed balloon when it was too late to jump, ended with Machin, this time with Oliver, falling in the basket into a clump of trees, which cushioned the impact.

Whereas a great many aeroplane observers applied for pilot training and re-emerged at the front as pilots, graduation from balloons to heavier-than-air craft was rare. This was partly because many had become balloonatics after failing the tests for aircrew. They were specially trained for balloon work and had to master varying skills, including the theory and practice of balloon flight. They were no more transferable than trained air mechanics. Also, having got used to the idea of escape by parachute, it may be that they didn't much fancy going without. But there were certainly balloon observers who transferred to aeroplanes. One who succeeded was the ambitious Leonard Field, who later enjoyed a distinguished career in Military Intelligence.

9

HAWKER AND STRANGE
AND THE FOKKER *EINDECKERS*

L IFE in the RFC squadrons in that summer of 1915 was toler-
able enough, with the newer squadrons gradually knuckling
down alongside the old. Setting off for France remained an
adventure, as one young second lieutenant on No. 7 Squadron,
Francis P. Adams, flying an RE5 (the first of a series of Reconnaissance Experimental types to go into production at Farnborough),
recorded in his diary. Delayed at Folkestone by bad weather, they
finally took off on 8 April, by which time they were so exhausted
by their celebrations over the Easter weekend that they were glad to
get away. Their early reconnaissances, flown at excessive heights,
betrayed their inexperience, and they were directed not to exceed
7,000 feet. They then became vulnerable to ground fire, of which
Adams wrote: 'Some of the Archies are quite white bursts, apparently
shrapnel, and some are black, evil-looking things. The bursts sometimes shake the machine and the shell fragments can be plainly
heard.' But by the end of the month he felt blooded. 'More holes in
the machine – this is now becoming a matter of course.'

So far as enemy aircraft were concerned, although there was a
noticeable increase in activity, there was little more than skirmishing
as yet. But it was inevitable that the Germans, too, would seek to
spy on the activities of their foes and, as the Army pioneer Bertram
Dickson had foreseen, sooner or later this kind of Intelligence-

gathering would attract armed confrontation. Yet both sides were sluggish in providing their pilots and observers with suitable weapons; rifles and pistols were still the norm in the early months of 1915. The obvious answer was the machine-gun, and on the British side the choice fell on the Lewis, which was lighter than the alternative, the Vickers: a bonus was that the chilling effect of the airstream provided an inbuilt cooling system and allowed radiator casing and cooling fins to be discarded. A drawback was that, until an efficient non-freezing lubricant became available, oil in the gun's mechanism was prone to congeal, causing stoppages. A further inhibition was that these guns were in demand elsewhere, Britain having contracted to provide a number to the French, who had been generous in turn in supplying aircraft and engines to Britain.

The problem of mounting and firing such a gun in a tractor machine to penetrate the propeller arc without damaging the propeller was shortly to be solved, though not, in the first instance – and to their cost – by the British. Meanwhile several improvisations were attempted. Louis Strange was a pioneer in offsetting the Lewis to one side, though heading in one direction and aiming in another required a freakish marksmanship. More effective was fixing the gun high enough above the top plane for the bullets to clear the propeller-tips. It was with a BE2c so fitted that Lanoe Hawker first went jousting into enemy airspace.

Although the new Fokker monoplanes fitted with interrupter gear, which synchronised the gun with the engine, allowing the bullets to pass between the propeller blades, made their first appearance that summer, they were too scarce and too cautiously flown as yet to cause alarm. 'Hun machines always over their own lines and generally much lower,' noted Adams on 29 May. 'They immediately run for it and dive to earth if one pursues them.' This was just as well as at this stage Adams and his observer still boasted nothing more lethal than a rifle and revolver between them. Their main concern was engine trouble, for which they frequently had to turn back.

Nevertheless newcomer Adams found many compensations, not least lunching with the artillery on his days off, discussing methods of co-operation, and getting to know the men on the ground and their problems. Like many others before him and after, Adams was conscious of the extremes of his own life, and especially of his home comforts, compared with the men at the front. 'It's exceedingly pleasant to return to an ideal billet, a hot bath and a shave and a leisurely breakfast, with a London newspaper only 24 hours old. Life is certainly quite pleasing.' If he reflected that it was likely to be short, he confided no such qualms to his diary.

By early June Adams's RE5 had been armed with a Lewis gun, operated by an observer named Meakin, and they soon had a chance to use it. 'Had an exciting time on June 5th', related Adams. They seem, on this occasion, to have been mixing business if not with pleasure then at least with some kind of prank: their reconnaissance was aimed at the railway junction at Valenciennes, but they were to drop a message bag addressed to the Hun Flying Corps on Lille aerodrome on their way home: in the bag was a copy of the squadron magazine, with some friendly taunts for German pilots. After being spotted by German observation balloons they were crossing Lens at their briefed height of 7,000 feet when Adams espied a Hun machine some way astern and shouted to Meakin: 'Get the Lewis gun ready!' Two abrupt left-hand turns brought them roughly parallel with what they took to be an Aviatik. 'At 300 yards she let off a belt from her machine-gun,' Adams wrote later. 'All the bullets were heard, but nothing seemed to hit. We held our fire, then let her have a couple of bursts.' The Aviatik was still circling threateningly when a second machine, of the pusher type, startled them by firing at them and scoring hits, Meakin being fully occupied at the time in changing a drum. Then an Albatros swung in underneath them, and bullets began to come up through the fabric from below.

These encounters, before the Fokkers got to work, were not as desperate as they sounded. Adams and Meakin completed their reconnaissance, by which time they were again being chased. Yet they were still doggedly determined to deliver their message. Over Lille aerodrome they were tagged by another hostile, but they dropped the message bag, a feat which would be wildly applauded over a couple of drinks in the Mess. 'Furious shelling greeted us near the lines,' noted Adams, which no doubt they deserved. 'Soon after that my engine stopped and I managed to land.'

Such combats, if they can be so called, were not untypical of the inconclusive nature of air fighting that summer. Nevertheless Adams felt a glow of pride at completing his mission. He felt warmer still after a few sets of mixed doubles at a nearby château. 'Extraordinary interlude, so near the war,' he noted. 'Started off with fizz!' Emotional warmth, though, seems to have been absent, due to the plainness of the mesdemoiselles. 'None very striking,' was his verdict, 'but some could play tennis rather well . . .' Like so many other front-line diaries, it was to end abruptly, the last entry being penned on 2 July. But the two men were safe, interned in Holland, and were repatriated after the war.

As the summer progressed, attacks on our reconnaissance machines, although still spasmodic, became more determined, and squadron commanders generally entrusted the more distant reconnaissances to the better-armed aircraft. This did not always afford them safety. A note dropped over the British lines from a German machine recorded the death of a British pilot and the capture of his observer on a lone long-range reconnaissance in a French machine. 'The German pilots have the highest praise for their opponent,' concluded the note, 'who died in an honourable fight.'

Better able to take care of themselves were the crews of the FE (Farman Experimental) 2b's, a pusher-type of pre-war de Havilland/Farnborough design, four examples of which were delivered to No. 6 Squadron in June. It was easy to fly, had a reliable (120 h.p. Beardmore) engine, and gave pilot and observer a wide view from a spacious cockpit. Two machine-guns, linked together and fitted to a pivotal mounting, could be fitted in the front cockpit, and the observer could stand up and fire to the rear over the top planes and over the pilot's head, giving some protection astern. This left the pilot free to fly the plane. But Lanoe Hawker still packed his rifle, getting his own back on his observer by firing it forward over *his* head. Here was a fighting machine well able to hold its own with the new and faster German machines then coming into service. Unfortunately, deliveries that summer were restricted to the four to

No. 6 Squadron, and the type failed to appear in any numbers before the end of the year.

Hawker's main interest at this time was the new Bristol Scout he had been allocated. Even in the virtually unarmed BE2c, as already mentioned, he had shown a flair for air combat almost before it was thought of, and he was soon evaluating, testing and stunting his new Bristol and designing, with the practical help of air mechanic E.J. Elton, with whom he shared the credit, his own front mounting for a machine-gun. After study and trials he arranged to fire the gun obliquely forward, crabwise, as Strange had done, to port of the propeller arc. A speed of 89 m.p.h., and a climb to 6,500 feet in ten minutes, against twenty in his previous machines, with a ceiling of 15,500, placed Hawker in his element. He knocked nothing down at first due to the inherent aiming difficulties, and he made no claims, but he forced several aircraft to spin down in confusion, trailing smoke. 'It's quite exciting, diving at 120 miles an hour and firing a machine-gun.' And of the Bristol Scout: 'She is a little beauty . . .'

Hawker had a habit of waiting on the ground, ready to start, until he got warning from ground observers or from pilots already airborne of 'hostiles'. Then he would take off and go hunting. But his exploits were not confined to air combat: he fitted his forays in the BE2c and later the Bristol Scout into his routine squadron work. When the Zeppelin raids began on England, 6 Squadron were given the task of destroying the lair of one of the raiders near Ghent, and Hawker was chosen as the most likely man to succeed. Floating menacingly over the target lay a captive balloon, manned by a machine-gunner, and Hawker decided to neutralise that first. He 'proceeded to execute some split-arse spirals round the balloon and heaved grenades at it', according to his report. Of the three bombs he subsequently dropped on the shed, two scored hits; but ironically the offending Zeppelin had been destroyed in the air shortly before-hand. Account was taken of his earlier work, however, and he was awarded the DSO.

Shot in the foot on one of his forays, Hawker had to be lifted in and out of the cockpit, but he continued flying although hobbling about with the aid of a stick. One day, enjoying the peace at high altitude, he had a revelation, soon to be confirmed, that his friend Bayly was indeed lost and would never return.

Palpably exhausted, with the carefree impetuosity of earlier days blunted, he was sent home on leave, where he renewed his friendship with the bereaved Baylys. Returning refreshed, he earned further plaudits from his squadron commander. 'He's now back,' wrote Gordon Shephard, 'flying as daringly as ever, and has inflicted damage on German aircraft by combat in the air.' Although Trenchard's policy kept Hawker's name unknown outside the RFC, his reputation within it as the outstanding scout pilot of his time was firm. His appearances over the lines in his Bristol Scout also won the respect of the enemy.

Early in July Hawker's fellow flight commander Louis Strange was posted to home establishment to form a new squadron after eleven months at the front, a record for any pilot at that time. Before he left he survived one of the most bizarre escapades of the war. No. 6 Squadron had also acquired a single-seater Martinsyde S1, which attracted Strange because of its machine-gun mounted above the centre section, and Shephard allotted it to him as his personal aeroplane. But it was slower than Hawker's Bristol Scout, and when they got news of an intruder, usually by wireless from Bron James, Strange sometimes used it as a decoy, enabling Hawker to attack unseen. The main problem with the Martinsyde was that to change the ammunition drum the pilot had to loosen his safety belt and stand up in the cockpit to reach it, a perilous procedure, especially during combat. Add to this the weight of the drum, the force of the airstream, and a machine that was sluggish, climbed ponderously, and was inherently unstable, and Strange's preference for it emphasises the faults of the alternatives. Its armament, and its top speed of 87 m.p.h., just about justified its label of 'scout'.

Strange was chasing an Aviatik from Lille, on his own this time, at 8,500 feet, both machines being near their respective ceilings. The German observer had been taking pot shots at the Martinsyde with a parabellum pistol, and Strange, having hitherto held his fire, replied with a drum from his Lewis. But when he tried to change the drum, it jammed.

[99]

Unable to remove it with one hand, he wedged the stick between his knees and tugged at the drum with both hands. When this failed he loosened his safety-belt and raised himself out of his seat to get a better grip. As he struggled, the safety-belt slipped down, he lost his knee-grip on the stick, and the Martinsyde, still climbing, stalled and flicked over into a spiral. As he was already more than half-way out of the cockpit, he was thrown clear of the machine, legs kicking, hanging on desperately to the drum.

A moment earlier he had been trying to free the drum with all his strength. Now its stubborn resistance was preserving his life. How long would it hold?

The edge of the drum was cutting into his fingers and he had to catch hold of something more permanent. The Martinsyde was now flying upside down, and he had the sense to realise that the top of the centre section strut must be behind and above him. Dare he let go of the drum with one hand to make a grab for it? There was no alternative. He groped for the strut and gripped it fiercely, transferred the other hand to it, and began kicking upwards until he got first one foot and then the other hooked inside the cockpit, thrusting around until he coiled his legs round the stick. He jammed on full aileron and rudder – and the machine obligingly rolled out right way up. Dropping into his seat with a bump, he grabbed the stick in shell-shocked triumph.

The crew of the Aviatik went home and claimed a victory: they had seen the British pilot thrown out of his cockpit. On the strength of this the Germans spent half a day searching in vain for the wreckage of man and machine.

Strange's departure two months later left the squadron short of a flight commander, and for a time Hawker took command of both A and B Flights. This was the prelude to perhaps his finest period. He continued to alternate scouting sorties on the Bristol with brilliant reconnaissance work in the FE2b, but it was on a designated offensive patrol that he set out in a new Bristol Scout (he had run out of fuel in the old one and crashed it), on the evening of 25 July. Soon after crossing the lines he spotted two enemy two-seater biplanes over the Ypres salient. Any chance of surprising them was defeated by Archie, whose pattern of bursts warned them of his approach. One of the hostiles stayed long enough to return his machine-gun fire, and the Bristol was hit, but Hawker discharged a whole drum at him with such accuracy that the German spun down. Twenty minutes later, still over enemy territory, Hawker intercepted another two-seater. This one, too, was armed with a machine-gun, but again Hawker's fire was the more accurate and he crippled its engine and forced the pilot to land.

The sun was setting and Hawker was conning the evening sky from 11,000 feet, nearing the end of his patrol, when he spotted an Albatros two-seater that had ventured over the British lines, confident in the power of its bristling machine-gun, palpably intent on some specific artillery spotting. Hawker had been obliged to seek his prey almost exclusively on the German side, where proof of his marksmanship was rarely available: here was a chance to provide the doubters – and there were always doubters – with the evidence.

Manoeuvring so as to put the apparently unsuspecting German a thousand feet below him down sun, scarcely daring to breathe, he dived on his target, holding his fire. When the Albatros filled his sights, a single burst sent it diving out of control. Seconds later it turned on its back, ejected the observer, and burst into flames. Exultation at this spectacular outcome would have been complete but for the pity aroused by the sight of a fellow aviator plunging puppet-like to his death.

Strangely enough, the body of the observer, thus preserved from the flames, yielded invaluable Intelligence. Not only was he carrying a map on which he had marked the exact location of a British battery that was firing at the time, the same map also showed the position of four German batteries, one of which, persistently troublesome for weeks beforehand, had long been searched for in vain.

This trio of victories in a single evening, climaxing in the swift and spectacular destruction, in a clear sky, of a high-flying and apparently invulnerable Albatros, witnessed by thousands of troops, together with its Intelligence bonus, coming on top of many months of unparalleled aggression against the enemy, surely called for some special recognition, and Hawker was immediately recommended for a VC.

[101]

Hawker had heard about the new Fokker *Eindeckers* with the synchronised forward-firing machine-gun, but so far he hadn't encountered one. He would hardly have chosen to do so near the end of a patrol in an FE2b, with fuel and ammunition – not to mention his own stamina – running low, nor would he have relished the thought of being dived on unawares on first acquaintance by what was fast becoming a dreaded antagonist. But it was as he and his observer, Lieutenant Noel Clinton, returned from a reconnaissance via Lille that a Fokker fired on them in what was becoming a typical swooping shock attack. Only Hawker's exceptional skill saved them from the *coup de grâce*, and eventually he so out-manoeuvred the German pilot that a point-blank burst from Clinton sent the *Eindecker* crashing down on the outskirts of Lille. This was almost certainly the first of the *Eindeckers* to be shot down in combat, justifying the phlegmatic Clinton in rating the patrol 'a nice little outing'. Hawker's reaction, as always, was ambivalent. Enthusiasm at his victory was tempered by fellow feeling for his victim.

Hawker's mood swings could be of some amplitude, and there can be little doubt that he was overworked that summer, with two flights to lead and run and two types of fighting aeroplane in which to take the war to the enemy. It was strenuous and nerve-racking work, and it was perhaps inevitable that the most capable and aggressive pilots should get the bulk of it, especially for anything non-routine. Gordon Shephard noted the dark rings appearing round Hawker's eyes, the unaccustomed gauntness, and the overall signs of strain, and he sent him on leave. Happily Hawker was home when his VC was gazetted. The award was a landmark, the first VC to be won for valour in air combat.

Shephard did not feel he could spare Hawker for long, and when he returned to France he was still tired. 'I'm not quite as well as I should like,' he admitted, 'and if I don't get better soon I shall apply for a home job.' But he didn't want to go just yet. 'I'm very keen on completing a full year out here, something no one else has done.' After the lay-off, work proved the best cure, and he was soon feeling 'much more chirpy', recording further successes and giving his mind to reorganising the technique of artillery co-operation in the FE2b.

But he was denied his immediate ambition. There were still only twelve squadrons at the front at the end of that summer, but the expansion that was in progress at home meant that Hawker was earmarked to command a new squadron, and on 20 September, five days before the start of the Battle of Loos, he was posted home, having completed all but seventeen days of the year he had set his heart on. He was the last remaining of the original pilots of No. 6 Squadron who had crossed the Channel on 6 October 1914; and he knew he had just about worn himself out.

Had he known what awaited him in England he might have preferred to stay where he was. He was ready enough for the challenge of forming and commanding a new squadron, No. 24, with the prospect of flying a brand-new single-seat pusher aeroplane, the DH2, designed by Geoffrey de Havilland (who had meanwhile left Farnborough and formed his own company, Airco). It would be the first single-seat scout squadron to be formed in the RFC. But he was unprepared for the situation that confronted him at the squadron training base on Hounslow Heath. Just as the demand for rapid expansion had bred hurried decisions on aircraft selection, so the training of pilots had had to be rushed. Most of the men joining 24 Squadron were raw and inexperienced; many were still in their teens. Hawker checked them out individually on the various hacks available at Hounslow and in most instances was obliged to instruct them afresh. He also assumed responsibility for their physical and mental fitness during the winter months, when they were awaiting delivery of the DH2s and when flying opportunities were few and boredom threatened. Leading the pack himself, he had them running round the Heath before breakfast. A saving grace was the personal interest he took in all their problems.

There was no chance of boredom for Hawker: the shortage of experienced leaders was such that he was placed in charge of two of the night-flying stations ringed around north-east London whose task it was to attempt to intercept raiding Zeppelins, a tiresome and, it was considered, almost hopeless assignment. Here again he found himself filling the role of instructor, and there was always competition to fly with him because of his reputation. He didn't even get a break at week-ends. 'They will have to give me leave soon,' he wrote on 27 November, 'or I shall collapse.'

Rejuvenation did not come until the arrival at Hounslow, on 10 January 1916, of the first de Havilland DH2 scout. Powered by a 100 h.p. Gnome Monosoupape of French design and manufacture, it was to earn a reputation, when first introduced, of a liability to spin. Hawker was kept busy convincing his pilots that this reputation, if not altogether without substance, was exaggerated, and that correct piloting could counter any such tendency. One of the problems was that those of his pilots who had trained on Stability Jane had to be retaught when they came to fly an unstable machine like the DH2. Farmans and Avros had to be nursed through every manoeuvre, whereas, with a BE, a touch on the controls and the machine did the rest. Trainees could be passed out more quickly on the Blériot, but their skills were strictly limited. Nevertheless a month later, on 7 February 1916, the squadron moved to France.

News of the further depredations of the Fokker *Eindeckers* had already percolated through. But FE2b's were also beginning to arrive in strength, and the crews of these, with Hawker's DH2s, and a third pusher type, the Vickers Gunbus, braced themselves for the task of neutralising what, in Hawker's absence, had become known as the Fokker Scourge.

Anthony Fokker, a Dutch aviation engineer, had had a monoplane built to his own design as far back as 1912. Of clean outline and fair performance for its time, it was very similar to the French-built Morane Saulnier monoplane, the main difference being that part of the structure was of welded steel tubing instead of wood. The Germans saw its potential, improved the design, and put it into quantity production. Powered by an 80 h.p. Oberursel rotary engine, its clean lines gave it the ability to make long almost vertical dives on a target. But this feature was not utilised immediately; it was employed at first as an unarmed reconnaissance machine.

The change came with the chance capture of a modified Morane Saulnier Type L parasol monoplane flown by the French pioneer aerobatic pilot Roland Garros, who in 1913 had been the first man to cross the Mediterranean by air. To solve the problem of aiming a machine-gun straight ahead, Garros and designer Raymond Saulnier had fitted wedge-shaped metal plates to the blades of Garros's propeller, believing that the proportion of bullets that would strike the blades would be small and would anyway be safely deflected. On 1 April 1915 Garros took off to try out this theory, and it worked. With no more than superficial damage to his propeller, Garros shot down a German two-seater in flames. After he had repeated the feat twice in the next seventeen days, the French began fitting the device to all similar aircraft, and very soon another pre-war stunt pilot, Adolphe Pégoud, was chalking up victories.

Failing to appreciate the immense advantage they had gained, the French seem to have made no attempt to safeguard their secret. Eventually the Germans must surely have tumbled to what was afoot and reacted accordingly, but engine failure in Garros's plane while on a bombing run over Courtrai, and the prevailing wind which carried him deeper than he intended into enemy territory, ensured that cognizance came sooner rather than later. Realising the implications too late, Garros tried to set fire to his machine, but was unsuccessful; he brooded on this so guiltily as a prisoner that he plotted to retrieve his reputation by escaping and rejoining the fight. He eventually did so, only to be killed in action. But he could not undo the damage he – or those who had countenanced his bombing mission – had done.

Gun, engine and propeller of Garros's machine were passed to Anthony Fokker, with orders to copy it for installation in his very similar monoplane. But Fokker and his staff went further; aware of a pre-war patent for a synchronised gun, they introduced a timing mechanism which allowed bullets fired from a machine-gun to pass between the blades of a revolving propeller, rendering deflector plates superfluous. In addition, bullets fed from ammunition belts removed the necessity for changing drums. Crude as the device was, and primitive as was its carrier, together they constituted the first efficient gun platform for scout pilots.

Yet the Germans, too, failed at first to appreciate how decisive the development was. The first Fokker E1s, as the armed machine was designated, were produced in small numbers and allotted in pairs in

July 1915 to various flying units, to operate as escorts for two-seaters. Although the Germans were already smarting under the unopposed bombing raids of the French, appreciation of the potential attacking role of the Fokkers came slowly, and then from the pilots themselves, principally from two men who were to become national heroes in Germany, Oswald Boelcke and Max Immelmann.

Boelcke, who was involved with Fokker in testing the E1 from its inception, was at least Immelmann's equal in flair and aggression, and he surpassed him in strategic and tactical vision. He laid down four basic principles of air fighting: height advantage; attacking out of the sun; the use of cloud for concealment; and close range. He also showed tactical awareness in choosing attacking positions where the target aircraft's guns could not be brought to bear on the attacker. Yet the 'Eagle of Lille', as Immelmann was dubbed, gained the greater immediate fame through his romantic appearance and his invention of the turn which bears his name.

The Fokker's hawk-like ability to dive vertically in surprise attack took the aggressor too far beyond his target for a quick follow-up strike; Immelmann's answer was to use his diving speed for a swift zoom to gain height, pulling up into a loop before a half-roll off the top so that he was upright and above his target, flying in the opposite direction. By falling away into a stall turn he was then ideally placed for surprise attack, or to escape if need be. And it was Immelmann who launched what was later to develop into the Fokker Scourge when he shot down a British two-seater bomber on the German side of the lines on 1 August 1915, the first officially confirmed Fokker victory.

The head-on form of attack, in which the aircraft itself was aimed at the target, revolutionised air marksmanship and with it air combat. Fortunately for the Allies, however, the initial impact was attenuated by a mistaken distribution of the new *Eindeckers* in penny packets, and it was not until that autumn and winter, rising to a crescendo in the New Year, that the successors of the E1s, the E11s and the E111s, with more powerful engines and concentrated into special units (though never totalling more than 50 at any one time and 300 in all), shot down several hundred Allied machines and reduced their principal victims, the unfortunate crews of the BEs, to 'Fokker Fodder'.

The day before Immelmann's first victory, and six days after Hawker's triple success, a third VC was won, by a man who was not an experienced flyer like Hawker, nor the callow youth that many newly-arrived pilots were beginning to be. At twenty-seven Aidan Liddell was two years older than Hawker, and his VC was remarkable not so much for the action itself, which was similar to many other brave attempts by mortally wounded pilots to coax a crippled aircraft home with their report (and often, as in this case, preserve the life and freedom of an observer), as for the man and his background. No conventional hero, he was an academic of delicate health and physique, with a first in zoology at Balliol, one whose exceptional gifts, it was said, would have brought him distinction in any pursuit. An Argyll and Sutherland Highlander, born in Newcastle, he had learned to fly in 1914 for his own interest, without thought of transfer to the RFC. He went to France in August 1914 with overall responsibility for the machine-gun sections of his battalion, and at Christmas 1914 he took part in the famous (or infamous) fraternisation, of which he wrote: 'On that day everyone spontaneously left their trenches and had a meeting half-way ... The Germans gave us cigars, and we gave them chocolates and tobacco. They seemed very pleased to see us! Some had lived in England for years, and were very bucked at airing their English again!'

Then it was back to the killing. 'You don't know how nerve-racking this trench business is, and how far off the end of the war seems. It would appear that it must go on until the Germans are quite exhausted, which might take a little time.' The flash of wry humour was typical, the reference to his nerves prophetic. A mention in despatches and a Military Cross (a DSO was recommended) confirmed his fortitude, but in February 1915 he was sent home on sick leave, and having already taken his ticket, a transfer to the RFC after six debilitating months in the trenches seemed natural. On 23 July he returned to France to join No. 7 Squadron, flew his first reconnaissance patrol on the 29th in an RE5 and his second and last two days later. It was for another astonishing display of fortitude, when he brought his crippled machine under control and made a forced landing on the Allied side despite hideous wounds, that his VC was awarded. He died a month later. Sadly the life that he saved, that of his observer, Second Lieutenant R.H. Peck, was to be sacrificed later.

Having been posted home from 6 Squadron in July, and finding the promise of a squadron frustratingly delayed, Louis Strange wangled himself a posting as a flight commander on 12 Squadron under Cyril Newall, and he was back in France by mid-September. Trenchard visited the squadron with Baring and expressed approval of the new gun mountings Strange had devised for the BE2c, but when he saw Strange he bristled. 'What are you doing here? I thought I sent you home to form a squadron.' Strange wisely kept his peace. 'You must go home. Make a note, Baring.' Strange thought his presence would be forgotten, but a few days later, after a Bristol Scout had been allotted to the squadron, a delighted Strange was fitting a Lewis gun to it when Trenchard appeared again with Baring. 'I thought I told you, Baring, to remind me to send Strange home?' Then he turned to Strange and boomed, 'Strange, go home at once.'

Surely he couldn't mean right this minute? But he said again, 'Go home at once.' Then, pointing to an old Maurice Farman, he added, 'in that machine, now!' There was nothing for it but to salute and order the machine to be started up. But with a 35-knot headwind Strange had no intention of crossing the Channel that day. Instead, he dropped down into Abeele and 6 Squadron, where his old boss Gordon Shephard accepted his excuses. But he had to promise to leave early next morning, after what he called 'a most hectic and hilarious night with my old friends'.

Strange proceeded to form a new squadron, No. 23, but the night before they were due to leave for France (16 March 1916) he went down with appendicitis, an overworked surgeon left a swab inside him, and he was fourteen weeks in hospital and unfit for flying for many months. When he recovered he went to CFS as a flight commander and instructor. But his operational career was not quite finished yet.

10

THE BATTLE OF LOOS: DERMOTT ALLEN AND A BOMBING CAMPAIGN: LIVES THROWN AWAY

GREAT hopes were pinned by the French General Joffre in a 1915 autumn offensive, starting in September, deploying the growing strength the Allied ground forces had accumulated that summer, and taking advantage of the known transfer of German divisions to the Russian front. Joffre's offensive was to be mounted on an ambitious scale: he planned to advance across the bare, undulating Champagne country and achieve a decisive breakthrough, developing an attack along the entire front which, if successful, would drive the enemy from French soil. Despite objections from Haig that ammunition was still short and the terrain unsuitable, the British, aware that failure to back up the much stronger French contribution could leave them isolated, agreed to develop a subsidiary attack in the region of Loos, directly north of Vimy Ridge and the important town of Arras. Haig's First Army was to push up between Lens and La Basée while the Second Army made diversionary attacks east of Ypres.

The RFC in France now comprised three wings controlling twelve squadrons, numbering some 160 miscellaneous aircraft, mostly BE2c's and Morane Parasols; there was still only a leavening of Gunbuses and FE2b's. And the RFC had its problems. 'We'll be in a chaotic state if we do advance,' wrote Dermott Allen, now a flight commander on 8 Squadron in Third Wing, after a spell of photographic work. 'It is pitiable how short we are of spares.' For weeks the bombing squadrons slaved day and night in preparation for the offensive, keeping their machines active on reconnaissance and artillery-spotting by day, devising and fitting bomb-racks by night. 'Life is very strenuous,' said Allen. His day began at 06.30, he had his flight to run, and to keep in touch he did a reconnaissance or artillery 'show' every second day. 'Yet one hears of railway unrest in England.' The jingoism of the early days, it seemed, had cooled, with strikes proliferating, arousing great bitterness in France. 'The British working man is really a swine of the first water,' wrote Allen intemperately, 'till he gets really properly hunted and straffed.' Social inequalities, exacerbated by wartime restraints and controls which bore most heavily on the working population, were largely to blame.

The First Wing was to be solely occupied in artillery co-operation with Haig's First Army; indeed the entire programme of artillery bombardment that was to precede and accompany the British attack would depend on their persistence and skill, first in locating enemy batteries and then in directing the fire that would aim to silence them. The Second and Third Wings were to delay and harass the expected flow of enemy reinforcements by bombing the important Lille–Douai–Valenciennes rail communications triangle. French bombers would be similarly active on the Champagne front.

'The first signs of the big push showed themselves on 20 September,' noted Allen. The preliminary bombardment began next day in a tense atmosphere but in good weather, and the bombing programme opened two days later. Then on the 24th it began to rain, and it was still raining on the 25th when the infantry went over the top. The corps squadrons, all visited and motivated before the attack by Trenchard, did well enough until the visibility deteriorated, but they failed altogether to provide information on the progress of the attacking troops, mainly through a breakdown in the primitive air/ground signalling methods that had been planned but insufficiently practised. There was also a failure to appreciate the value of low flying to observe changes and gaps in the dispositions of the enemy force, so that, as it afterwards became clear, golden opportunities were missed.

In the opening attack the British used gas for the first time, and

Lieutenant J.G. Selby, seconded to the RFC from the gunners and observing from a Morane Parasol of 3 Squadron, applauded at first: we were giving the Germans a taste of their own medicine. But he soon changed his mind. 'We were flying at about 8,000 feet. The wind had changed and we could see the gas visibly drifting back over our own trenches. My pilot throttled down and turned round and said: "Thank God we're in the Flying Corps, old boy!"' It was a moment of ambivalence for Selby, his relief at his good fortune being balanced by guilt.

The aerial bombardment enjoyed some spectacular successes, among them an attack, on the 25th, by a BE2c of Allen's squadron from a height of 150 feet, on a bridge which carried a light railway over the main line in the Valenciennes triangle. The pilot succeeded in cutting the one and blocking the other; this was Sholto Douglas. Next day, despite appalling weather, an attack on the locomotive sheds at Valenciennes blew up two ammunition trains and exploded twenty trucks of shells, halting all traffic at this vital junction at a critical time. Reconnaissance flights, too, bore fruit, pioneer air photographer Darley reporting rail activity further south near Cambrai which stimulated raids in which the permanent way was cratered by direct hits. (Soon afterwards Darley was shot down by Immelmann, but he survived as a prisoner.)

'My special job', wrote Allen, 'was to interrupt communications on the Valenciennes–Douai line. Any train but Red Cross was to be bombed from low altitude, which meant going down to 7–800 feet, although the bombsight, except when used in the vertical plane, was not much good at this height.' Flying without an observer, he carried one 112-pounder and six 20-lb anti-personnel bombs. Going in second of three, he dropped his 112-pounder 'on or near' a busy junction north-west of Valenciennes, obliterating the area round the points with dust and smoke. But much to his disgust, four of his 20-pounders failed to explode.

Allen believed that the bombing campaign was proving effective: the Valenciennes–Douai line had been continually blocked and traffic held up. At the very least the enemy must have been caused great inconvenience, forcing him to employ batteries of rockets and reinforcements of troops in an effort to protect the route. The Germans were also going in for camouflage, daubing their trains and suppressing tell-tale emissions of smoke. The result, for the RFC, was prohibitive losses, largely from ground fire but also from the increasing aggression of units of the German Air Force, particularly the Fokkers, which emerged for the first time as more than a threat. 'It's hard to believe that I've lost every single officer that I had a month ago,' lamented Allen. 'They simply disappeared one after the other.' Yet the daily routine continued. 'I'm afraid one gets very callous to this sort of thing. It all happens so quietly and unobtrusively. A machine goes out and does not return. It is shown on the daily state as missing for a couple of days and is then struck off charge. I tell someone to take an inventory of the missing officer's kit. A new pilot or observer arrives and has to be trained. Then one gets a letter from the relatives of the missing. These have to be answered. War is a beastly business. I can't conceive any normal person liking it, and yet one could not dream of remaining at home.' (After a short break at home through illness, he had agitated to return to a squadron.)

Yet the losses in the air paled before the slaughter on the ground. Rumours, all too accurate, were reaching the squadrons of a total of 50,000 casualties. Most of the flyers had been regimental officers, and they rated their own sacrifices as nothing compared to those of the fighting troops.

Assessing the impact of the bombing was difficult. Brancker, talking to Allen at the height of the campaign, thought that although German communications had been disrupted, the lines had never been completely cut. German records later revealed that substantial damage was wrought but that debris was quickly cleared: all reinforcements were said to have reached their destinations on time.

The Germans demonstrated the truth of this by launching fierce counter-attacks, and when the reserves requested by Haig were delayed, due reputedly to French's desire to keep them under his own control through jealousy of his subordinate, the British were forced to pull back. Meanwhile in Champagne the Germans, having had advance warning of the French attack through their Intelligence agents, and enjoying the advantage of higher ground, held on.

The Allies also used agents, or 'spies', but information from behind enemy lines was scarce, and assaults tended to be continued even when failure seemed inevitable. 'Tomorrow I am for a bombing show,' noted Allen. The target was the same, but losses had bred caution: there was to be no low flying unless trains were actually seen.

'The First Army is going to attack,' noted Allen on 12 October. 'I hardly think they seriously think they're going to get through. It's awful to think of the lives that are going to be lost tomorrow to gain a few hundred yards . . . If only we had the ammunition to absolutely annihilate the Bosch batteries and trenches.'

Allen realised that the material damage his squadron could inflict was small, but he had been indoctrinated with the Trenchard dogma. 'It is a means of forcing the Hun to come up and fight us at our own time and choosing.' The Fokker pilots, led by Boelcke and Immelmann, were all too ready to oblige, even sometimes crossing the Allied lines – unusual for the Germans – and the vulnerability of the BE2c was ruthlessly exposed. Allen still believed in the doctrine of attack, but he was begging for faster machines and stronger escorts. 'Once you have the Hun in the air he must not be allowed to get away.'

From 30 September the bombers were given an escort, generally one for one, Third Wing being fortunate in having the only Vickers Gunbus squadron so far formed (No. 11) to protect them. Alternatively, two or three bombing machines might be sent together while Gunbus patrols endeavoured to keep the air clear. The corps squadrons, too, found themselves obliged to fight for the information they sought, necessitating escorts.

'Bombing seems to be off for the present,' noted Allen later that month. He saw this as a bad sign: bombing and the ground offensive went hand in hand, so there must be a lull in the fighting. Rumours, mostly of a discouraging nature, were rife. 'Two more fellows missing from the squadron,' Allen recorded on 12 October. 'They went on a long recce in one of my "spot" machines and unfortunately didn't come back. One is affected by one's own show a great deal.'

[113]

Immelmann recorded his fourth victory (a BE2c) on the 10th, yet the Germans, by continuing to split the Fokkers up into penny packets, still failed to maximise their advantage. And to give the crews of the outclassed British machines their due, it was amazing how well most of them held their own.

The wintry weather that set in as October advanced came as a blessed relief. Haig's casualties, as was usual for the attacking force, were more than double those of the enemy, the French lost 190,000, and by early November Joffre had finally abandoned his plan, anyway for the time being. He was still convinced that, although his losses were half as many again as the German, the Allies could stand it and the Germans could not: he believed he was wearing them down. On the British side, Sir John French got the blame for the débâcle, especially for the delay in providing reserves, and he was replaced as commander-in-chief by Douglas Haig.

'Life,' wrote Maurice Baring, presumably thinking of those who survived, 'resumed its normal course.' Allen wrote with equal fatalism. 'One has now quite fallen into a groove. This war has quite become part and parcel of one's existence.' Peace was a thing of the dim and distant past, and no one cared to guess when it would return. Leave, which was the one thing everyone longed for, was something it was better not to contemplate: one only started counting the days. Yet the idealism with which Britain had begun hostilities remained strong. 'If it is left to the folk out here, I don't think there would be any thought of chucking it until the Bosch has taken it properly in the neck.'

Allen was one of the few who tried to keep the many facets of the war in perspective. 'It always strikes me as peculiar how really little interest nearly everyone takes in the war in general. We each have our own little job, such as servicing engines or procuring spare parts. We are dominated by our own little corner.' Absorbed in the task in hand, people just didn't concern themselves further. As for the flyers, survival was a consideration but not an obsession. 'Personally I admit I never worry. As for the big issues, one knows practically nothing.' The gap between the brass-hats and the men at the sharp end, despite Trenchard's frequent visits to the squadrons, remained wide.

Nevertheless Allen retained his critical faculties. Several more of the originals were booked for a return to France in charge of squadrons or flights: Brock was to lead 15 Squadron (BE2c's), Carmichael 18 Squadron (Gunbuses), and Borton 27 (Martinsyde Scouts). The policy was that no one could command a squadron in France until he had first commanded a reserve squadron at home, which meant that Allen could not be promoted direct in France. Mapplebeck, too, was wanted as a squadron commander, and he went home to take over a reserve squadron at Joyce Green, near Dartford, where, with few Zeppelins to intercept, he spent much of his time making night flights over defended points around London to give practice to the searchlight and gun crews. Perhaps he got bored with this, as there are accounts of low level stunting over the houses of some particular friends in Shooters Hill. 'We lay flat on the grass and were quite sick with fright,' was one comment. This exuberance came to a tragic end when, having called at Shooters Hill unexpectedly on 24 August to persuade them to come and watch him try out a recently acquired Type N Morane monoplane known by the British as the Bullet, difficult to fly because of its high wing loading, he descended in a succession of spirals which steepened until the machine hit a hangar roof, the whole ghastly sequence being watched by his horrified friends. It looked like a typical show-off misjudgment, in a machine in which the pilot was inexperienced; but a doubt was later expressed about this particular model's basic airworthiness. It was ironic that Mapplebeck, whose scepticism about the glib assumption of pilot error had been so well founded, should have a similar question mark surrounding his own death.

Even amongst his larger-than-life contemporaries Gibb Mapplebeck had stood out, and he had had so many narrow escapes he had seemed indestructible. 'There are few of the early pilots,' wrote Strange, 'whose loss was felt as deeply as his.'

Operational experience was also a requisite for appointment to command a squadron, but Allen saw this rule being manipulated to give preference to favourites at home. 'People who've done very little

operational time are being promoted immediately to flight commander, and after a couple of trips over the lines are being sent home
to form new squadrons.' This was galling for a man like Allen, who
had pressed for a return to the front line but could not be appointed
to a squadron while in France. Even if these men were outstanding,
he reasoned, surely it would be better to put them in charge of an
existing squadron rather than expect them to form and train a new
one from scratch.

Allen was also critical of the amount of flying the squadrons were
required to do that winter, with several reconnaissances daily, often
when the weather was not really fit, two or three machines on artillery ranging, and two or three bomb raids a week. It was right to
maintain the offensive spirit, as Trenchard demanded, and it looked
good in the summary of work; but it seemed to Allen that flying
time was often being amassed with an eye to the summary alone.
Reconnaissances often took off as soon as possible after dawn, and,
with myopic regularity, followed a well-worn route, inviting interception. Bombs were dropped for the sake of bombing something.
'Wouldn't we have done better to husband our resources?' asked
Allen.

It was not until January 1916 that the Fokkers 'really took the
game up seriously and made our lives unbearable', according to Lieutenant H.B.R. Rowell (later knighted after a career in shipbuilding):
he arrived on 8 Squadron in October. Nevertheless Allen recorded
that by Christmas 1915 his original group of pilots, four to a flight,
had been replaced three times over. Forty-nine RFC pilots and
observers were lost in action in the last two months of the year,
partly owing to the standard of the replacements, who usually arrived
with no more than twenty hours' solo flying, often less, and who
displayed a woeful lack of flying expertise. They had no idea how
to avoid trouble, or how to extricate themselves when they got into
it, only underlining the case for a period of consolidation.

Experienced crews, too, were needlessly over-exposed, often in
atrocious weather, leading to gaps not easily filled. Lieutenant H.W.
'John' Medlicott, of 2 Squadron, one of the few genuine 'aces' so
far, had five victories, three in a Bristol Scout and two in a BE2c;

with him on 10 November 1915 as observer was Lieutenant Arthur Whitten Brown, almost equally experienced. They were on a reconnaissance to Valenciennes when their escort lost them in a snowstorm: typically, they continued with their mission. By all accounts it was absurd weather for such a long reconnaissance to be attempted, but after ten blank days urgent orders had come through from wing headquarters to get the job done. Under fire, they were eventually forced to crash-land, and Brown, having already sustained a bullet wound, was badly hurt as they crashed. Both men survived as prisoners, but Brown spent many months in hospital. They had prepared themselves well for escape in case of capture, but Brown had to give up the idea. Medlicott made several attempts, only to be shot dead with another escaper in the last of them, in May 1918. Brown lived to navigate John Alcock, in 1919, on the first direct air crossing of the Atlantic.

11

SCRAPS WITH BOELCKE AND IMMELMANN: McCUDDEN AND PORTAL AS OBSERVERS: HARVEY-KELLY AGAIN

INSULATED though they were from the carnage in the trenches, news of the death of erstwhile comrades at the front upset them almost as much as the daily recital of fellow pilots and observers missing or killed, and this stimulated their resolve. When an aeroplane did not return there was always hope, postponing or alleviating shock. Pilot and/or crew might well have survived to be taken prisoner. Most such incidents occurred out of sight over enemy territory. Crashes on the aerodrome were not infrequent and could be nasty, but more often than not they were survived. Even when German infantrymen fell wounded or killed during bombing and strafing there was something impersonal about it. This protective cocoon, though, could be rudely sundered, as Allen found on a long reconnaissance in the middle of the battle. He had crossed the lines just south of Albert on his way home and was looking at the statue of the Virgin on the church when a German two-seater dived to the ground in front of him. He noted the spot where it crashed and was sent out afterwards with a mechanic to land nearby and guard the wreck until a ground party arrived. Artillery and a Gunbus were sharing the credit. A crowd had gathered round the wreck and there had already been some souvenir hunting, but Allen recovered most of it. 'I just glanced at the bodies,' he wrote. 'The two poor Huns were riddled with bullets and one was horribly mutilated. I felt most awfully sorry for the poor devils . . . I don't think I will forget the sudden glimpse of that machine crashing through the air . . . When I tried to shave on my return my hand shook so much that I nearly had to give it up.'

Allen was pained to see that whereas the national papers summed up the work of the bombing squadrons in the Loos battle in a couple of lines, they gave colourful accounts of the depredations of the Fokkers. It was bad for morale, as were many of the rumours and counter-rumours from home. He heard of one raw pilot in No. 4 Squadron who sighted three hostiles on his first trip over the lines and at once headed for home. 'They say he is now in bed with nervous prostration and has acquired a bad stutter. I'm not surprised. Officers come out here with an exaggerated idea of Hun frightfulness and not having much experience sometimes get a bit panicky.'

Propaganda excesses at home left the front-line flyers sceptical: they had a healthy respect for the Hun, with whom a chivalrous enmity was still being maintained. When Allen heard, as he later did, that some of his crews had survived to be taken prisoner, the first tidings, in at least one instance, came in a message dropped on the aerodrome by the enemy.

Allen had learned to fly at Hendon in 1912, graduated on the first course at CFS, joined 3 Squadron under Brooke-Popham in January 1913, flown to France with the armada on 13 August 1914, and remained until January 1915, when he was injured in a crash. He managed to get himself posted back to reconnaissance work in France three months later and thence to 8 Squadron as a flight commander under Lionel Charlton; but his health broke down again in March 1916 (he was then twenty-five). After running a training squadron in Scotland he was appointed to develop major training schemes overseas as senior staff officer, first in Canada and later in Texas. The Canadian scheme had first been examined by 'Pregnant Percy' – Lieutenant-Colonel C.J. Burke – in 1915, but it was not until 1917, under the pressures of expansion, that a school was established in Canada. More than 4,000 pilots were trained under these schemes, and Allen, on his return to England, was awarded the Air Force Cross.

When Willie Read returned to France in June 1915 to join No. 5 Squadron (Avros and BE2c's) as a flight commander, he had virtually commandeered the squadron's only Bristol Scout, which he christened 'Priscilla'. And when, in mid-December, he was posted home a second time, he announced that he 'must have one more go with Priscilla'. The two enemy machines that he intercepted returned his fire, penetrating his fuel tank, and he only just got back. It was nearly the end of Priscilla, if not of Read, who left for home next day with a Military Cross for 'conspicuous gallantry on several occasions'. 'It was an easily won MC,' he said, 'as I could not recall any conspicuous gallantry.' This was typical of Read. Next time he returned to France he would be commanding a squadron.

The fraternisation of the first Christmas of the war was frowned on as liable to weaken resolve and was discouraged in 1915, but there was tacit agreement to do no more that day than go through the motions. 'Only three machines from 8 Squadron [BE2c's] left the ground,' recorded Robin Rowell, who led them. 'I wandered over the lines just to see that all was quiet, when Brother Bosche started firing at us with anti-aircraft guns.' But the firing, like the flying, was more festive than furious. 'These three machines were then seen to turn round towards the lines and fly homewards in a series of loops and other stunts,' recorded a witness. 'Archie stopped firing at once, and loud cheers were heard from both sides of Nomansland.'

It was the BE2c crews, partly because they were still the most numerous, who suffered worst at the hands of the Fokkers, and indeed the German pilots seemed intent on picking them off. Thus they became known as Fokker fodder. The best way of countering the Fokker's advantage of having synchronised guns firing forward through the propeller arc became a subject of lively debate among the Blériot crews.

Four days after Christmas, as they walked out to their machines to look for enemy reinforcement activity between Cambrai and St Quentin, two of the best pilots on 8 Squadron found themselves in disagreement. 'If a Fokker dives on you,' said Scotsman David

Glen, 'the best thing to do is to fly straight on. That's the only way to give your observer a chance.' Glen's observer had already shot down a Fokker using these tactics, which gave weight to what Glen said. But his companion, Sholto Douglas, another Scot, while admiring Glen's nerve, was far from convinced. 'I prefer to turn in underneath them. Your method may work against the rank and file, but you wouldn't stand a chance against men like Boelcke and Immelmann.' The adulation heaped on these two men in Germany had become well known.

The air was clear, but from 6,500 feet they could spot no special activity, they had seen no enemy planes, and they were not far short of the limit of their reconnaissance when they saw six tiny, thin black lines suspended in the sky in the direction of Douai. The *Eindecker* was notoriously difficult to spot, especially head on, but Glen and Douglas saw them simultaneously. 'I was thoroughly frightened', said Douglas afterwards, 'and I longed to turn and run for it. We were outnumbered by six to two, and it might have seemed prudent to turn back, but then we would have failed to complete our task and the German scout machines would have achieved their object. Someone else would only have had to try again later.'

As he kicked the rudder and thrust the stick hard over to port, turning towards and under the attack, Douglas saw Glen bravely holding his course. When he straightened out, four of the Fokkers were pulling out of the dive, but two others were hurtling downwards, whether in pursuit of Glen or having been hit he could not tell. Then, far below him, he saw Glen's BE2c spiralling down in flames.

The four remaining Huns were now turning to him. 'In the heat of the fight I was too busy to feel frightened. Mostly I felt angry, furious with these Huns who were undoubtedly trying to kill me. There was only one thing to do, and that was to kill them first.'

As Douglas turned and dived underneath his attackers he heard the racket of the Lewis gun immediately above his head and smelt the choking stench of cordite. Then his observer, James Child, waved excitedly and pointed to one of the Fokkers. 'I've got him!' Douglas looked up just in time to see another Fokker pull up in front of him in a steep climb prior to beginning a loop. 'At the top of the loop he seemed to twist on to one side, reverse his direction, and come straight for me. Immelmann!'

The man who had executed that spectacular manoeuvre was indeed Max Immelmann. And one of the pilots who now sought to finish Douglas off, as he afterwards learned, was Oswald Boelcke.

Douglas's mad, writhing helter-skelter to get back to safety prostrated his gunner with sickness, leaving them easy meat for the Fokkers. Douglas – and his pursuers – thought Child was dead. But Douglas's fear of his plane breaking up was less than his fear of being shot down, and he went on rough-handling his machine in desperation. As the Fokkers attacked in succession, one of the German pilots – in fact it was Boelcke – came in so close Douglas could almost feel the bullets spraying into his back. Boelcke had indeed fired at point-blank range, only for his guns to fail. He had run out of ammunition.

As the Fokkers forced him nearer the ground, Douglas feared his loss of height and therefore manoeuvrability would prove fatal. But making a virtue of necessity, he sacrificed his last 300 feet or so, letting the plane fall out of the sky for the sake of the protection he hoped he might get from the ground itself. Now they could not execute their favourite diving attack without flying straight in.

For a moment, thinking their adversary was about to land, Boelcke and Immelmann chivalrously held off. Or that was how it seemed. Then Child, recovering now they were flying more or less straight and level, surprised Immelmann with a burst that seemed to come from a corpse, forcing him to retire to 1,000 feet.

Douglas was still about ten miles from safety when one of the Fokkers overtook him in a shallow dive, banked steeply, and turned back towards him on a collision course. Again it was Boelcke. His aim was to flush the BE2c up like a pheasant, where Immelmann and the remaining Fokker pilots would be waiting for it. But Douglas's hunch was that the instinct of self-preservation that demanded he hold his course would force Boelcke to break off.

With the slower flying speeds of the time, a collision course was not a sudden moment of involuntary terror but a deliberate span of hypnotic tension. Both men were under a spell which might lock them into immobility until it was too late. The ultimate moment seemed almost to have passed when Boelcke broke off.

The Germans kept up the chase until Douglas was within a mile of the front line. Then they gave up. Soon afterwards Douglas's engine seized and he landed in the middle of a gun battery south of Arras.

Douglas described his escape as his most hair-raising experience of the war, and the story made the headlines at home, embarrassingly so as it was written up by an Army Intelligence officer who knew very little about flying. Trenchard was to blame for this, for not appointing an RFC Press liaison officer to ensure accurate reporting.

The German Air Force were said to be out of sympathy with the 'playing fields' attitude attributed to RFC men, the outlook of their own pilots being presented as fearless but clinical. They did not see air combat as some superior form of school sports. Boelcke's comments on the Douglas incident, however, seem at variance with this view. He saw it as a fine fight and a 'joyous scrap'.

Of the two pusher types, the Vickers Gunbus and the FE2b, the Gunbus was effective at first, but its origins dated back to 1912, and it was too limited in speed and ceiling to stand up to the Fokker, while there was still only one flight of FE2b's at the front for the Battle of Loos. In time the FE2b's were to work out a method of frustrating their attackers by forming a defensive circle, but the Gunbus was soon to be withdrawn from the front. It was powered by the 100 h.p. Gnome Monosoupape, which behaved erratically in the Gunbus, as the experience of an eighteen-year-old named Oscar Greig confirms. Commissioned in May 1915, he arrived in France in July with fifteen hours solo on the Gunbus and, like many other eighteen- and nineteen-year-olds of his era, under twenty hours in all. Whereas most of the pilots who fought and flew in 1914 and early 1915, young though they were, had attained maturity, most of those now arriving at the front had come straight from school via the training stations and were little more than schoolboys. Yet with their physical and mental vitality they were ideal recruits to the air war. Theirs was the age group notorious for risking life and limb on motor-bikes, and their contempt for death made them formidable fighters. Unfortunately, because of the demand for expansion at all costs, they were inadequately trained and poorly served by their machines, and often by their seniors.

Again and again young Oscar Greig had to return to base with a dud engine, but his persistence soon earned the respect of his fellows, and his extreme youth was more apparent when he put pen to paper. 'The major has sent in my name for a decoration,' he recorded. 'I do hope I get it. It would please Mummy so. Anyhow it would be topping!' But he had been in action barely a month when he had a cylinder blow, and this was the beginning of a loss of confidence. In October he got into a horrific spin from high level, and although the Gunbus eventually came out after falling for many thousands of feet, both Greig and his observer were left with shattered nerves. Soon afterwards a sensitive commanding officer, recognising good material when he saw it, posted them home for a rest. Greig's observer went on to pilot training, and Greig became an instructor, to return to France in 1917 for a short and unpleasant spell on FE2b's.

Another newcomer in the same month was an army despatch rider who had applied successfully for transfer to observer, RFC. This was Charles 'Peter' Portal, who was to become the most distinguished of all chiefs of air staff after Trenchard, holding that appointment from 1940 to 1945. Although 22, he qualified under the motor-bike test: despatch riders were notorious for speeding. When he reported to No. 3 Squadron (Morane Parasols) at Auchel he had never been in an aeroplane nor seen a Lewis gun, but he had learnt the morse code, and as a despatch rider he could read a map. No doubt this was why, posted to A Flight, he was at once selected to observe for the new flight commander, Captain T. O'B. Hubbard. Or perhaps, since 'Mother' Hubbard, as he was inevitably dubbed, seemed too gentle a character for the role, had only just arrived, had only once flown a Morane, and had crashed it at that, Portal was ripe to be sacrificed. He soon learned that the Morane was treated by pilots with great respect: the old hands assured him, just to cheer him up, that he had much more chance of being killed by a Morane than by the enemy.

Portal was disappointed that no one attempted to instruct him in his squadron duties. He would have much to say on the subject of training. But Hubbard did tell him to find out how to work a Lewis gun. 'We'll do the early tactical reconnaissance', he said, 'the day after tomorrow.' Portal spent several hours dismantling and reassembling the Lewis and learning how to clear stoppages, only to be told when the time came that the Morane couldn't carry both him and the gun. He did the tactical recce with a stripped rifle and a hundred rounds of ammunition.

On this first flight with Hubbard, the 80 h.p. Le Rhone engine kept missing, the Archie was alarmingly accurate, and Portal confessed to being 'very afraid'. Yet he soon became inured to the Archie. Unlike the BE2c, the Morane had to be 'flown' every minute, but Portal soon realised that Hubbard, for all his gentle nature, was an excellent pilot, while the observer's position behind the pilot made the Morane superior to the BE2c as a fighting machine, with some pretensions to defending itself from stern attack. The main drawback, as Portal saw, was that few of the observers really understood the Lewis gun – another black mark against training.

When a Morane was shot down by Immelmann over Valenciennes, three more were sent off together for mutual protection. Portal was allotted to Harvey-Kelly, by this time with 3 Squadron as a flight commander, and he persuaded H-K to let him mount a Lewis. The second Morane, whose observer also carried a Lewis, managed to reach the briefed height of 10,000 feet, but H-K and Portal could get no higher than 8,000. The third Morane, which held Jimmy McCudden, now a sergeant observer on C flight, staggered along behind them at 6,000. McCudden, with fantasies of flaming Fokkers, had packed not only a Lewis but also enough ammunition for a brace of dog-fights. Tight lateral formations were in any case considered unsafe because of the risk of collision, several hundred feet often separating one machine from another; here the height separation made mutual protection impossible. But H-K was not a man to turn back. Immelmann duly appeared and was recognised by his antics, and he attacked the top Morane, leaving McCudden and

Portal, for all their obvious potential, impotent. But the unknown observer drove Immelmann off.

In November 1915 Captain Edgar Ludlow-Hewitt, whose work with the artillery as a flight commander on No. 1 Squadron had been outstanding, assumed command of No. 3 Squadron on promotion to major, and for his observer he chose McCudden. An application for pilot training had been made by McCudden in July, but he had been told he was too valuable as an observer. Yet he knew a safe pilot when he saw one, and he developed a great admiration for Ludlow-Hewitt 'for his coolness under fire – not batting an eyelid when shells burst around him continually.' McCudden, although he had done a lot of flying as corporal and sergeant observer, had not, it seems, yet acquired this degree of serenity. 'As for myself, I was in a terrible state of funk.' If this was true, it clearly did not affect his performance. More revealing of his character was his admission that he 'didn't much care for the dashing, extrovert type of pilot; all right for him but not much good for the passenger.' (He had been flying earlier with Harvey-Kelly.) But the more he flew with Ludlow-Hewitt, the more intensely he disliked flying with anyone else.

Many of Harvey-Kelly's contemporaries were now commanding squadrons, and H-K appears to have been passed over because of his unpredictability: his exploits, and his manner of relating them, had become legendary. 'The funniest man I've ever met,' was the opinion of Archibald James. 'He kept one in roars of laughter the whole time.'

Many of H-K's stories were told against himself. On leave from France, he failed to report back at the due time. Orders sent to various leave addresses in England and Ireland went unacknowledged, and hotels and bars in London where RFC men congregated were combed unsuccessfully. When he eventually turned up at the War Office he followed his combat philosophy: get your blow in first. He flung a sheaf of telegrams and letters on the table and demanded to know how the hell he could go to all these places at once. He added that he was already fed up with England and wanted nothing more than to be sent back to the war. As usual he got away with it; but it may have delayed his promotion to squadron commander. This came, with No. 3 Squadron, in the New Year.

The enforced delay to the development of McCudden's career was ended in January 1916, when Ludlow-Hewitt unselfishly granted his wish to be sent home on a pilot's course. Now twenty, he had already been awarded the MC and the Croix de Guerre. His elder brother, Flight Sergeant William, had been killed instructing in March 1915, but a younger brother, John Anthony, had applied for a transfer from despatch riding to the RFC. Jimmy was back as a pilot in time for the Somme battle that summer.

12

AGENTS AND PIGEON FANCIERS:
A SPY IN THE MOTOR TRADE

BEFORE the two warring armies became entrenched, secret agents had little difficulty in passing from one side to the other, to gather information, and to report back. But as the front line consolidated, and parallel trenches were dug in close proximity, crossing the strip of neutral earth known as no man's land became perilous. At a conference attended by the three RFC wing commanders at Trenchard's headquarters shortly before the Battle of Loos, Trenchard told them he had a job for them, specially requested by GHQ. They wanted him to send an aeroplane to land behind the German lines, dropping an agent at a secret rendezvous near Courtrai. The agent's mission, it was stressed, had an important bearing on the forthcoming battle. 'The French have already done this sort of thing 28 times,' Trenchard told them, '27 times successfully.' The wing commanders would love to have known what had happened the twenty-eighth time, but they knew that Trenchard would never say no to an earnest request from the Army, and they were not disposed to argue, especially when they learned they would not have to despatch a second aeroplane to pick the agent up afterwards – an altogether trickier assignment. He would be armed with carrier pigeons who would home back to GHQ with his reports. When his task was finished – if he survived it – he would work his way back, normally through Holland or Belgium.

The task was allotted to No. 6 Squadron, the pilot chosen being one of the contemptibles who had crossed the Channel with 4 Squadron and, by nursing his aircraft right through the retreat, rightly gained a reputation for reliability and resource. He had force-landed his machine many times in ticklish situations but never broken it, though it had sometimes needed running repairs, which he had performed single-handed before taking off again, just the sort of coolness under pressure that might be required. This was the 25-year-old Captain T.W. Mulcahy-Morgan, formerly of the Royal Irish Fusiliers, and few could match his record. His brief was to land the agent, name of Van de Leene, at dawn on the edge of a village known to the agent, a suitable field being indicated adjacent to a wood, into which the agent would beat a hasty retreat.

The chosen field turned out to be small and enclosed by trees. Even in the slow and stable BE2c the glide before landing had to be judged to a nicety, and at 04.45 on 13 September, twelve days before the battle opened, in the poor visibility of first light, Mulcahy-Morgan had the misfortune to leave his port wing behind in a tree. Both pilot and passenger were badly hurt, Van de Leene, in the front cockpit, being saved from mortal injury by the bulky pigeon basket he carried in front of him. He broke both legs and suffered internal injuries, while Mulcahy-Morgan broke his jaw. The pigeons survived unhurt. First on the scene were some friendly civilians, who seized and secreted papers and pigeons, but the two men were too badly injured to be hidden, and eventually the Germans arrived and took them prisoner.

A pilot captured at the moment of setting down his spy was liable to the death penalty. The spy would be shot for sure. And when they were interrogated, in hospital in Courtrai, their chances looked bleak. But threats were accompanied by the usual blandishments – the more help they gave, the better would be the prospects of leniency. Mulcahy-Morgan got the impression that things weren't going too badly for Van de Leene, who he guessed was probably being 'turned' – if he wasn't a double agent already. His own position looked the more precarious, and he took refuge in his broken jaw, feigning dumbness, and got away with it. Five days later another agent sent

[129]

back news of the crash, and of the safe custody of papers and pigeons.

After two years in captivity Tom Mulcahy-Morgan escaped, returning to England in April 1917. He was awarded the MC and Bar.

The first successful spy-dropping attempt by the RFC was made a fortnight later, on 28 September, the pilot being Captain G.L. Cruikshank of 3 Squadron, the machine a Morane Parasol. Guy Cruikshank, aged twenty-five, and a Cambridge graduate, was also one of the contemptibles, highly regarded by Trenchard and already holding the MC. Thanks to Cruikshank the drop was a model of its kind and he was awarded the DSO. But the third of these adventures, five days later, was anything but trouble-free. The pilot this time was Lieutenant J.W. 'Jack' Woodhouse, of 4 Squadron; even at twenty-seven he passed the motor-bike test, having before the war won over a hundred British and Continental motor-cycle events including the International Race at Le Mans.

Woodhouse seems to have had by far the most meticulous preparation of the three. At a conference in the office of his CO, Charles Longcroft, at which a number of staff officers were present, large-scale maps were produced and various landing fields considered. This time the drop was to be made at dusk, so that the agent could escape in darkness, although for Woodhouse this meant a night landing back at base.

Over a period of several days Woodhouse made a number of flights to memorise landmarks, while light bombing took place simultaneously so that his familiarisation flights should not be conspicuous. The agent, a middle-aged French ex-army NCO named Le Marrier, tough, gregarious and immensely popular, arrived in time to get to know Woodhouse, not to mention the whole of the Sergeants' Mess, where he was accommodated before the drop, a security risk that accorded ill with the otherwise secretive preparations. Then at last, with tanks half full and the BE2c stripped of all impedimenta to improve its climbing rate and reduce landing and take-off runs, Le Marrier squeezed his swollen bulk (plain clothes underneath French uniform, one pigeon basket on his lap and a second strapped to the wing, pockets bulging with personal gear and a large bottle of Sergeants' Mess wine), into the front cockpit and Woodhouse climbed to 7,000 feet and waited for dusk.

Descending to 1,000 feet, they were approaching their recommended field when they saw lights and heard the crack of a rifle, and Woodhouse instinctively opened up and started to climb. He decided to give Le Marrier the chance to abort, but Le Marrier shook his head and pointed north, where an alternative field was located, alongside a wood like the first, about eight miles south of Cambrai. As dusk fell, and with a ground mist aiding concealment, Woodhouse made an even more silent approach than he had planned, his switched-off engine failing to pick up as intended just before landing, but the touch-down was smooth and the run short. He helped Le Marrier out of his cockpit with his many accoutrements and waved him off towards the wood. So heavily laden was Le Marrier that he dropped one of his baskets of pigeons and didn't notice it at first, then had to turn back to retrieve it. Meanwhile Woodhouse had set the throttle, switched on, and swung the propeller. He had prepared the tail skid to hold the ground as firmly as possible when the plane started to move; but now the engine, over-rich from the windmilling descent, backfired.

Woodhouse switched off, opened the throttle fully, and started to turn the propeller backwards to clear the surplus petrol that had accumulated during the descent. Suddenly he was shocked to see a figure emerging from the wood, coatless and empty-handed: he was considerably relieved to recognise Le Marrier, who had seen his pilot's predicament and come back to help. He tried to grab the propeller, but Woodhouse, anxious not to be found in the company of a spy, chased him off. 'He laughed,' said Woodhouse afterwards, 'but I don't think I did.' After pulling the prop backwards a few more times Woodhouse sat down for a rest. At last, after he had stuffed his gloves into the air intake for the 'suck in' sequence, he again swung the prop and this time the engine fired. He scrambled back into the cockpit as the machine moved forward.

It was now pitch dark, the engine was missing badly, and soon he had to land again, fortunately in a level, deserted area. After running

[131]

the engine in short bursts to burn out the surplus oil he got off again, and the engine behaved rather better, but he was hopelessly lost. When he was sure he had crossed the lines he put the machine into the slowest possible glide, lit a cheroot to steady his nerves, and waited for the bump, hoping to see enough at the last moment to flatten out. The landing was heavy and the machine came to a halt on its nose, but only the propeller was damaged. He had been away nearly two-and-a-half hours.

'I consider,' wrote Brancker, commanding Third Wing, 'that Lieutenant Woodhouse deserves very high commendation.' For this and other stirring exploits, he too was awarded the DSO.

Selection for the task of dropping agents was haphazard at first, though some preparation was given. Sergeant Sidney Attwater, a skilled toolmaker and A.V. Roe apprentice from Preston who had inevitably been enlisted as an air mechanic, had graduated to air observer and finally, after training, to pilot on FE2d's (250 h.p. Rolls-Royce engine). 'I received orders to report one morning at 2 a.m. to my flight commander,' he recorded. It was a perfect moonlit night, and he had to do three night landings without flares, which he accomplished safely. Next day he was sent on a trial run in daylight to a small German aerodrome, and on the next moonlit night he was introduced in the CO's office to a French agent. At 01.15 'Monsieur Victor' boarded the FE2d with a large basket containing pigeons, ammunition, money etc., which was duly affixed to the starboard wing. He also carried an old-fashioned string bag which he revealed was full of dainties and gifts for his wife and family. Spies were generally natives of the district they were being dropped in, with special knowledge of the country, more often than not civilians, but 'Monsieur Victor' wore French uniform, and Attwater noted with some disquiet the number 13 on his cap. 'How are you going to get away after I've landed you?' asked Attwater. This was not answered until after the landing, when the agent asked to be taxied to a wood at one end of the aerodrome. 'Turn round ready for take-off,' said Monsieur Victor, 'and wait for another agent to come back with you.' Attwater agreed to wait for a minute or so. 'I was getting a bit windy', he admitted, 'by the time he arrived.' To Attwater's alarm, the replacement let off a few rounds at a solitary hangar as Attwater prepared to take off. There had evidently been some answering fire, as he later found several bullet-holes in the FE2d. But to Attwater's enquiry about the fate of Monsieur Victor, the reply was: 'It is impossible for him to be caught.' There is some evidence that these two agents were identical twins, working a familiar deception. Attwater rated these agents 'the most courageous men in the war'.

Once the agents had despatched their reports back to GHQ by pigeon post, a re-supply operation was required to furnish them with more pigeons. How were these pigeons to be dropped? A pilot named Edward Pennell was assigned to the task of concentrating on methods of pigeon dropping. Reflecting that it was pigeons themselves which generally did the dropping, he braced himself to become the first of the pigeon droppers.

In conjunction with an unnamed airman from Hartlepool, who was an expert on homing pigeons, and an air mechanic named Callender, Pennell began his experiments. The valuable homing pigeons had to be settled at GHQ so they would return there, and they could not in any case be risked on practice drops, so the barns in nearby farms were scoured for wood pigeons. Two of these pigeons, each wearing a tiny harness, were tied together with a six-foot cord, on the principle that when tethered and released they would fly against each other and gradually descend to the ground. In practice the unfortunate birds became hopelessly entangled and died. A better method was evolved, using the same principle, in which four pigeons were placed in separate compartments in a rectangular metal box fitted in the bomb rack under the fuselage, with doors opening earthwards. When the release cable was pulled by the pilot, the doors opened, the pigeons fell out individually, flew off in different directions, and, being tethered, slowly fluttered to the ground.

The operation was to take place in daylight when there was good cloud cover interspersed with clear patches: on crossing the line, Pennell was to climb above the cloud, fly for a given time on a prearranged compass course allowing for drift, descend through a clear patch on estimated time of arrival, and look for six large hay or straw stacks in a field which would also contain a herd of black and white cows. After releasing the pigeons at the lowest height consistent with safety, Pennell was to seek cloud cover again as quickly as possible.

Cruising around at 5,000 feet on ETA, Pennell searched for a break in the cloud. 'I had now got the wind-up pretty badly,' he said afterwards: he was expecting the whole German Air Force to be waiting to pounce. Diving through a convenient gap, throttling down as he did so, he circled at 1,000 feet, looking for hay stacks and cows, but there was nothing to be seen. It suddenly occurred to him that his chances of finding his target must be hundreds to one, and that a protracted search would give the whole show away as well as attract opposition. It was not long before he turned for home. When the pigeons were offloaded back at base it was found that the cold and perhaps the height had been too much for them; half were dead.

Another attempt a week later, when the pigeons were actually dropped, was no more successful, the agent reporting that they mostly died before reaching the ground. For the next attempt the pigeons were fitted with small parachutes, but it was no more successful.

As the number of agents proliferated, a special flight of four BE2c single-seaters was formed by Guy Cruikshank under Biffy Borton of 27 Squadron to land them at chosen rendezvous, the agent being strapped to the lower wing, close to the fuselage, shielded by a strip of three-ply wood. The front cockpit was simply faired over. After Woodhouse's experience the timing of the drop reverted to early morning, with the pilot taking off shortly before dawn. Successful drops were made, but after an occasion when pilot and machine failed to return, suspicion fell on the agent, and Cruikshank decided to take the next flight himself, fully prepared for skulduggery. Immediately he landed, the agent turned a gun on him and fired, but Cruikshank was quick enough to get in a single shot which proved fatal for the agent. Although wounded in the arm, Cruikshank brought the plane back safely and with it the revelation of the agent's treachery.

By 1916 a Special Duty Flight, now transferred to Headquarters

Wing under Cyril Newall, was formed by Jack Woodhouse, Cruikshank having been appointed a flight commander on 70 Squadron (Sopwith 1½-strutters). Meanwhile Woodhouse had greatly augmented his night-flying experience by attacking raiding Zeppelins while based at Dover. As before, the job was to drop spies behind the German lines, but this time by parachute, 'much more pleasant for the pilot,' wrote Woodhouse, 'but I suspect rather dicey for the spy.' The parachute selected was of the C.G. Spencer type, the one used by observers in kite balloons, and it was carried in a casing under the fuselage. The agent wore a harness which was attached to the parachute by a line: when he jumped his weight pulled the parachute from its casing and it opened immediately and automatically. Or so the agent was assured.

Woodhouse, flying a BE12a (a single-seater with 140 h.p. RAF engine), carried the agent very much as in the BE2c, lying flat on the strengthened wing. But shortly before he was due to jump, the agent would naturally peer down into the darkness to try to recognise the dropping area. On one occasion the agent, transparently doubtful of Woodhouse's navigation, stood up reluctantly when alerted, steadied himself in the airstream by gripping the side of the cockpit, and stamped about uncertainly on the wing, showing a marked reluctance to leave. Woodhouse had already throttled back, they were barely above stalling speed, the fellow's movements were upsetting stability, and soon control would be lost and they would spin in. 'I had to help him to make up his mind,' was Woodhouse's masterpiece of understatement. He had the man on his conscience afterwards and was relieved to hear some time later that his reports were duly arriving.

When there were no agents to drop or to supply, Woodhouse was employed in bombing specially selected targets from a level impossible in daylight. This, with the agent-dropping, meant a lot of night flying, and as landing behind the lines was not involved any more he chose to fly with full tanks and cruise about waiting for dawn to find his base aerodrome. Returning early one morning with a French cheroot stuck in his mouth, he found Colonel Newall sitting on a shooting stick waiting for him and his report. 'Smoking in open cockpits was definitely not done,' recorded Woodhouse later, 'but the future chief of the air staff never turned a hair.'

For the agents themselves, the actual descent was only the beginning, their fate often depending on an accurate drop. The use of parachutes introduced an assumption of pinpoint accuracy which it was not always possible to achieve. And however remote the rendezvous, there was always the danger that the passage overhead of an aeroplane would alert ground observers. The facility with which agents merged into the background on the enemy side of the lines, and passed back their reports, is explained by the fact that they were mostly operating in home territory that had been overrun by the Germans but remained friendly to the Allied cause.

This certainly helped another agent dropper, Claude Ridley, of 60 Squadron, to 'do a Mapplebeck' during the Somme battle, when he force-landed with engine trouble with his passenger still on board. The agent told Ridley to hide in a ditch, disappeared, and returned with civilian clothing and money, after which Ridley had to shift for himself. 'I am a British officer trying to escape,' he told any locals he met. 'Will you help me?' They always did. Challenged aboard a tram, he punched his way clear and jumped, crossed an electrified fence at the Belgian frontier, and arranged his own passage back into France, bringing with him much useful Intelligence. Welcomed back at 60 Squadron, he was awarded the DSO.

Some years after the war, Jack Woodhouse renewed acquaintance, quite by chance, with a man in the motor trade against whom he had raced at Brooklands pre-war. 'It's a long time since we met,' was Woodhouse's greeting.

'Not so long as you think,' was the reply.
'Oh?' queried Woodhouse. 'How's that?'
'Do you remember a night at Auchel when you took off to drop a spy by parachute?'

All Woodhouse could remember of Auchel was of dropping a man with a shockingly untidy beard. This fellow was clean-shaven. But he went on to describe precisely what had occurred prior to take-off, even to the extent of what Woodhouse had said in his halting and indifferent French. 'Not all agents', he added, 'were Frenchmen – but keep what I've said under your hat.'

There the conversation was interrupted, leaving Woodhouse to ponder whether his old racing antagonist had been an Intelligence Officer involved in the drop, or the agent himself, minus a very untidy false beard.

1916

13

FOKKER FODDER – 'MY GOD! IT'S MURDER!': HAWKER AND 24 SQUADRON: THE LESSONS OF VERDUN

T HE Allied Strategy for 1916 aimed at something far more ambitious than the costly but disappointing engagements of the previous year. At Neuve Chapelle, and again at Loos, breaches had been made in the enemy lines, but the exploitation of these breaches had been frustrated by the enemy's ability, rapidly and decisively, to draft in powerful and seemingly inexhaustible reserves. It was clear that before any deeper penetration could be achieved, those reserves must themselves be eroded. This was the objective of a joint Allied offensive planned for the summer of 1916 in which the initial breakthrough was to be made by the British, with the French following up to soak up the German reserves and inflict a crushing blow. The assault was to be preceded by a massive bombardment intended to annihilate the German first and second line trenches and open the way for the infantry. The Somme was chosen as the battleground because the Allied armies could fight there side by side: this was at the insistence of the French, whose army was double the size of the British and whose scepticism about British reliability was ingrained.

There were thirty-eight British divisions in France by January 1916, and nineteen more would have arrived by mid-summer: Haig expected to be ready to mount his assault by that time. Would the RFC be ready to play its part? It was now accepted that the role of air forces in visual and photographic reconnaissance, in spotting for and directing the artillery, and in denying these facilities to the enemy (by bombing their airfields and intercepting their intruders), was of paramount importance, and each of the four British armies now in France was supported by an RFC brigade. Each brigade had two wings, one for the corps (army co-operation) squadrons and one for the army (bombing and fighting) squadrons, and each squadron, on paper at least, was brought up to a total of eighteen machines from the previous twelve. By mid-summer, all being well, the RFC would have doubled in size in the space of nine months to twenty-six and a half squadrons, which looked impressive; but many were still equipped with the same basic BE2 machine, and not all the new squadrons were yet up to strength. Against this, the delivery in quantity of the Fokker EII, with its more powerful engine, and the EIII, with a further speed increase, in recent months had added to the disastrous inferiority from which the RFC aircraft had suffered since the introduction of the Fokker EI. The German pilots still operated almost exclusively over their own side of the lines, but Trenchard's insistence on maintaining an aggressive posture – anything else, in his book, spelt disaster – inevitably meant that whenever a penetration of any depth was attempted, either for reconnaissance or bombing, the Fokkers were waiting. No longer distributed in penny packets, they now operated in groups of three or four, and of the machines they ambushed, most were shot down and the occupants killed. As the carnage reached crisis point, Trenchard was obliged, on 14 January 1916, to issue an order whose effect was to weaken his force dramatically just at the moment when the demands made upon it seemed likely to increase.

The order began with a humiliating admission of inferiority. 'Until the RFC are in possession of a machine as good as or better than the German Fokker it seems that a change in the tactics employed becomes necessary.' Trenchard proceeded to lay down as a hard and fast rule that any machine employed on reconnaissance must be escorted by at least three fighting machines. 'These machines must be flown in close formation and a reconnaissance should not continue if any of the machines become detached.' Since it was rare for any group of aeroplanes to escape fragmentation, if only through engine trouble, this was an operational restriction of extreme severity. The ruling was to apply to both short- and long-range penetrations, and the implications of the obvious tactical reversal were acknowledged and even emphasised. 'Flying in a close formation must be practised by all pilots.' Hitherto, as already indicated, formation flying in anything like close proximity had been shunned as dangerous.

As it happened, the RFC already had in prospect the introduction of machines which it was hoped would prove as good as or better than the Fokker. These were the DH2 and the FE2b, and later the FE2d, already mentioned. Both types were designed by Geoffrey de Havilland, the Fee, as it came to be known, originating as early as 1910, and both had the open lattice-work fuselage, beam spars and bracing wires of the period. But being of the pusher type, they were not dependent on interrupter gear for firing straight ahead.

Led by Lanoe Hawker, No. 24 Squadron (DH2s), Britain's first single-seater scout squadron, arrived in France on 8 February 1916 in great excitement but was immediately absorbed in a crisis of its own. The day after their arrival, one of the flight commanders, on the first flight of a DH2 from a French airfield, got into a spin and failed to recover. Five days later, another pilot spun in, and this time the machine caught fire. It had happened before, earning the DH2 the grisly sobriquet of the 'spinning incinerator'. With the morale of his pilots, all inexperienced and nearly all under twenty-one, severely shaken, Hawker responded by taking up a DH2 and, according to his biographer, spinning it from every conceivable angle, engine on and engine off, and demonstrating how, with correct remedial action, and provided there was sufficient height, it always recovered. 'It's all right, you fellows,' he is reported to have said after landing. 'You can get the DH2 out of any spin. I have just tried it out.'[1]

The mysteries of the spin had not yet been solved, and Hawker's discovery – on the face of it – was a momentous one. Apparently his pilots 'gathered eagerly around . . . while he explained the correct manoeuvres until they all understood them clearly . . . Out they all went to follow his example.' But what these manoeuvres were is not

1 Hawker, Tyrrel M., *Hawker VC* (The Mitre Press, 1965).

[143]

specified, nor was the discovery publicised, which seems inconceivable. Another pilot on Hawker's squadron is said to have been the first man to stunt a DH2, but neither man was mentioned when an investigation into spinning and those who solved its secrets was later published (see Chapter 18).

Within its limitations the DH2 was to prove an agile little single-seater, wonderfully manoeuvrable, almost capable of turning on the proverbial sixpence. But its time was not yet. The first bulk delivery of the two-seater FE2b's, too, with its spacious front cockpit in which the observer could move about freely and enjoy a wide field of fire, aft over the top planes and in a wide arc ahead and abeam, had reached No. 20 Squadron in January, but like the DH2 it had yet to establish itself. Meanwhile, despite a marked improvement achieved by the introduction of tighter formation flying and the provision of escorts, losses mounted.

Bitter criticism of the War Office for its general failure to design and supply suitable modern machines for its air crews, and in particular of its apparent tolerance of the shortcomings of the BE2c, was shrugged off by the routine appointment of a committee. This did not divert a flamboyant, egocentric but far from uninformed ex-RNAS pilot named Noel Pemberton-Billing from pressing charges in the House of Commons of criminal negligence by RFC commanders. Pemberton-Billing had earlier distinguished himself by his brilliant planning of an RNAS bombing raid on the Zeppelin sheds at Friedrichshaven: he had since resigned his commission to stand (and be elected) as a member of Parliament, posing, with some authority, as an expert in air matters. On 22 March 1916, two years ahead of his time, he demanded the creation of a single force that would consume what he called the inertia of the RNAS and the blunders of the RFC. He particularly stressed the over-ordering of the BE2c (of which over 2,000 were built), which he claimed the pilots themselves were stigmatising as Fokker fodder. Continuing what amounted to a blistering attack on the RFC leaders, he went on to suggest that 'quite a number of our gallant officers in the Royal Flying Corps had been rather murdered than killed'. This latter calumny referred to accidents in training rather than in action, which he attributed to faulty construction. Certainly it was true that the majority of fatalities were occurring at the training stations rather than at the front.

The outcome of Pemberton-Billing's charges was a judicial inquiry, a first step on the road to amalgamation of the two air services. But its immediate impact was small. Trenchard's fury was directed at the alarmist insinuations of Fokker invincibility, which were taken up enthusiastically by sections of the Press (especially by the trenchant C.G. Grey of *The Aeroplane*), and the effect this was bound to have on the morale of his pilots. There might also, it was feared, be a knock-on effect on recruitment.

Judging from the quality and lack of experience of new pilots arriving in France, it was clear that reorganisation of the entire training programme was urgently needed, and on 16 February Trenchard sent Jack Salmond home to undertake this task. One young man, perhaps hardly typical, reporting for duty at St Omer that spring was the seventeen-year-old Cecil Lewis. There was certainly no faulting his enthusiasm. 'In those days,' he wrote later, 'I lived for the air. There was nothing in life to compare with taking a machine off the ground, wheeling away into the sky, trying turns, spirals, dives, stalls, gliding, zooming, doing all the stunts a pilot needs to give him confidence and nerve in a tight corner.'[1] But he recognised that as yet he was hopelessly ill-equipped for action. Even after being given a BE2c, told to regard it as his own, and to do all the flying he wanted, he confessed a day or so later that his total flying time was fourteen hours. 'It's absolutely disgraceful to send pilots overseas with so little flying,' he was told by his flight commander at St Omer. 'You don't stand a chance.' Perhaps his obvious youth had aroused his mentor's pity. 'I'll speak to the major and try and keep you here for a bit . . . another 50 hours and you might be quite decent, but 14! My God, it's murder!' In two quite separate contexts the same crime was being alleged.

At this time, replacement pilots were arriving at St Omer at the rate of about ten a week, an insufficient number inadequately trained. The deficiency was caused partly by the winter weather, which had

1 Lewis, Cecil, *Sagittarius Rising* (Peter Davies, 1936; Greenhill Books, 1993).

[145]

delayed and truncated training programmes, partly by an inevitable failure to fulfil over-optimistic estimates, and partly because,
in the phenomenal expansion being attempted, new squadrons
were being formed and sent out before they were ready. Despite Pemberton-Billings's calumnies there was in fact no shortage
of volunteers, rather the reverse. '... to belong to the RFC in
those days was to be singled out among the rest of the khaki-clad
world by reason of the striking double-breasted tunic (the maternity
jacket, as it was known), the wings, and the little forage cap
set over one ear, but more than this by the glamour surrounding
"birdmen"', wrote Cecil Lewis. 'Flying was still something of a
miracle. We who practised it were thought very brave, very daring,
very gallant: we belonged to a world apart.' The shortage was
not of young men willing to chance their arm but of instructors,
especially of men of the right calibre. Pilots sent home on rest from
France were not always temperamentally suited to so specialist a
task.

In those early months of 1916 the crews of the new pusher-type
fighters were granted an unexpected hiatus in which to work up: on
21 February 1916, with the Fokker menace at its height, the planned
Allied offensive was pre-empted by a massive German assault on a
nine-mile front in north-eastern France along the banks of the Meuse,
opposite the ancient French town and fortress of Verdun. The German objective was to bleed France white in a war of attrition, forcing
the British to take over more and more of the line; they would deal
with them later. Meanwhile they relied on the French co-operating
in their own destruction by defending the fortress, for reasons of
national pride, to the bitter end. Meanwhile the bulk of the German
fighter force under Boelcke would be concentrated in the skies above
Verdun.

In the longest and bloodiest battle of the war, repeated German
assaults were met by sacrificial French resistance in what became
known as the 'hell of Verdun'. Joffre, having decided to hold the
fortress at all costs, placed Pétain in command on this front, and in
establishing a supply route, and by frequent rotation of units, Pétain
contributed decisively to the failure, despite recurring crises, of the

(*Above right*): Lanoe Hawker, VC, DSO. His motto, posted on the squadron notice board, was 'Attack EVERYTHING'.

(*Above*): 'She is a little beauty'. The Bristol Scout with the obliquely-mounted machine-gun in which Hawker won his VC.

Jack Woodhouse with the agent, a French ex-army NCO named Le Marrier, whom he dropped from a BE2c behind the German lines.

C.F.A. 'Peter' Portal. Astounded at the ignorance of his instructors.

Gwilym H. Lewis. 'You have no idea how scared I am.' Yet he found dogfights 'wildly exciting'.

Hugh Dowding. 'Pernickety, interfering, querulous' . . . but not easily shaken from his convictions.

Lionel Rees, VC. 'Everyone knows that the major is mad . . . I told you he was the bravest man in the world.'

'Willie' Read. Looked after his men – but kept himself warm.

Read with Leslie Porter. 'I lost my best flight commander.' Read blamed Dowding.

The Sopwith 1 1/2-strutter. Flown by 43, 45 and 70 Squadrons.

S.F. Vincent. Overheard Smith-Barry 'as good as tell Trenchard he was a butcher'.

George McCubbin. Crashed his machine showing off – but later, with observer Corporal J.H. Waller in an FE2b, accounted for Immelmann.

Harold Balfour in the cockpit of a Caudron trainer at the Ruffy-Baumann School of Flying at Hendon

Roland Garros in the box-like Type L Morane Parasol monoplane in which he scored his victories and was himself shot down.

The Morane Parasol Type LA, with rounded fuselage. 'It was a machine you could never relax in,' wrote Cecil Lewis – but it took him right through the Somme battle.

The Morane Type N, which the British called the Bullet. 'They were tricky little brutes to fly,' wrote Harold Balfour. Mapplebeck killed himself in one.

Sidney Attwater when a corporal observer on 8 Squadron (BE2c's). Later, with his fellow Lancastrian Tom Mottershead, he was nearly court-martialled.

Tom Mottershead, DCM, VC. Set on fire b an Albatros DII, he got plane and observe back safely.

An FE2d of the type flown by Attwater and Mottershead.

Ball's Nieuport – showing the contrasting wing chords.

Albert Ball, VC, DSO and two bars. 'A quiet, shy, simple little chap', he protested that he 'did not think anything bad about the Hun'.

Flight Sergeant James McCudden as an observer, 1915. Whereas Ball was the gifted amateur, McCudden was the seasoned professional.

Ewart Garland. An Australian who 'kept on flying to the limit of endurance and beyond'.

Arthur Gordon-Kidd. A classic opportunist bombing on the first da on the Somme.

18-year-old Harold Tambling during training on the Bristol Fighter.
'We have a completely new squadron every few weeks.'

German assaults. These culminated in a final abortive bid on 11 July. By that time, Pétain's appeals to the British to relieve the pressure at Verdun by opening the planned campaign on the Somme had borne fruit.

For Trenchard and the RFC – and for Commandant Paul-Fernand du Peuty and the *Aviation Militaire* – the lessons of Verdun were starkly clear. Du Peuty was already sympathetic to Trenchard's doctrine of the offensive, of the absolute necessity of dominating the enemy's air space or he would dominate yours; but if he harboured any doubts, the experience of Verdun would have quelled them. To begin with, the *Aviation Militaire*, keeping on the offensive, attained a marked superiority, so much so that the Germans were forced to deploy their Fokkers to protect their air reconnaissance machines. Nevertheless the German two-seaters were sometimes able to penetrate French air space and harass French troops, leading to complaints that the only aeroplanes ever seen over the battle area were German. Weakening under intense pressure to provide protective patrols for the French infantry and artillery, du Peuty surrendered the initiative, allowing the Germans, under Boelcke, to move in quickly and bomb the ground troops, shoot them up, bomb their installations, inflict increased casualties, and generally gain the ascendancy, even to the extent of shooting down French reconnaissance machines. The more the army demanded direct air support the more the Germans dominated, both on the ground and in the air. Finally, ignoring the blandishments of the generals, du Peuty reverted to his original tactics and proved to his detractors that he had been right in the first place. Aiding him in this demonstration were new types of machine, the latest Morane and particularly the Nieuport 11 or Bébé, a single-seat V-strut sesquiplane (biplane with the upper wing-span – or wing-chord, as in this case – greater than the lower), small in size but speedy and with a good rate of climb, and with a Lewis gun on the top wing firing over the propeller arc. It was in machines of this type, superior in most respects to the Fokker, that reputations were made above the Verdun battlefield by the first clutch of French aces – notably Charles Nungesser, Jean Navarre and René Fonck. And it was in a Nieuport Bébé, one of a number received by the RFC in March 1916, that the first of the publicised British aces, Albert Ball, scored his first successes.

Meanwhile Hawker was cementing his reputation within the service as a tactician and leader, although, inhibited by the restrictions placed on squadron commanders, he rarely led his men into combat. But unlike many in his position he flew regularly, allowing one of his flight commanders to lead. Despite the numerous administrative and personnel problems involved, he found running a squadron in France much easier than he had found the working-up period at home, and he accepted that his job now was to drive and inspire. When called upon to send his pilots on risky assignments in which he had been ordered not to take part, he felt the moral authority granted by the VC and DSO ribbons on his tunic and was glad of them, and he took part when he could in order not to lose touch. He was aware that many of the orders he received from wing head-quarters, especially for providing escort for deep reconnaissances designated urgent despite poor weather, resulted from insistent and sometimes unreasonable army demands which Trenchard would not deny. Above all he remained an operational pilot, improvising and inventing, popular with his own squadron and with the squadrons they were escorting, a model for every DH2 pilot, several more of whom were now arriving in France with new squadrons.

Expectations of a protracted tussle with the Fokker *Eindeckers* for supremacy did not at first materialise. With the majority of Boelcke's men engaged elsewhere, Hawker's pilots were given time to accustom themselves to the formation flying ordered by Trenchard, patrolling the lines north of the Somme. Meanwhile a second FE2b squadron, No. 25, arrived from England. Both FE squadrons, when called upon to provide escort beyond the lines, found themselves under surveil-lance, but when challenged they generally gave as good as they got. Often, by retaining close formation, they deterred attack altogether. They also developed the frustrating defensive tactic of forming them-selves into a circle, which meant that no Fokker pilot could get on the tail of one FE2b without coming under direct fire from one or more of the others.

14

THE ARRIVAL OF BALL:
THE DEPARTURE OF IMMELMANN

B Y April, Hawker's DH2s (No. 24 Squadron) had perfected their tactics and had begun escorting reconnaissance and photographic machines beyond the lines. The Fokkers tried to get at the two-seaters, but they were confronted by the DH2s before they could do so. On 24 April, a group attack by Fokkers on five reconnaissance BE2c's was effectively repulsed by four escorting DH2s, and next day another succession of determined Fokker attacks on a reconnaissance machine was beaten off by two of Hawker's pilots. These two engagements finally confirmed that the manoeuvrability of the DH2 was more than a match for any Fokker pilot, Boelcke and Immelmann included. The Fokkers still tried to interfere, and although the DH2 also proved superior in speed, climb, and general fighting efficiency, the Fokker pilots could always escape by diving, so not many were actually shot down.

Because of the penetration attempted daily on behalf of the army, RFC losses were always greater than those of the enemy, but not a single machine was lost when under escort by Hawker's squadron. And the contrast between the massive information gleaned by the RFC, against the trickle obtained by the few enemy planes that ventured over the British lines, was immense.

Of particular value was the work of the photographic crews, who, as always, were obliged to fly straight and level while operating the camera. In the FE2b the work was done by the observer; in the BE2c, still far more numerous in this period, the observer, sitting in front of the pilot under the small centre section, top plane above, lower plane below, could see little. Thus the pilot, sitting slightly aft of the mainplanes with a fair downward view, had to operate the camera, which was clamped outside the fuselage beside him. To sight it he had to lean over the side and direct his gaze through a ball-and-crosswire finder: controlling the machine with his left hand, he then selected the area he wanted to photo, put his right arm out into the 70-knot wind, and pushed the camera handle back and forth to change the plates, pulling a ring on the end of a cord for each exposure. It was a tedious process, and, with escorting machines similarly obliged to fly straight and level to maintain protection, a hazardous one. Losses there certainly were, and at times the Fokker pilots operated with all their old panache; but in the course of four consecutive days in mid-May the whole of the enemy's trenches facing the Fourth Army – the first line, the intermediate line, and the second and third lines – over a front of more than twenty miles, were successfully photographed without any interference from the Fokkers. The Fokker threat had been repulsed, and command of the air, so essential to the forthcoming battle, had been secured.

Similarly reassuring were the dummy combats staged against a Fokker captured intact on 8 April, which revealed it as outmoded except for its interrupter gear and 500-round belt-fed machine gun. All the current machines performed well against it – except, of course, the BE2c, which 'just wasn't in it', according to one of the test pilots.

There were two especially notable personnel occurrences to report in the months before the Somme battle. On the British side it was a unique acquisition; on the German side it was a tragic depletion. First, on 18 February, the nineteen-year-old Albert Ball, described as a 'quiet, shy, simple little chap', but with a chin that suggested a stubborn, rebellious streak, arrived at No. 13 Squadron on BE2c's, where he was engaged on artillery work and occasional bombing missions. Ball not only disliked twin-seat flying, he hated being

responsible for another man's life; nevertheless his aggressive potential emerged and was recognised, and on 7 May he was posted to
11 Squadron. Here the basic machine, recently replacing the Vickers
Gunbus, was the FE2b, but this heterogeneous squadron also boasted
three Bristol Scouts and three of the tiny Nieuport 11 single-seaters,
offering Ball a taste of the aerial freedom he craved. It did not take
him long to make his mark. Four days later, while flying a Bristol
Scout, he scored a probable victory over an Albatros two-seater and
was mentioned for the first time in an RFC communiqué, bringing
his name to more general notice. It was with 11 Squadron, under
the benevolent eye of his new commander, 'Mother' Hubbard, and
with the help of his mechanic, F.J. Land, that he built the small
wooden hut, surrounded by flowers, on the edge of the aerodrome,
near the hangar where he housed the Nieuport Bébé he was now
allotted, and where he lived on his own and stood immediately ready
for action. It was here, too, that he delighted in lighting a magnesium
flare outside his hut at night and walking round it in his pyjamas
playing the fiddle. No doubt this was a contributory factor in his
desire for solitude – and in the granting of it.

A practising mechanic even as a boy, Ball had volunteered for
army service with the Sherwood Foresters, transferring to the RFC
after learning to fly privately during the summer of 1915 – necessarily
at dawn so as to be back on parade at 6 a.m. Already commissioned
as a second lieutenant, he was awarded his wings on 26 January
1916 and posted to France three weeks later.

Ball is reputed never to have flown for amusement: but he neglected no opportunities for practising his stalking talents, putting the
wind up many a BE2c pilot he happened to encounter on his own
side of the lines. One day Lanoe Hawker, whose habit it was to
make flying visits to the corps squadrons to discuss escort problems,
was airborne in the only machine that could be spared, a BE2c, when
he spotted a Nieuport Bébé. The pilot started stalking him at once,
and Hawker, the finest of all handlers of the BE2c, thoroughly
enjoyed the battle of wits that followed. Neither man knew who he
was up against, but Ball, in the far superior fighting machine, could
never quite attain the position he wanted and eventually conceded

defeat. But he noted the BE's identification markings, and he rang up the squadron after he landed to find out who it was. He was considerably mollified to learn that it was Hawker.

Despite his quiet simplicity Ball was highly strung, and for all his eccentricities he suffered from acute nervous tension, so much so that in no time at all he asked for a rest. This unseemly request was referred to his brigade commander, none other than Josh Higgins, who noticed, while inspecting the squadron machines, that Ball's gun wasn't mounted as ordered. 'Put it lower,' ordered Higgins. 'Take it off and put it lower.' Ball had his own method of operating the gun, but he was in no mood to explain. 'Who has to fight it?' he demanded. 'You or me?' For this piece of insolence, and the premature request, he was punished by being sent back to BEs, this time on 8 Squadron.

Ball described this as a cad's trick, but he still seems to have been treated with an amused and even respectful tolerance, as someone altogether out of the ordinary, and on 27 June his first decoration, a Military Cross, was gazetted. Meanwhile Patrick Playfair, now commanding 8 Squadron, gave him plenty of interesting work, including night bombing and spy-dropping. After landing his passenger safely on one of these nocturnal spy-dropping trips he couldn't get the man to leave, so he threatened to shoot him if he didn't go at once, before they were discovered. Ball eventually 'helped' the man out of the cockpit.

Among the new FE2b pilots was an eighteen-year-old South African named G.R. McCubbin, survivor of an episode in his training that verged on the farcical. While a pupil at Joyce Green, George McCubbin force-landed his machine in the grounds of an officers' convalescent home, though without doing himself any damage that might have qualified him for admission. His machine too was undamaged, and next morning, after being entertained overnight by the nursing staff, who proved appreciative of the company of an able-bodied visitor, he took off safely but could not resist executing a few stunts in salute. Losing control, he crashed in almost the same spot as before, but this time smashed up his plane and broke a leg, qualifying for admission after all. When he joined 25 Squadron in France some time later, however, he and his observer, Corporal J.H. Waller, were responsible for the tragic depletion of enemy strength already mentioned – or so the British have always claimed. Of seven FE2b's which took off on an offensive patrol over Lens in the late evening of 18 June, two, piloted by Second Lieutenants J.R.B. Savage (leading) and McCubbin, sighted three Fokkers some distance below and immediately dived to the attack. In the mêlée that followed, the precise manoeuvres of each of the combatants remain typically obscure, but certain it is that the pilot of one of the Fokkers was Immelmann, and that he turned the tables on Savage by rolling into a steep climbing curve that brought him above and behind his target, and that Savage was mortally wounded by a burst from Immelmann's guns and dived away out of control.

Seeing that McCubbin was already seeking revenge, and aware that he was vulnerable, Immelmann broke off his attack on Savage, but too late. Corporal Waller opened fire point-blank, and the Fokker failed to recover from its dive, careering on down until it crashed. McCubbin and Waller did not know it until later, but they had removed a major threat to the supremacy Trenchard was demanding. A second FE was shot down by the other Fokkers and its crew taken prisoner, but the Eagle of Lille was dead.

The Germans could not believe that their hero had been outfought, and they attributed his last despairing dive to a defect in his interrupter gear damaging his propeller; it was a fault that had occurred before. He would not be the only 'ace' about whose death an air of mystery was to linger. The evidence appeared to be conflicting, although later it was reported that the Fokker's control wires had been shot through. More immediately, Immelmann was accorded the tribute of having a memorial wreath dropped by another South African pilot over a German aerodrome, with a message of condolence. McCubbin got the DSO and Waller the DCM.

The drawback – perhaps the folly – of according extravagant praise and publicity to a few outstanding pilots was the blow to morale when their invincibility was seen to have been illusory. This could well be why reasons other than enemy action were found for Immelmann's death, although reports of the action left the British in no doubt. The Germans decided not to risk a second similar blow, and Boelcke was withdrawn from the line.

Two of the scout squadrons attached to the Headquarters Wing under Dowding, No. 27, (flying Martinsyde G100s, which featured a much larger wing area than the S1 and a Beardmore 120 h.p. engine), and No. 60 (Moranes under Ferdy Waldron), reported no interference next day during escort work and offensive patrols. The G100, a single-seat tractor biplane designed as a long-range escort fighter, was quickly dubbed 'Elephant', or 'Jumbo', for obvious reasons, and it did not last long as a fighter. Its weight and size made it sluggish in combat, and 27 was the only complete squadron so armed. Yet Oliver Stewart, the aviation commentator, thought its good qualities were underestimated, while air mechanic C. Callender said it did 'yeoman service' as a fighter and bomber on the Somme. 'The majority of machines turned out by factories at this stage of the war', added Callender, 'were not up to standard, but many modifications and improvements were made in the field.' This was often at the behest of disgruntled pilots, and the work of the ground crews in refining and rearming unsatisfactory machines often went unsung – but not by Trenchard. 'These men,' he repeatedly emphasised, 'are the backbone of all our efforts.'

Equally remarkable was the composition of 60 Squadron, both in personnel and equipment. Old Etonian Ferdy Waldron had enlisted three more OEs as flight commanders, the senior being Bob Smith-Barry. Other squadron pilots included Peter Portal and the eighteen-year-old Harold Balfour. Each flight sported, at first, a different type of Morane Saulnier. First was the Type N monoplane, adapted from a pre-war racing machine, with a maximum speed of 90 m.p.h. at sea level and a good rate of climb. Because of its superior streamlining, the British christened it the Bullet. Second was the Type L (later LA), the first of a series of 'Parasol' monoplanes, so named because of their umbrella-like single wing. Third was the BB, a two-seater biplane otherwise resembling the Bullet. Only the Parasol, the type to which Raymond Saulnier fitted deflector plates and in which Roland Garros was captured, was much used by the French.

Trenchard was especially wary of the Bullet because of its high wing loading, high landing speed and extreme sensitivity to elevator control, but in the build-up to the Somme battle he was glad of what he could get. 'They were tricky little brutes to handle,' according to Balfour, and Mapplebeck had killed himself in one. But shortly before the battle the Parasol flight on 60 Squadron was re-equipped with them.

Meanwhile No. 3 Squadron, now commanded by Harvey-Kelly, was still flying the Parasol. 'It was a machine you could never relax in,' wrote Cecil Lewis. It needed the greatest skill and care and a light but accurate touch. 'People killed themselves on Moranes with alarming rapidity.' But it was to carry him right through the Somme battle, during which he won an MC and was mentioned in despatches. *'Good old Parasol!'* Anything he flew after that, he wrote, was child's play.

15

THE SOMME – A COMPLETE WASH-OUT: BOMBER LOSSES: A WELSH VC

ALTHOUGH the original plans for a combined offensive on the Somme had been pre-empted by the German assault on Verdun, the British for their part continued to prepare for a summer campaign, while continually under coercion from the French to act as early as possible to relieve the pressure on them. On 21 May, and again on 21 June, the situation at Verdun impelled Pétain to plead for Haig to start a diversionary action. Haig's plan was for the British Fourth Army under Rawlinson to develop his main assault on an eighteen-mile front stretching from Maricourt, north of the Somme, to Gommecourt. On Rawlinson's left, in support, was the right-hand corps of the Third Army under Allenby: nineteen British divisions in all. South of the Somme, eight French divisions were to hold a ten-mile front opposite Peronne. Opposing these armies, and holding strong positions on high ground, well protected by deep dug-outs, was the German Second Army under von Below.

Haig's plan was to subject these fortified positions to eight days of crippling bombardment beforehand, using a massive concentration of artillery on targets registered in previous weeks by air observation. Stunned and bemused, the enemy would then have to face the advance of the British infantry across no man's land. Meanwhile the RFC, in addition to its routine work, was to mount an assault on enemy kite balloons, which now stretched away 'like a palisade', it was said, on the German side of the lines (and were duplicated on the Allied side), while the bombers would aim at air-fields and communications targets. Working back from a D-Day of 1 July, the bombardment was to start on 24 June. But, incon-veniently, a thunderstorm on the 23rd wrought havoc to prep-arations, the damage being specially severe to the British kite balloons, several of which were struck by lightning and destroyed. One unfortunate crew, when their balloon was wrenched from its winch in an electric snowstorm, were blown across the lines and whirled up to 13,000 feet before being blown back and deposited safely but miraculously behind Arras. And on the 24th, although pilots flew low in order to direct the artillery, the planned opening bombardment was hindered and curtailed by rain.

Thus the softening-up barrage that was to shatter the resistance of the German front-line troops got off to a dismal start. On the 25th the RFC did well in destroying five German balloons, four by *Le Prieur* rockets attached to interplane struts and fired electrically by the pilot (the eponymous inventor was a lieutenant in the French navy). Meanwhile the barrage rose at last to an awesome crescendo, exceeding anything in military experience. Things went well again on the 26th, when the bombardment was halted for a time so that its effectiveness could be judged from air photographs, corps com-manders finding this visual evidence 'of the greatest value'. Then, for four days, although the barrage continued, nearly all air work was hampered by fog.

So to 1 July, by which time the RFC's total active aeroplane strength in France had reached 421, plus over 200 in reserve at the depots and parks; this was an increase of some 150 since March. And on that first day the corps squadrons embarked for the first time on a systematic attempt to provide regular contact patrols. In previous battles, advancing troops had frequently found themselves cut off from their support, commanders sometimes being unaware of their precise whereabouts. The contact patrol, flown at heights of 500 to 1,000 feet, and lower when necessary, aimed to provide liaison between the front line and the battalion or brigade headquarters, closing the Intelligence gap. 'A pilot patrolling at low level,' wrote Cecil Lewis, 'could see the red flares which the Tommies carried and were instructed to light at different times.' The observer marked the position on the map provided, recorded the co-ordinates, and put a message in a weighted bag; the pilot then swooped low over the relevant headquarters and dropped the bag. By this method, pin-pointing of the flares fixed the movements of the forward troops for the commanders hour by hour.

This was the principle of the contact patrol. It had been tried briefly but unsuccessfully during the Loos battle, and now the same understandable inhibitions on the part of the ground troops contrib-uted to another disappointing result. For them it was against nature to reveal themselves so openly. All too often their flares remained unlit, and Cecil Lewis described the intended air co-operation on the first day as 'a complete wash-out'; indeed he saw 1 July as 'an entire failure'. There was, he wrote, 'no co-operation from the very men we were there to help'. As for the air crews, they found themselves weaving through the shells of their own guns to get the information they sought. Operating for five and six hours a day, sometimes more, for days on end, they flew so low they could soon distinguish which side was which from the colour of their uniforms. Co-operation with the ground troops improved within a day or so, the use of klaxons by aircraft proving audible and mostly translatable, but Lewis blamed the sequence of frustrations that followed on the disastrous start.

The Allied troops began to advance across no man's land at 07.30 that morning. But the plan to destroy the enemy's first and second line trenches had been only partly successful, and it was the French, whose heavy artillery was the stronger, who achieved an early suc-cess. The Germans, forewarned by the barrage, and with their natural topographical advantages, put up such a fierce resistance that the British were mown down, making minimal progress. Again and again the tidings brought back by the corps squadrons were grim. Any element of surprise had been forfeited, and the result was 57,000 casualties, among them 19,000 killed, the biggest loss ever suffered by a British army in a single day.

In the first few days of the battle the RFC also suffered serious losses, if not in quite the same proportion. It almost seemed as though

Trenchard was determined that they should. If soldiers died, so must airmen. He continued to pursue his two-pronged policy of, one, continual aggression, and two, never failing the ground forces whatever the odds. Still most numerous among the squadrons were the BE2c's (and its refinements d and e), whose crews, scarcely resting, varied long hours spent on artillery control and photography by loading up a few 20-lb bombs and heading for enemy aerodromes, railheads and sidings. Meanwhile FE2b's; Martinsyde and Morane scouts; two flights of Sopwith 1½-strutters lent by the Admiralty after an appeal from Trenchard, the first two-seater to mount a synchronised gun; and two more squadrons of DH2s (No. 29 under Eric Conran and No. 32 under a pugnacious Welshman named Lionel Rees), joined No. 24 in escort work and in long offensive patrols to re-affirm air superiority and make the work of the corps squadrons possible.

Noticeable was the extreme youth of many of the newcomers. Each was given a fitter and a rigger to look after his machine and was made 'absolutely responsible for them', according to the eighteen-year-old Gwilym Lewis, the youngest pilot on 32 Squadron. Lewis's virile, Clark Gable-ish looks would have been identified with that actor in a later era. Now his natural fears were considerably attenuated by the reluctance of the enemy scout pilots to challenge intrusions; he was much more scared of the German two-seaters. He found it astounding how many RFC machines crossed the lines and how promptly the Huns turned tail. It was reassuring to find that the enemy had the wind up just as much as he did. An awful lot of hot air, he thought, was talked and written about pluck. He would love to bring a Hun down – but when the scrapping began he was scared to death. 'You have no idea,' he wrote, in a letter home, 'how scared I am when I go for these brutes.' Yet he found dogfights 'wildly exciting'.

Of Lionel Rees, his squadron commander and a fellow Welshman, he wrote: 'Everyone knows that the major is mad. He is never happier than when attacking Huns. I wouldn't be surprised if he comes home with a VC.' But he reserved his greatest admiration for the crews of the FEs of 25 Squadron, whom it was often his job to escort. 'They recce and bomb all day long.' Of his own morale he admitted: 'A nice cushy wound would suit me all right,' but that otherwise, even if he had the chance, he wouldn't go home. Despite frequent losses, 'it's not such a bad little war if it wasn't so cold.' This, in open cockpit pushers like the DH2 and the FE, was a daily affliction, even in mid-summer.

Of the bombing, much was opportunist, and even when major raids were attempted, although the concentration on a single target was greater than hitherto, machines still tended to be despatched in dribs and drabs. Most of these raids were calculated to delay enemy reinforcements. Of the twenty-eight BE2c's which took off on specific bombing missions on 1 July, beginning soon after midday, only one hit its target. Of six machines that set out to bomb the well defended town of St Quentin, only three got back.

One who didn't, Second Lieutenant Laurie Wingfield, had enjoyed the variety of his corps squadron existence, knowing that by comparison with the infantry he was living in luxury. But he recognised the bombing of the railway station at St Quentin, thirty-five miles beyond the lines, as a special job. 'The "eggs" we were carrying were large ones,' he wrote later, 'weighing 110 lbs each full of TNT and I had to carry two.' This meant sacrificing all superfluous weight – which included an observer. Even a machine-gun was thought an unjustifiable load, but Wingfield decided to take one – and regretted it when it reduced his rate of climb. He was told he would be escorted by a squadron of DH2s, but when he arrived at the line and they failed to appear, he set course alone. When he reached St Quentin he dropped his bombs on the railway station as briefed and was rewarded by a huge column of smoke, rising, as he looked back, to 2,000 feet. 'On the way home,' he wrote later, 'I met a Fokker, and that was the end of the story.' Completely outclassed though the BE2c was, Wingfield put his six months' experience to good use and it took the Fokker pilot fifteen minutes to shoot him down.

It was still not the end of the story. The bombing of St Quentin that day had not only been costly, it had also, like so many of these attacks, been abortive so far as Headquarters knew. And Wingfield, now a prisoner, could not enlighten them. But German prisoners captured later that month revealed the spectacular truth. Having received urgent orders to entrain that afternoon for the Somme front, two enemy battalions had been crammed into the station, arms piled up and transport standing by to be loaded on to a train, when one of Wingfield's bombs hit and exploded in an ammunition shed. There were two hundred ammunition wagons lined up in the station sidings, the fire spread to them, and sixty were destroyed before the rest could be got away. More than that, the fire destroyed the train and the whole of the equipment of the two battalions. Men fled panic-stricken in all directions, leaving 180 dead and wounded, and the regiment which suffered most had to be sent back to be re-equipped.

Even then Wingfield's story was only half told. Fifteen months later, in October 1917, he escaped from prison camp, crossed the Dutch frontier, and returned home, to begin a distinguished career in the aviation industry.

The BE2c's and d's of No. 7 Squadron, under Major F.J.L. Cogan, were directed to railway targets in the Cambrai area, where the station was hit for the loss of one machine. But it was a classic opportunist attack later in the day which brought the best results when Second Lieutenant Arthur Gordon-Kidd spotted a train on the line approaching Cambrai. The train was nearing a cutting situated on a curve, and Gordon-Kidd was well aware that such enclosed areas gave exceptional force to bomb-blast if the weapon could be accurately aimed, with wreckage sometimes blocking a cutting for days. Coming down to 900 feet to give himself every chance, he approached the train head on, timed his run perfectly, and scored a direct hit on the middle carriages, which caught fire and exploded. For this exploit he was awarded the DSO. Later a pilot of 16 Squadron (also BEs), found the train still burning and dropped two more bombs on the rear coaches. Further massive explosions confirmed that the train was carrying ammunition, and it was still blazing fiercely that evening.[1]

---

1. In August 1917, flying Spads of 19 Squadron, Gordon-Kidd was mortally wounded.

All day, standing patrols of DH2s and FE2b's went out in pairs to cover specific areas, waiting over the lines until they were relieved by the next pair. Although their primary job was to fight, they watched for enemy movements, and, in the case of the FE2b's, carried 20 lb bombs for targets of opportunity. These patrols engaged in many scraps, and two FE2b's were shot down, but they helped to keep enemy aircraft occupied while the corps machines, at lower altitudes, carried out their tasks for the army.

When targets were attacked in sufficient numbers, with a strong escort, the German pilots rarely interfered. This was demonstrated on 2 July, when six RE7s (developed from the RE5 and capable of carrying a 336 lb bomb) set out with an escort of four Martinsydes to bomb an enemy infantry headquarters and ammunition dump at Bapaume: six Moranes of 60 Squadron patrolled the area while the attack was in progress. The heavy-cased bombs carried by the RE7s started a fire which, it was said, 'grew in intensity and still coloured the eastern sky when darkness had closed over the day's fighting'.

Euphoria at the occasional bombing success, however, was tempered by dismay at the losses suffered in those first few days of low-level attacks on rail targets. Reconnaissances on 3 July reported many troop movements in the neighbourhood of Cambrai, but the bombing of trains, which resumed early that morning, met with sterner opposition. Some of the bombers were shot down, others were forced to turn back, few reached their primary targets. Bombing raids on St Quentin also suffered losses and rebuffs. Throughout these days Trenchard was continually touring the squadrons, inviting the men to 'gather round', encouraging and, according to the crews, inspiring by his presence, and he turned up with Baring at 60 Squadron that day in time to wish Waldron luck on an offensive patrol. Waldron, evidently not under an embargo, believed in leading his men, and on this day five Bullets were required to act as a decoy for the BE2c's bombing St Quentin. Among the pilots were Smith-Barry and Balfour. Not only were they unable to help the bombers, they were soon hard pressed themselves, running into a dozen enemy machines at 8,000 feet twenty miles beyond the lines, several Fokkers among them.

In armament and manoeuvrability the Fokker was superior to the Morane, but Waldron attacked at once. Balfour spotted a Fokker on Waldron's tail and forced it to break off, but soon afterwards he saw Waldron going down, apparently under control. Smith-Barry drove the other Fokkers east, but his Morane too was badly shot about and he and his colleagues were forced to return. There was no further sign of Waldron: he had been shot down and killed. 'One of the best men we ever had,' was Trenchard's verdict. Although losses were a daily occurrence, somehow it struck home more forcibly when it was one of the original few. Smith-Barry was appointed to take his place.

The tally amongst the bombers, on those first three days, was eight missing, with many others out of action for varying periods, if repairable at all. The inescapable conclusion was that deep penetration by BE2c's, flying without close escort and without observers, and with their performance, such as it was, further restricted by bomb-carrying, was unsustainable. Even the successes were rarely quantifiable, and Trenchard, whose daily tours of the squadrons revealed the bomber crews as being, in his own phrase, 'a bit rattled' (with good reason), acknowledged that the BEs would be more usefully employed in their routine corps duties, to which they were returned. Trenchard considered putting in for a couple of VCs to sustain morale: meanwhile, when switched to bombing, the BEs were ordered to fly in formation under escort.

If Trenchard did in fact recommend any pilots on this front for VCs, they weren't granted, the only VC of the opening days of the battle being won in the Loos area, by a squadron commander subject to the normal embargo that he must not cross the lines. Yet no one was unduly surprised – least of all Gwilym Lewis – at the name of the recipient. On the morning of 1 July a formation of ten enemy bombers crossed the lines near Festubert. DH2s of 32 Squadron under Lionel Rees had been airborne in this area since 03.40, but it was not until Rees himself took off with Lieutenant John Simpson, a 26-year-old Canadian, at 05.55 that contact was made with the German formation, and it was Simpson, who had lost touch with Rees, who made it. As was not unusual in German formations, the leader was an observer, Leutnant Erich Zimmermann. Despite the odds against him, Simpson attacked immediately. Three of the hostiles broke towards him, and after a sharp exchange Simpson's machine was hit. Watchers on the ground saw the DH2 descend some 5,000 feet, apparently under control, but in fact Simpson had sustained eight bullet wounds in the head and was already dead. Rees had seen nothing of this, but he now caught sight of the enemy formation. It was so unusual for hostiles to penetrate to any depth that he took them for a British patrol – until he spotted their markings through binoculars.

When the Germans saw a second DH2 climbing towards them they were confident of scoring a second victory, but Rees, holding his fire, splintered the fuselage of one hostile from short range with his first burst and then attacked another, which wobbled crazily before going down apparently under control. When the leader and two other machines turned away, Rees began chasing them and was soon overhauling them, only to be hit in the leg by a burst fired from long range, losing proper control of the DH2s rudder. Yet he still bore down on the leader. His subsequent account concluded: 'I finished firing about ten yards away, and saw the observer sitting back firing straight up in the air ... He was firing an immense amount of ammunition. Just before he reached the lines I gave him one more drum. Having finished my ammunition I came home.' Rees had scattered a major German bombing raid single-handed, and German records confirmed in detail his account of the fight. One German crew actually jettisoned their bombs over their own lines. The observer firing so blindly into the air had indeed been the leader, Leutnant Zimmermann: it had been a dead man's hand on the trigger. The pilot, although wounded, got the plane down.

Gwilym Lewis, in a letter home, wrote: 'Archie batteries say they have never seen anything so gallant or comic in their lives ... I told you he was the bravest man in the world.' But the leg injury proved worse than feared, and it was the end of Rees's operational career.

Here was another man, like Hawker, whose watchword was 'Go in to attack! Whenever you see the Hun, no matter where he is, be he alone or accompanied, go for him, and shoot him down.' It was an attitude that, once inculcated, it was hard not to follow, costly though it often was, as in the case of the Canadian Simpson. No scout pilots of this or any period adopted this attitude more enthusiastically than the Canadians, but none excelled the Welshman Lionel Rees, who had earned his reputation – and an MC – as a flight commander on Gunbuses with 11 Squadron. Together with men like Hawker, Harvey-Kelly, Don Lewis and Bron James he exerted an almost messianic influence on the ethos of the RFC, long before the advent of the aces.

16

FLAMERS AND FROSTBITE:
NO EMPTY CHAIRS

T HE first phase of the battle, in which the British, at enormous cost, gained a six-thousand-yard footing on the main or Bazentin ridge, despite stubborn German resistance, lasted a fortnight. During that time, and beyond, Trenchard's declared objective of keeping the German Air Force too preoccupied in defence either to interfere significantly with the work of the corps squadrons, or to intrude effectively over the British lines, was achieved. General von Below later complained of three areas of dominance by the RFC in these early weeks. First: 'The enemy's aerodromes enjoyed complete freedom in carrying out distant reconnaissance.' Secondly: 'With the aid of aeroplane observation the hostile artillery neutralised our guns and was able to range with most extreme accuracy on our trenches.' And thirdly: 'By means of bombing and machine-gunning from a low height against infantry, battery positions and marching columns, the enemy's aircraft inspired our troops with a feeling of defencelessness.'

This dispassionate summary was supported with some vehemence by the German troops themselves. 'The English are always flying over our lines directing artillery shoots,' was the burden of one lament, 'thereby getting all their shells right into our trenches. This moral defeat has a bad effect on us all.' As for their own air force, the letter continued: '. . . one must be too ashamed to write, it is simply scandalous. They fly as far as this village but no further, whereas the English are always flying over our lines.' German records subsequently described July and August 1916 as 'the blackest days in the history of the German Air Force'.

The second phase of the battle, which lasted for two months, until mid-September, settled into a tense and debilitating struggle for possession of the main ridge. Most significant for the RFC was that the German Air Force began to show signs of a recrudescence. To match German expansion and reorganisation on the ground, which included, on 29 August, the appointment of Field Marshal von Hindenburg as Chief of the German General Staff, assisted by General von Ludendorff, General von Hoeppner, until recently chief of staff of the von Below's Second Army, was made responsible for the centralised administration of the German Air Force. Meanwhile Boelcke was brought back to organise the formation of *Jagdstaffeln* or *Jastas* (pursuit or hunting squadrons), each to consist of fourteen newly-developed machines, namely the D-type Albatros and Halberstadt. Both mounted two fixed machine-guns firing through the propeller arc, and all would be flown by carefully selected pilots who had been through advanced air training schools. Command of *Jasta* 2, which was formed on 30 August, was given to Boelcke, who invited a two-seater pilot and former observer whose enthusiasm had impressed him, Manfred von Richthofen, to join him. The first batch of new machines was delivered on 6 September, and Boelcke's first combat mission was flown on the 17th, two days after Haig renewed the assault in what became the third and final phase of the battle.

For most of that summer, however, the RFC enjoyed an air superiority they were never to know again, and life in the better equipped squadrons seemed ideal, so far as soldiering could be ideal in wartime. Visits to artillery units, partly to talk shop, partly to kill time in bad weather, and partly for good will, offered continual reminders of how lucky they were. Gun emplacements and dug-outs under fire, existence on hard rations in the midst of shell-holes and mud – this was indeed a different world. By comparison the RFC lived a civilised life, still to some extent officers and gentlemen, comfortably housed in farms and sometimes châteaux, or in Nissen-hutted camps, with three-course meals in the Mess, and even, in the quieter sectors, the correct wines and the traditional circulation of port, coffee and liqueurs. Many, like Captain P.N. 'Puggy' Shone, a newly-arrived observer, had experienced both worlds, and after ten months in the trenches he felt he had moved from an East End dosshouse to the Savoy. 'Five minutes behind the lines,' he noted, 'you were in complete safety,' while, with the help and ingenuity of ground tradesmen, the functional hut furnishings were transformed. 'In our hut we had running water,' boasted Shone, 'and to sleep in a camp bed – amazing!'

Another man with dual experience was Sergeant-Observer H.G. Taylor, of 25 Squadron (FE2b's): Taylor, after a boyhood in rural Surrey, had served with the Machine-Gun Corps on the Somme and would never forget the appalling conditions. 'In the trenches you faced death every second, not knowing when it might come; in the RFC you could certainly say between flights that you had so many more hours to live. On the other hand, in the air, you could see death coming, especially if you caught fire at height. With no parachutes, whether you stayed in the machine or jumped, the result was the same.'

Some people believed that only those airmen who had once fought on the ground and retained an indelible impression of that experience could ever have a proper sense of responsibility towards the men in the trenches. But the evidence, from Trenchard down, is that this was not so, and that all were fully aware of their luck. Even in Messes close to the front there was almost always a piano, and a gramophone playing the latest London theatre hits, as well as newspapers and the companionship of kindred spirits. Parties and binges, and the horseplay of Mess games, were discreetly encouraged, as a release from the perpetual strain of facing Archie and a highly skilled and courageous adversary, not to mention the missing faces and the perpetual fear of a 'flamer'. 'Once you see a machine fall from the sky in flames, especially when it contains your friends,' wrote H.G. Taylor, 'you always have this fearful picture in your mind.' This was the unmentionable dread, which only surfaced in ghoulish ditties that were rendered with frenetic gusto as comic songs.

Volunteers from overseas often formed a grudging admiration for the atmosphere created in RFC messes: one who commented on it approvingly was Canadian Harold E. Hartley. He noted the studied avoidance of controversial subjects, the understatement, and the absence of selfishness and swank. The habit of sleeping in hutted dormitories he found far preferable to single rooms or bunks, making for closer companionship, and he relished the clubbable blend of leg-pulling and old-fashioned courtesy which was extended to new-comers. He likened the ambience to that in a college fraternity. If at first it was dominated by the public school element, it was beginning, by 1916, to be democratised as casualties increased and men from all walks of life, not to mention 'colonials', as they were still apt to be called, contributed their own distinctive aura to the mixture. Hartley was also pleased – and perhaps surprised – to find his commanders understanding, helpful, and fair.

If there was one discomfort from which the airman suffered to a greater degree than the soldier it was the cold. One of the first to arm himself with fur-lined thigh-boots was Hawker, and even in the FE2b's, which rarely reached a height above 8,000 feet, the spacious but draughty and exposed open cockpit became a refrigerator. The wearing of silk underwear, silk gloves, leather gauntlets and a leather face-mask, with fur-lined garments from head to foot, was never proof against 70- and 80-knot winds at temperatures far below zero. It was worse still for the pusher crews, where any warmth from the engine went to waste behind them, and where the crude bombsight necessitated the setting of a stop-watch with bare hands. 'I got frost-bite setting that stop-watch,' said Sidney Attwater when still a corporal observer, 'and so did many others.' An issue of whale oil to protect exposed facial areas proved unpopular because of its revolting smell, and most men substituted cold cream.

Patrick Playfair and his observer, after landing from three hours at 7,500 feet in a Gunbus, were unable to move from their cockpits for several minutes, and when they did manage to climb out they were unable to straighten their legs. Both collapsed and had to be helped to their feet and supported to the rest hut. The problem was quite fortuitously solved by an Australian RNAS pilot named Sidney Cotton (later a pioneer in aerial survey and air spy photography). In the very cold winter of 1916/17, Cotton was tuning up the engine of his Sopwith 1½-strutter, dressed in dirty, begrimed overalls, when he and others were despatched in a hurry to intercept an intruder. They saw nothing, but when they collected together afterwards, everyone was frozen stiff except Cotton. 'That's funny,' he said, 'I'm quite warm.' He hadn't had time to don flying kit and was still wearing his dirty overalls. On examining them he found they were saturated with oil and grease and must have acted as an airtight bag and kept the body heat in. He asked for leave, went to London, and had a flying suit made up to his own design. It had a lining of thin fur, then a layer of airproof silk, then an outside layer of light Burberry material, the whole being made up in one piece like overalls. The neck and cuffs had fur pieces sewn inside them to prevent the warm air escaping. Deep pockets just below the knee allowed pilots seated in cramped cockpits to reach down into them easily for maps and accessories. After searching tests the Sidcot suit, as it was eponymously known, came into general use, replacing the old-fashioned boots and coats. Frostbite sufferer Sidney Attwater wrote: 'They were splendid.' They were still widely used in World War II.

Many squadron commanders found the restrictions placed on their flying distasteful, and Hawker still flew on patrols, regularly if not frequently. This was how he kept in touch. He shared the problems of most squadron commanders in that his seniors, under pressure from army or corps commanders, often exaggerated the urgency of their requirements, forcing him to order his pilots out when the odds against them could have been improved given more time.

Planning was a feature of Hawker's leadership, and after a show there was always a de-briefing – an innovation then – and a lively discussion. There were many anxious days for Hawker that summer as he waited for his pilots to return from patrols. Men who were overdue were not necessarily missing: Hawker could still hope for a phone call to say they had got down elsewhere. When a man was confirmed as missing there were letters to write, effects to be sorted, replacements to be requested. Trenchard's dictum, for reasons of morale, was 'no empty chairs at the breakfast table', and sure enough another raw newcomer would arrive the same day. None of Hawker's young pilots was married, but there were families and girl friends to be advised and, if possible, soothed. Sometimes he could truthfully say there was a good chance of the man being a prisoner; sometimes he would know with virtual certainty that the man was dead. Sometimes there would be debts, even pregnancies. Next day there was a new man to be trained.

One replacement, who had only recently taken his ticket, was awakened by his batman on his first morning to be told that 'Mr A has been shot down and Mr B has crashed in flames in the village'. That morning Hawker put the newcomer through his paces and ticked him off for 'showing off, and for losing height in the turn'. These unfortunate fledgelings were the inevitable result of expansion outstripping supply, and their shooting, like their flying, was often appalling. One man arrived never having seen a Lewis gun before.

Nevertheless it was the DH2 squadrons, with No. 24 in the vanguard, which largely defeated the Fokkers. The FE2b's contributed, giving the German pilots some nasty surprises at first by their wide field of fire, and so did the Moranes, though the latter suffered a disastrous July. Smith-Barry was not one to mince words, and he complained to Dowding, at wing headquarters, of one batch of replacement pilots: 'They've only seven hours flying, sir, it's bloody murder.' He refused to send anyone out on patrol until he'd brought him up to a standard that he felt gave him a chance; according to one recruit, nineteen-year-old S.F. (Stanley) Vincent, when Trenchard visited the squadron Smith-B 'as good as told him he was a butcher'. Another new pilot, Peter Portal, recognised his commander as a daring and spectacular airman, despite the embargo on his leading the squadron into action, and noted how he encouraged individuals and tolerated no divisions of race or class. Portal also thoroughly approved of the care Smith-Barry took of his pilots: they 'had a good chance to learn the real principles of safe flying from precept and example'.

Yet Smith-Barry was intolerant of anyone he suspected of over-caution. Borrowing the Morane of a new flight commander, he found a neatly rolled package stowed in the cockpit. 'Emergency rations,' he was told by a mechanic. Examination disclosed silk pyjamas, razor, toothbrush, 500 cigarettes, and other insurances against mis-fortune. Tearing the parcel open and scattering its contents for all to see, S-B shouted: 'One of my pilots is preparing to be a prisoner!' Many would think such preparations prudent, and they were widely popular, but S-B wouldn't have it. His attitude was on a parallel with that of the Air Board over parachutes: that given a possible alternative to fighting to the death against the enemy before coaxing his machine home, a man might choose it.

For all Smith-Barry's professionalism and paternalism, not to men-tion his eccentricities, one thing he could not change was the basic inferiority of the Morane. By 3 August half the squadron's original pilots had been killed or wounded or posted missing, and he requested that the squadron be taken out of the line to recuperate. He had scarcely made the request when he lost yet another pilot, Claude Ridley, missing from a spy-dropping mission. (In fact, as already recorded, he turned up later.) Dowding supported the request, and Trenchard, belying Smith-Barry's accusation, told Haig: 'I have had to withdraw one of the GHQ fighting squadrons from work temporarily ... This squadron, since the battle began, have lost a squadron commander, two flight commanders and one pilot – all killed or missing, and yesterday it lost two more machines and two pilots and two observers by anti-aircraft fire. Besides this, they have had several officers wounded. They have a very difficult machine to fly, and I think a rest away from work is absolutely necessary.'

Three weeks later, when the squadron resumed operating, there was only one flight of Moranes remaining: the other two had been replaced by the Nieuport 17 or Super-Bébé, far and away the best single-seater scout at that time. Their arrival coincided with the post-ing in of Albert Ball. Given a free rein by Smith-Barry, Ball made an immediate impact. Roderic Hill, who joined the squadron a month earlier with an exceptional rating, but was still confined to Moranes, clashed with his commander on being thus restricted, but made the best of the Morane and soon earned S-B's respect. He described Ball as 'sitting in his hut on the aerodrome, gramophone going, working out schemes'. Although a boy of a kindly nature, he was 'uncannily swift and sure' according to Hill. 'He had one idea, to kill as many Huns as possible.'

Contemporary sources emphatically deny that the appellation Hun was derogatory or derisory. 'I would go as far as to say,' wrote nineteen-year-old Australian pilot Ewart Garland, 'that flying men on both sides felt less personal antagonism than say footballers in the heat and excitement of play ... There was no hate between enemy airmen, and quasi-affectionate references to German airmen were quite usual.' Cecil Lewis wrote: 'They were our friends the enemy. We treated them well when they were captured, and they us.' Only when the Zeppelins and later the Gothas were bombing London did Lewis experience a brief access of rage. He spoke of a strong magnetic attraction between airmen matched against each other at altitude. 'I have felt this magnetism engaging an enemy scout three miles above the earth.' When Ball's father wrote to him to say 'Let the devils have it,' Ball replied: 'I do not think of them as devils. I only scrap because it is my duty, and I do not think anything bad about the Hun.'

The speed and manoeuvrability of the Nieuport 17 soon attracted basic tasks like photography: by putting a camera in a Nieuport, photographs could be taken more quickly and more safely than in a slower machine. With malice aforethought, Smith-Barry had a camera installed in the machine of the one man on the squadron whom he suspected of being a shirker, sent him on a photographic sortie with an escort of three of his colleagues, and awaited results. Sure enough the pictures revealed the tentative nature of the flying: the pilot had tried, by tilting his machine, to cover the area without penetrating it. Smith-Barry called the four pilots in and told them they had wasted everyone's time and would have to go again. To the escort pilots he then proposed a novel method of ensuring success: two of them were to fly one on each side of the leader and a little behind, with the third astern. 'If Blank leaves what you consider the correct line or height, you have your guns to remind him to get back into position.'

Stanley Vincent was on the leader's right, and he was soon putting a burst of fire, 'with tracer bullets much in evidence', past the leader's wing-tip. Both the other escorts had occasion to fire off similar reminders, the one astern going into action when the leader began climbing above the height for which the cameras were focused. 'The photographs were quite satisfactory this time,' said Vincent. However he added: 'The very next day this chap, then well over the German side of the lines, had engine failure and went down and landed behind the enemy lines and failed to destroy his machine. The Germans thus found out that the Nieuports were carrying cameras, and their guns paid that much more attention to us.'

As for the faint-hearted leader, although he could expect to survive the war, he would, when repatriated, have to face searching interrogation by a specially appointed committee, in common with all former prisoners.

On another occasion Vincent was one of three on an offensive patrol when they clashed with five of Richthofen's *Jasta* and had to fight for their lives. When it ended, as suddenly as it had begun, and the sky was clear, the leader, exhausted and slightly airsick as they all were, turned for home. In effect they were cutting short their patrol, and when they landed S-B was furious. 'We'd deserted our post, we'd left a gap in the sky where the enemy could pour through and attack our corps machines, we'd let ourselves down.' Smarting under this tongue-lashing, the nineteen-year-old Vincent retired to his tent in suicidal mood. Some time later, in came S-B with a bottle. 'Hello Vincent,' he said. 'Have a brandy.'

17

BALL AND McCUDDEN: THE CONTACT PATROL: THE MEN OF THE FE2b's

OFFENSIVE patrols, photography, escort work – all these were the daily diet of the Nieuports, and Albert Ball, for all his individualism, could be an asset on bomber protection. Accompanying the FE2b's of 11 Squadron, he was confronted by about twenty assorted hostiles in three groups. He crashed one, sent another down in flames, and, with the last of his ammunition, downed a third. Returning to the nearest aerodrome, pursued by the enemy for much of the way, he rearmed and returned to the scene, only to find it deserted. Short now of fuel, he was attacked by two hostiles on the way back and his Nieuport was riddled. Compelled to land away from home, he slept by his machine, organised repairs, and flew back next morning. Six days later, when the bombers he was escorting came under attack, he drove two hostiles down, forcing them to land, and crashed a third on its nose. No wonder he loved his Nieuport.

Intolerant of help and advice himself, Ball never sought to advise or correct others, disliked anyone flying with him, and, with Smith-Barry's connivance, enjoyed a roving commission. In a description of Ball's method, Hill wrote: 'There was a curved rail down which the gun had to be run to change drums. By exerting pressure on one side of the stock, Ball held it rigid when nearly down, pointing up at about 80 degrees. [Curiously Hawker had done something similar in the DH2.] By skilful manoeuvre he was able to zoom up underneath his victim, then by a slight oscillation of the control stick cause his guns to rake the target fore and aft at a range of about 30 feet.' This approach, often unseen, was just as often fatal for the victim.

Ball fought with his head, according to Hill, who called him 'the offspring of a vixen and a lion'. He was not all blind aggression. As an instance of his animal cunning – Hill dignified it as astuteness – he related an incident when Ball flew most of the way to Cambrai just under one of the Moranes, totally unsuspected by the pilot. 'His security', said Hill, 'lay in the fact that he fought at such close range that the rest of the hostile formation dare not fire at him for fear of hitting each other.' In a hectic six weeks with 60 Squadron, from 23 August to 4 October, Ball increased his tally of victories to thirty, higher than anyone on the Allied side except the Frenchman Guynemer with thirty-seven. The sight of the red spinner on Ball's propeller boss so terrorised the enemy that there were times when even the pilots of the new *Jastas* shrank from attacking him. 'Figuratively speaking,' wrote Hill, 'he did the work of a whole squadron, setting the model of courage and determination, though not of leadership; we were instructed in formation flying by others.' A short leave, the award of a DSO, and promotion to captain, which placed him technically in charge of a flight, didn't change him. When he saw a flock of Huns he opened his throttle and flew straight at them, using his guns in hosepipe fashion, and leaving his flight to fend for themselves.

Meanwhile Jimmy McCudden, having completed his pilot training, had returned to France on 8 July as a flight-sergeant pilot on FE2d's on 20 Squadron. Of four NCO pilots who arrived that day, none was to survive the war, although two were to win the highest award. McCudden himself was one, the other was a Lancastrian named Tom Mottershead, also bound for an FE squadron, No. 25.

McCudden's ambition to join a single-seater scout squadron was satisfied four weeks later when he was posted to 29 Squadron on

DH2s under his old pilot Eric Conran. But he was confined mostly to escort work, and it was another month before he scored his first victory. Even then his diffidence prevented him from making a claim, and he was credited with the two-seater Albatros he attacked on 6 September on the evidence of ground witnesses who saw it crash.

Jimmy McCudden's long apprenticeship – two years as air mechanic, gaining the rank and responsibilities of sergeant at twenty, with occasional opportunities to fly, and then six months as air observer, followed by pilot training, was in striking contrast to the meteoric rise of Albert Ball. Indeed in most ways they were totally dissimilar. Ball's dark, unruly mop was the extreme opposite of McCudden's flaxen thatch, smarmed down close to the scalp. Ball was instinctive and impetuous, the typical street fighter, prodigal of his energy; McCudden was measured, percipient, calculating. Ball was brash but introspective, McCudden modest but anxious to be sociable. Although Ball was mechanically minded, he had not served in the ranks or trained as a technician as McCudden had, and although both men were individualists and loved nothing better than hunting alone, Ball knew only one way to fight whereas McCudden knew many. In sporting parlance, if Ball was the gifted and dedicated amateur, McCudden was the seasoned professional. Yet it was the combination of Ball and his Nieuport which now grabbed the headlines, and when he was finally posted home for a rest on 4 October he had earned himself two bars to add to his DSO and MC, making him the first triple DSO in the British Army. His fame had gone before him and he went home to a hero's welcome, to be mobbed in the streets in his native Nottingham. Meanwhile McCudden, in his now obsolescent DH2, opposed from mid-September by the new German scouts, was struggling to survive.

Trenchard was much too alert not to know that the air superiority enjoyed that summer was ephemeral, and with the Germans, by the third week in July, suspending their Verdun offensive and concentrating the majority of their strength on the Somme, his demands for still greater expansion excited dismay at home. 'With regard to the number of pilots we have had and are asking for,' he explained, 'I admit the demand is enormous.' But he couldn't understand the protests. 'We are fighting a very big battle, and fighting in the air is becoming intense. The fighting will increase, I regret to say, not decrease, and it is only a question of keeping it up longer than the Hun.' Trenchard was again emphasising the numbers game, the war of attrition which, by the brutal arithmetic of casualties, the Germans must lose. 'If we cannot do that, then we are beaten; if we do it, we win.'

As successive assaults, in the months leading up to the final phase, gained little, and the blood-letting continued, Trenchard amplified his worries to Brancker: 'I must warn you now that in the next ten days, if we get fine weather, I anticipate a very heavy casualty list . . . But what is to be chiefly remembered is that whatever we suffer, the Huns are suffering more . . .'

The results of Allied bombing in this period – the delay and damage caused, and the effect on ground troops – may best be judged from the response of the German defences. The normal load for a bombing machine was two 112 lb bombs or eight 20-pounders, with escort machines often carrying a few 20-pounders for good measure, and there were some spectacular successes; but the Germans reacted so aggressively that although escorting DH2s, FE2b's and Sopwith 1½-strutters generally held their own, bomber losses increased.

The 1½-strutter, so called because of its short centre-section struts, was a two-seater originally ordered by the RNAS. Its Scarff Ring mounting, which allowed the observer in the rear seat to swivel and fire his gun in any direction easily and quickly, was the invention of a back-room boy in the Admiralty Air Department, Warrant Officer (Gunner) F.W. Scarff, RN. It was so successful that it was incorporated in other types of machine. Scarff also had a hand in producing the Scarff-Dibovsky interrupter gear for firing through the propeller arc, also used in the Sopwith.

*   *   *

The third and final phase of the Somme battle began on 15 September. Haig still believed that the elements of shock and surprise might achieve a breakthrough, and these elements were represented in a new weapon, the tank, of which thirty-six were now available. Impatient to deploy them, Haig ignored advice to wait until they had been delivered in greater numbers, making the same mistake the Germans had made with their Fokker *Eindeckers*. The plan was to keep the tanks clear of observation until the night before the attack, when they would move into position under cover of darkness. The RFC were to co-operate by night-flying over the lines to drown or camouflage the noise of the tanks moving up, and by shooting down all kite balloons whose observers might be in a position to spot the build-up.

The best weapons for destroying kite balloons remained the *Le Prieur* rockets, and the only squadron equipped with them on this part of the front was No. 60. The massed batteries protecting these balloons made rocket attack especially hazardous as the rockets could only be fired accurately in a steep power-dive. Early on the morning of 15 September Trenchard and Baring drove up to the 60 Squadron Mess in their Rolls-Royce and told the pilots who had 'gathered round' that the balloons must be destroyed before the ground assault commenced. He then called for volunteers. In deathly silence, according to Baring, three were chosen, and Trenchard spoke to each one. After he had wished them luck he revealed the true extent of what he expected of them: it was to be a suicide raid. 'Remember this. It's far more important to get those balloons than to fail and come back.' With this stark invocation resounding in their ears, the three pilots took off.

Their vulnerability had not been exaggerated. Two balloons were shot down, but the two pilots who returned had met fierce opposition and their machines were riddled, while one pilot was missing. Since German Intelligence had in fact been aware that tanks were to be used, it was the familiar story, in the air as on the ground, of a sacrifice in vain.

While much of the work of the RFC preserved lives indirectly, there were times when the saving was immediate and obvious, as during the opening assault on the 15th, when the crew of a BE2e of No. 34 Squadron on a contact patrol reported three knocked-out tanks, one ditched and lopsided in our own trenches, one upended against a tree, and one in flames straddling the German trenches. These losses left the attacking force exposed to a potentially murderous machine-gun barrage, and a weighted message bag was dropped to corps headquarters to warn them. Further reconnaissance, and a verbal report made after landing, averted a pre-planned frontal attack, which, it was said, 'would have resulted in the complete wiping-out of the attacking force'.

A contact patrol observer on No. 9 Squadron whose reports were models of accuracy and tactical acumen was Second Lieutenant T.E.G. Scaife, a 24-year-old South African farmer, born in Leicester but educated in Cape Town. Seeing about 50 British infantrymen pinned down by a German machine-gun nest, Tom Scaife and his pilot used their Lewis guns so effectively that the barrier was removed. Of these contact patrol crews it was written: 'They, alone, were the witnesses of the whole titanic struggle, and through their eyes the army commanders could follow the fortunes of their troops.' Air to ground communication was often by klaxon horn, which could be heard above the din of battle, and which asked the infantry to indicate their positions by ground signal. Scaife and others flew as many as eight hours on that first day, and failures of the ground troops to achieve a particular goal were often traceable to poor visibility hampering or grounding these patrols. If the work was unspectacular and the crews largely anonymous, they were at the vortex of the fighting and their exposure to danger was unsurpassed. Scaife himself, with his pilot, was shot down and killed on 26 September at the climax of the battle.

Every kind of show had its own particular perils; the grass seldom looked much greener elsewhere. Roderic Hill was a great admirer of the FE2b crews of 11 Squadron, with whom 60 Squadron shared an aerodrome, and whom they often escorted. Of the observers he wrote: 'They were not strapped in, and they had to move around their roomy cockpits, oblivious of their safety, standing up on their little boxes, firing now forwards, now rearwards over the top plane, wielding their Lewis guns in the icy blast as though they weighed no more than rapiers. They also operated the bombsight and released the bombs. Although sluggish and unmanoeuvrable, the machine was sometimes thrown about in combat, and then the observer sat on the floor, with both legs from the knees down hanging over the outside of the cockpit, gripping the edge with the back of the knees and at the same time gripping the gun with both hands to hold on.' At the best of times they had little more than a strong grip and a Lewis gun to hold on to, yet they claimed to have no fear of falling out. The airstream held them in.

FE2b's and d's were still flying offensive patrols, generally in pairs, and Lancastrian Sidney Attwater, now a pilot on 25 Squadron, records how he and his Lancastrian 'pal' Tom Mottershead, whose sustained courage had already earned him a Distinguished Conduct Medal (Attwater had a Military Medal from his earlier work as an observer), made a pact to stick together whatever happened. They had much else in common. Mottershead's fighting spirit was undimmed despite his maturity and his dependants – he was twenty-four, with a wife and baby son. Attwater had married while home on pilot training. They were reconnoitring a German airfield, inviting a scrap, when Mottershead began pointing down and signalling to Attwater to follow. He did so, down to 500 feet, and still Mottershead went on down, finally landing on the airfield. 'By the time I got down,' said Attwater, 'he and his observer had already opened up with their guns at the hangars, so we did the same. I know we used about 200 rounds of tracer, and one hangar was on fire. So I pointed up, and off we went.'

Back at base, and anticipating a reprimand for exceeding their brief, they resolved to say nothing of what they had done. But when the squadron commander sent for them and asked: 'What have you done with your ammo?', they had to own up. Threatened – tongue in cheek – with a court martial, they were given seven days' early parades, 'which meant nothing,' according to Attwater, 'because we were up in the air most mornings. But we felt much better for not just wasting petrol, but really having had a bash.'

Hearing some weeks later that Mottershead, transferred meanwhile to another squadron (No. 20), was in hospital, Attwater visited him to find him badly burned but remarkably perky. On a fighting patrol, his observer, Lieutenant W.E. Gower, had repelled one Albatros, sending it spinning down, but they had been set on fire by another, their fuel tank ruptured. Gower had played a fire extinguisher on Mottershead's clothing, and somehow Mottershead had flown the burning aeroplane home. In the inevitable crash-landing Gower was thrown clear, and he had helped to extricate his badly scorched pilot. Surgeons then began the fight for his life.

While Attwater was at his bedside a kite balloon was seen falling in flames in the distance, and Mottershead got out of bed to watch it from the hospital window — and got back in again when a nurse came in to scold him. He died next day, leaving Attwater to ponder whether his visit, and the episode of the balloon, had contributed. It seems not: his burns were too extensive for him to survive. The award of a posthumous VC underlined yet again the importance attached by the authorities to getting man and machine home. Clearly Tom Mottershead was one of the men whose desire to take the offensive inspired and even incited his fellows. Gower, who was one of them, was awarded an MC. Attwater, who was another, was later shot down on a dawn reconnaissance and taken prisoner; he survived into his eightieth year.

Throughout that summer the BE crews snatched a few hours from their corps duties to load up with bombs and distribute them over enemy airfields, railheads and sidings, protected more by the offensive patrols of the army squadrons than by direct escort. And long before the infantry attack on 15 September the bombers were at work. No. 27 Squadron, where the avuncular Sidney Smith, a founder-member, had succeeded the extrovert Borton, hit General von Below's headquarters that morning, together with rail centres and rolling stock, but their best work was done in the afternoon, after crews of 70 Squadron (1½-strutters) had reported forty trains on the lines in the Cambrai region, seeming to presage the arrival of an entire division. Eight Martinsydes took off, and three of them, seeing a train approaching Gouzeaucourt station, dive-bombed in turn. The first bomb stopped the train, bombs from the second machine blew up the rear truck, and the pilot then turned and dropped a 112-pounder on the troops as they evacuated the train. The third Martinsyde pilot hit an ammunition truck in the middle of the train, which blew up and started a succession of explosions in adjacent trucks. The remaining pilots hit trains and a supply dump nearby.

One of the flight commanders on 27 Squadron was the inventive Robert Bourdillon, who will be remembered as one of the architects of the CFS bombsight. He had meanwhile transferred to the RFC and qualified as a pilot. He studied the problems of flying in cloudy conditions, introduced more sophisticated methods of time-and-distance navigation to help his crews on long-distance missions in bad weather, and designed an effective 40-lb phosphorus bomb. Finally he pre-empted Leonard Cheshire by initiating target-marking attacks from low level to guide his fellows, becoming the first of the Pathfinders. His work was recognised by the awards of an MC and an AFC. (He survived to pursue a distinguished post-war career in medical research.)

Most of the day's air fighting took place above the region of Bapaume, which itself was bombed by BEs escorted by FEs. All the fighting took place behind the German lines. 'It was a terrific day in the air,' wrote Baring, and it was another year before so much flying was done again. Twenty-four German machines were brought down, against six RFC machines lost, with nine crew members missing. But four officers and a sergeant gunner had been wounded, all but one dying subsequently of their wounds.

The heaviest casualties that day were suffered by 70 Squadron, where an early morning patrol of seven 1½-strutters led by Guy Cruikshank was engaged in 'some of the bloodiest fighting of the day' (H.A. Jones). Cruikshank, a Gordon Highlander, and one of the pioneers of August 1914, will be remembered as the first Britisher to disgorge an agent successfully behind the enemy lines. He was 'a great and loved pilot,' according to Maurice Baring, 'with a sublime belief in his own invulnerability.' Another tribute spoke of him as 'one of the greatest pilots produced by the war'. He had been making a name for himself in the Sopwith two-seater as a scout pilot, with an ambition to try conclusions with Boelcke himself. When, unknown to Cruikshank, the opportunity came, Boelcke was patrolling alone in one of his new hunting machines, for which the Sopwith was no match. Yet witnesses of the spectacular duel between the two machines that followed, lasting a quarter of an hour, were enthralled by a mutual exhibition of flying skills. Eventually, after a lethal machine-gun burst from Boelcke, Cruikshank's machine disintegrated, and he and his observer fell to their deaths. The day's losses so distressed 70 Squadron that Trenchard sent Baring along to give a day's outing to any young pilots or observers whom the squadron commander deemed to be in need of a boost.

THE NEW GERMAN SCOUTS:
RICHTHOFEN'S FIRST:
CRITICISM OF TRENCHARD:
SMITH-BARRY GETS HIS WAY

O N 16 September, the first bulk delivery of the new Albatros and Halberstadt pursuit planes enabled Boelcke, having trained his men in the preceding fortnight, to plan a patrol on the 17th with a select few of his *Jagdstaffel 2*, five machines in all. Meanwhile the British were planning a raid on the same day on one of their principal objectives in the German rail communications system. Neither side knew of the plans of the other.

Beyond the Bapaume–Peronne road ran the two great feeder lines serving the enemy front, heading south from Cambrai. At Marcoing, six miles south-west of Cambrai, a branch line left the main Peronne line for Bapaume, and it was this junction, and the adjacent station, that the British chose, on the morning of 17 September, as the target for eight BEs of No. 12 Squadron, each carrying one 112-lb bomb and four 20-pounders, which meant leaving observers behind. They were escorted by six FE2b's of No. 11 Squadron. Taking off at 6 a.m., the formation had reached its operating height of 6,000 feet when a ground mist so hampered navigation as to rule out any chance of accurate bombing, and the formation returned.

By 09.30 the mist had cleared and take-off was again ordered. Similar conditions may well have delayed the take-off of *Jasta 2*; but however that may be, the scene was now set for tragedy on the one hand and prestigious victory on the other. It was a victory accomplished in machines that had only arrived at the front the previous day, flown by pilots, among them Manfred von Richthofen, who were eagerly awaiting their first clash with the RFC.

After forming up and gaining height, the British formation, soon to be reduced to six through various defects, crossed the lines at 10.30, in air that had become so clear that the cliffs of Dover were plainly visible. For some it was to prove a farewell glimpse of home; and the chances of survival – and of serenity – were not improved for BE pilot Robert Money when his petrol pump broke. But he still had his hand pump, and rather than abort he continued, as the good soldier-turned-airman he was. But as the pump was situated outside the fuselage, rather too far forward for comfortable working, he found the burden too great to enable him to keep in formation. Sickeningly aware that he was gradually losing height and speed, he found himself well adrift of the others as they approached Marcoing.

Ahead of him he saw the leader turning for home, evidently having dropped his bombs. There were three more BEs with him, but the fifth had disappeared. Money realised that he was going to be very lucky to get home; but it still did not occur to him to turn back. Ignoring Archie, which was becoming intense, he dropped his bombs and watched them fall; he was waiting for the last bomb-burst when he was startled by a crackle of machine-gun fire. The BE was involuntarily borne upwards, and in the next instant the engine stopped and he was enveloped in a cloud of smoke and flying fragments. Half the engine seemed to have gone, but by pushing the stick hard forward he managed to keep straight and level.

Again he heard the rattle of machine-gun fire, and looking up he saw one of the escorting FEs, having evidently hurried to his assistance, going down in a steep spiral, with two Huns on its tail. Cursing his own impotence, he got off a few rounds from his Lewis in the general direction of the hostiles, then realised it was hopeless. Another FE was going down, and he saw a third try to intervene although itself under attack. It seemed to Money that the air was thick with Huns.

Bunched together on the horizon, apparently out of harm's way, was the little group of four BEs, their escape apparently dependent on the sacrifice of the FE crews. (In fact, Moranes of 60 Squadron were about to arrive on the scene.) Meanwhile Money's emotions fluctuated between desolation and rage as Boelcke's five were joined by at least seven more enemy scouts, and the FE pilots, always vulnerable directly astern, fought a losing battle. Descending haphazardly earthwards, almost stalled, Money was the unwilling witness of their fate. Finally, almost as he crash-landed, he saw another BE, presumably the one that had been missing from the group, hit the ground nearby and pitch forward on its nose.

He was welcomed into enemy territory by the usual cliché: 'Well, the war is over for you!' The speaker was an officer, and Money was taken to a nearby Mess and given a drink, after which a doctor came and cleaned him up; he had suffered only superficial cuts and bruises. It was the base of a fighter unit, and they had witnessed the scrap. Several spoke English, and Money asked what had happened to the FEs. 'Two, three, four – finished,' they said.

'And the tractor biplane – the BE?'

'He too is finished. Boelcke himself shot him down.'

The figures were accurate: four of the six FEs and two of the eight BEs were lost. The pilot of the other BE, Second Lieutenant Aubrey Patterson, died a week later.

For the pilots of *Jasta 2*, other than Boelcke, this was their first victory against the RFC. One of them took pains to record particulars of his victim. It was an FE, and the pilot crash-landed in a field. Learning his trade quickly, principally from Boelcke, Manfred von Richthofen had crept up underneath the FE's blind spot, and he could not resist landing beside the wreckage of his victim. He was just in time to see pilot and observer being lifted out of their cockpits. The observer is said to have opened his eyes as Richthofen bent over him, smiled, and succumbed to his wounds. The pilot died on the way to hospital.

To celebrate this first of his victories, Richthofen wrote to a jeweller friend in Berlin and asked him to engrave a small commemorative silver cup with the date of the action and the type of machine. The jeweller obliged and forwarded the cup. He could hardly have imagined that this ritual would be repeated sixty times in the next few months – and indeed would have extended further had the supply of silver in blockaded Germany not run out.

Trenchard immediately sensed that the Germans had brought a new fighting squadron, or squadrons, into action on this front. These were not his only casualties that day, and he was quick to realise that the pendulum was swinging against him. The new German scouts, faster and more manoeuvrable, with their two fixed machine-guns firing through the propeller arc, and fighting in formation, out-classed anything the British had. But as yet their numbers were small, and Trenchard resolved to stick it out. He would not easily abandon his policy of aggression.

As for Richthofen, a cautious and calculating approach, a refusal to engage the enemy unless the circumstances were favourable, and the somewhat ghoulish collecting of trophies, rendered him less attractive as a hero to the British than to the Germans, but his methods made sound military sense. Yet he couldn't have succeeded as he did but for Trenchard's policy. 'Let the customer come to the shop' was Richthofen's motto. By operating over his own territory he faced no dangers from Archie, and with the prevailing winds in his favour he could never be trapped or caught out, as the British often were, on the wrong side of the lines.

In the month of September the Germans destroyed 127 British and French machines for the loss of twenty-seven, and although this partly reflected the natural advantages of defending, the air superior-ity of the Allies was put under serious threat. On 29 September Trenchard warned the War Office that he would be looking for a doubling of the number of fighting squadrons working with each army, and next day Haig backed him up, writing of 'the urgent necessity for a very early increase in the numbers and efficiency of the fighting aeroplanes at my disposal.' After paying glowing tribute to three summer months in which the RFC had maintained 'such a measure of superiority over the enemy in the air that it has been enabled to render services of incalculable value,' he warned that all but a few of the fighting machines at his disposal were 'decidedly inferior' to the improved machines of the enemy, leading to a marked increase in casualties and threatening a very serious situation unless adequate steps were taken. Whereas practically no German machines had crossed the lines in the first two months of the battle, they were now venturing up to the lines and across them. He then echoed Trenchard's conviction that 'it is the fighting far behind the enemy's lines that tells most.' Trenchard then put forward a statement of estimated requirements. When the massacre of the RFC that followed in the spring of 1917 earned the appellation of 'Bloody April', no one at home could say that they hadn't been warned.

Meanwhile the Allied armies, because of a break in the weather, were unable to exploit the undoubted advantages they had gained, at enormous cost. Even the RFC, which had fought a new type of warfare with courage and distinction, without rest and often with grievous losses, was so impeded by the conditions that army commanders had to report that the number and accuracy of air reports was 'not up to the usual standard'. In summary, a crescent-shaped area about six miles across at its widest point had been gained, but the battle, conceived as a diversionary attack to relieve the French at Verdun, had burgeoned and had seemed to promise a breakthrough that had not materialised. British casualties, killed and wounded, amounted to nearly 419,000, the French 194,000, with the grim consolation that the Germans, already outnumbered, lost 650,000. Taking 22 November, when winter finally set in, as the end of the battle, the RFC from 1 July lost 308 pilots, 191 observers, and 782 aeroplanes. German losses were less than half that number, yet the RFC still controlled the air above the battlefield. This they achieved by never forgetting their fundamental *raison d'être*; working for the army. By taking the fight to the enemy even when losses seemed prohibitive, Trenchard stuck to his principles, relying on the tenacity and resilience of his air crews. They never failed him.

Yet there was certainly criticism from within the Corps. The most outspoken, as already quoted, was Smith-Barry, who was contemptuous of the whole basic philosophy and psychology of the training organisation, quite apart from his reluctance to put half-trained men into battle. Trenchard openly apologised to his pilots for asking them to fight against a better-equipped enemy with obsolete weapons and machines, but he demanded it just the same. The BE2c remained the maid of all work, but employing it would have been suicidal but for the Moranes, the FEs and the DH2s, and finally the Nieuports, and their offensive patrols. Then had come the *Jastas*, of which by November there were seven, to disturb the equilibrium.

When Eric Routh, who had learned the hard way that summer with 34 Squadron under the analytical Major J.A. Chamier, was posted to 16 Squadron as a flight commander in November, again on BEs, he was introduced, as the composition of his flight, to one surviving pilot and one surviving observer. 'Reinforcements are on their way from England,' he was told. But when they came they proved to be worse than novices. Routh was allowed a period in which to train them, but their quality depressed him. There was one newcomer, he wrote, who 'looked more intelligent than most, but that is not saying a great deal'.

Born in Malta twenty-one years earlier of a naval family, Routh was mature enough to cope without being driven either to despair or drink, but he did occasionally find relaxation in the Mess with the adjutant, who provided a shoulder to cry on. '"Uncle" Davidson and I have a drinking bout. He put down eleven liqueur glasses of neat whisky, I beat him with twelve of brandy. I had the pleasure of seeing him carried to bed.' He added, with pardonable pride: 'I put myself to bed.'

Robert Money, from the comparative safety of POW camp, also found much to reflect on. He was especially critical of what he characterised as the 'flying for the sake of flying' mentality, even flying for the sake of kudos. It seemed to him that the RFC squadrons were often asked to do work of doubtful utility in unsuitable machines, something which he believed other nations eschewed. 'The British seemed to have less regard for air casualties than the French or the Germans.' He was trenchant, too, on the subject of throwing raw recruits into the fray. 'The practice we followed of sending pilots over the lines semi-trained – which cost us so heavily in lives and machines – was not followed by the French or the Germans, whose pilots had usually completed at least fifty hours in the air, were masters of their machines and had had some practice in navigation and air tactics.'

Ewart Garland, the Australian who had been so emphatic about the term Hun, was another BE pilot with few illusions – unless he imagined that his château billet on No. 10 Squadron was typical. Occupied that summer in artillery work, contact patrols, and bombing, he rated the bombing as mostly casual and random. It went on all day and every day along the whole length of the front, penetrating anything from ten to forty miles beyond the lines, each squadron looking after selected targets in a designated area. Strong headwinds remained a perpetual hazard, and Garland felt that higher authority took a sadistic pleasure in sending them out on suicidal missions, sluggish and overladen and at the mercy of machines which were twice as fast and twice as handy.

Garland himself had had only five hours solo when he was posted to 10 Squadron at the start of the battle: he had put up his wings eight days' previously. He shared a general cynicism among BE pilots about the faith placed by Trenchard in the scout pilots and their offensive patrols, believing that bombing by the BEs would be much more effective given close escorts. It was an eternal argument. 'Our fighter squadrons always went well into enemy territory,' he wrote later, 'deliberately provoking the Hun fighters to join battle. Our Higher Command held to the theory that this policy drew the enemy fighters away from our slow bombers and photo and observation aeroplanes; but we slow and more or less defenceless chaps disagreed violently with such policy, and urgently wanted our fighters to "look after us" on all our missions. I well remember how safe and happy we felt on the rare occasions our bombing formations were escorted by fighters, which buzzed all round us like hornets while we plodded along in fairly tight formations at half the speed of the fighters. On these happy occasions enemy scouts kept a respectful distance, and we usually got back unscathed. How it warmed our spirits to have the fighter boys with us!'

[191]

As Trenchard had feared, there was bitterness at the publicity now being accorded scout pilots. Twenty-five-year-old Lieutenant John Quinnell, an Anglo-Irishman who spent a year on No. 10 Squadron (and much later became an air commodore), felt that because corps work was unspectacular it was underrated. The scout pilots were magnificent and deserved their decorations, but he knew of two corps recce squadrons which got one decoration each at the end of six months of hard flying. 'All other breasts', noted Quinnell, 'were as bare as a sparrow's.' Although mentioned in despatches, he was not decorated himself until late in the war, and he complained that however conscientiously they worked they got no word of appreciation, yet they should have been sharing in the distinction and the glory. Their task was the prime one, yet it was made to seem subordinate. Weary, but too proud to ask for a rest, many corps pilots asked to be recommended for transfer to an army squadron.

Garland, while conceding that the scout pilots did great things, saw them as the darlings of the service, searching out the enemy high above the corps squadrons like knights of old, not to be bothered with escort work. He was happier with night bombing, which came to be regarded as a useful adjunct to the work of the BEs. It did not require escorts, and there was no interference from Archie, though there were dangers enough in the crude facilities for take-off and landing, the rough surfaces of aerodromes, and the primitive cockpit instruments available.

Throughout that autumn Smith-Barry continued to complain to Trenchard about the inadequacy of replacement pilots and to disparage the whole system of flying training. Whereas, in peacetime, young flyers had persistently begged for opportunities to fly, men straight from training school, although young and fresh, showed little enthusiasm for flying and had to be virtually ordered into the air. They rarely sought permission to go for a practice flight. S-B blamed the instructors: pupils were discouraged through being taught by instructors who lacked a sense of vocation and whose indifference was contagious. The mental attitude of the instructor – who often regarded his stint of instructing as a chore – was reflected in every pupil he trained.

One of S-B's hobby-horses was that a pilot under training should always sit in the pilot's seat, not, as was general, in the passenger seat, obliging him to make his first solo flight in an unaccustomed position. He wanted a standard type of machine, suitable for every kind of manoeuvre, and certainly not a type as inherently stable as the BE, which corrected most mistakes and gave the pupil a false sense of security. The pupil must learn to be master of both himself and his machine. As it happened, the ideal machine for practising manoeuvres was about to become available in the 100-hp Monosoupape-engined Avro 504J and later K.

S-B had another slice of luck at about the same time. The greatest fear of pilots was of spinning, and a great many lives were lost because the technical reasons for spinning were not fully understood and the corrective action was not known. It was a very lucky pilot who survived a spin. One who did, as early as August 1912, was a naval lieutenant named Wilfred Parke, who recovered from his spin accidentally by, as he put it, 'doing everything wrong'. His experience naturally aroused interest, but the control movements which brought about his escape, although analysed, were never confirmed for circulation to all pilots and instructors. The reluctance of pilots to experiment further, in the absence of parachutes, is understandable.

The pilot's instinct, when he got into a spin, was to pull back on the stick to bring the nose up: it went against nature to push the nose forward. This, however, with some application of rudder, must have been what Parke did.

A post-war investigation attempted to summarise what was known of the spin and the history of attempts to control it.[1] The first man to set down the procedure for getting out of a spin appears to have been Major Frank Goodden, test pilot at Farnborough, who, in August 1916, 'in view of recent accidents', spun an FE8, the last of the Factory's pushers, and summarised his method of recovery:-

1. Glauert, H., *The Investigation of the Spin of an Aeroplane* (Advisory Committee for Aeronautics, June 1919).

1. Switch off motor.
2. Control stick put central and pushed forward.
3. Rudder put in centre.

This, explained Goodden, resulted in a nose-dive, from which the aeroplane, having once got up speed, could easily be pulled out with the control stick pulled back slightly. Sufficient height was assumed.

Frank Goodden's test flights predate a scientific investigation carried out in 1917 by Dr (later Professor) F.A. Lindemann, who learned to fly to prove his theories. Several other pilots, including John Chamier and a New Zealander named Balcombe-Brown, made similar discoveries in the autumn of 1916, convincing a sceptical Smith-Barry. The work of another Hawker, Harry, Sopwith's test pilot, is referred to; but there is no mention of Lanoe and the DH2.

Meanwhile S-B's ideas had crystallised into a belief that his best course was to start a school for instructors, with the intention that all instructors should eventually pass through it. Only by standardising pilot training throughout the service could there be any real long-term benefit.

Finally Trenchard's patience cracked. 'Don't worry us any more with your complaints. If you think you can do better, go and do it.' But the irritation was as much counterfeited as real; he appreciated that Smith-Barry's *métier* was instructing. 'It's time you tried out all these ideas you've been pestering me with. I've told the training people, so don't let me or yourself down.' He was to take over the Gosport School of Flying, where he had previously served as an instructor under Ferdy Waldron, and the scene was set for the revolution in flying training which was to spread worldwide. 'The number of lives he saved', proclaimed Stanley Vincent, who later became his deputy at Gosport, 'is incalculable.'

19

THE BREEZE VERTICAL

'We were never far from our fears.'

S o wrote Thomas Traill, a pilot on 20 Squadron who, although only eighteen, had seen action as a naval cadet in the Dardanelles in 1915 and who, in a future war, would become an air vice-marshal. What were these fears?

During training, the fear of failure was paramount, eclipsing the fear of being killed or maimed. For most trainees, this was their first chance of measuring themselves against their peers in a man's world, and many who suspected they were unsuited to flying and had no aptitude for it persisted with their training until they were forced to abandon it, either by their instructors or because of an accident. Such accidents were all too often fatal.

Once posted to a squadron in France, the fears multiplied. Forced landings during training could be negotiated safely: the English countryside presented ideal surfaces for landing light aeroplanes. But forced landings in or near the front line might offer a choice between one maze of shellholes and another, often in a crippled machine. There was no such thing as a nice smooth belly-flop: all machines had fixed undercarriages, ready to snag on any declivity or protrusion. Engine failure, gun stoppages, navigation in cloud or bad weather, the incessant exposure to Archie, not to mention enemy scouts, the prevailing wind that always fettered the homeward flight, the long, unrecoverable fall to earth in a doomed machine, above all the 'flamer' – these were daily physical hazards, which most people succeeded in putting to the back of their minds. But added to all this was the abstract fear of fear itself, of letting the side down, of being found wanting. What held a man in the line, according to Traill, was the fear of being exposed as one who would leave his comrades to carry the can, with the burden of living with oneself thereafter.

Every man had his own reservoir of courage, which might be dissipated slowly, quickly, or suddenly: the difficulty, for squadron commanders, lay in judging the rate of evaporation. Doctors attached to operational bases were not necessarily skilled in monitoring flying fitness, and some squadron commanders were remote figures, but the best of them watched closely for that haunted look which was euphemistically known as staleness. Such paragons might send a man on leave whether it was his turn or not. There was an awareness from the top down of the effects of protracted combat flying, and in 1916 Henderson recommended the formation of a Special RFC Medical Board. But it was 1917 before flying fatigue cases were sent away for special study and treatment, and even then, when so many were weary, who could be spared? Experienced men had to be retained to protect the beginners.

The medical officer in charge of RFC patients at the General Hospital at Étaples, Captain Dudley Corbett, RAMC, listed the symptoms to watch for. They began with a general lassitude. Sleep did not come so easily, or would be troubled when it came, interrupted by nightmares, often hysterical: anyway it would cease to be refreshing. While airborne a man might recover his keenness, but he would take less trouble with himself and his machine and might fly erratically, attacking recklessly or not at all. He would be preoccupied and irritable beforehand and exhausted afterwards. Smoking could be so incessant as to become neurotic. Some, to keep going, relied on alcohol, but in Corbett's experience this was rare.

Tommy Traill was aware of men on 20 Squadron who had to prime themselves beforehand, and even take a bottle up with them. A stiff drink, they found, stiffened resolve. But Traill and his colleagues were too preoccupied with their own nervous tensions to feel compassion for those who couldn't cope. For Traill, the men who took to the bottle were infinitely to be preferred to those who shirked in the air but talked themselves into the scrap at debriefing. 'It was usually impossible to know what others were doing during a dog-fight,' conceded Traill, 'but you soon got to know these people. There were only a few of them.' Squadron commanders had the same difficulty, when making judgements on fitness to fly, in sorting the fake from the genuine. As for alcohol, 'we did have periodical binges when the weather permitted,' wrote one pilot, 'but ours was a pretty sober squadron, for we all knew that alcohol and flying don't go well together.'

Arthur Gould Lee, like Traill a future air vice-marshal, often referred in his letters home to squadron parties. 'Binge last evening – thick head. Sing-song round piano. But about ten o'clock, chaps on dawn patrol "sent" off to bed by their flight commander.' The inverted commas were Lee's: it wasn't an order. 'Another binge developed last evening.' And later: 'You ask about the frequent binges we have. But we don't have them that often ... Otherwise there's not a great deal of drinking. I drink nothing but lime juice at meals, and the others do the same.' Again: 'The binge went on riotously until midnight, but I packed up at eleven because of the early job.' 'Rowdy binge 11.30 p.m. Sunday. But I'm on early patrol and felt I'd had enough to drink.'[1]

Robert Money, recalling a Mess party, wrote: 'I don't want to convey the impression that we drank excessively or regularly.' The heavy drinkers, he thought, were not to be found at the front. Life was eventful and exciting enough without stimulants. And for most of these youths, a single drink brought exhilaration, two and they were ready to smash the place up – which they often did. Money disagreed with the impression given later by the American Elliott Springs, in his book *War Birds*, of RFC men drinking themselves silly to anaesthetise their nerves. 'I'm certain that kind of thing didn't happen in 1915 and 1916.'

Gwilym Lewis extended this view to later years. 'A great thing is that there is practically nothing drunk but soft drinks, so that the Mess is always full of spirit without any artificial stimulants.' But

1. Lee, Arthur Gould, *No Parachute* (Jarrolds, 1968).

consumption varied, and there were exceptions. Of a colleague of whom he was clearly fond, a Canadian who made him laugh, he noted: 'He drinks too much.'

Parties were an occasion, sometimes started to relieve the gloom after losses. When they developed, the damage was to property rather than to person, though a raid on an adjacent squadron could get out of hand and result in real injuries. With alcohol so freely available, inevitably there were abuses, but over-indulgence was rare. 'Dawn patrol with a hangover?' wrote one pilot, 'No thanks!' But those not on the detail might be less abstemious. Jack Slessor admitted: 'We used to drink a good deal.'

Major F.J. Powell, MC, when commanding an SE5 squadron in 1917, thought the centre of his squadron was the bar. It was not something he discouraged. He always carried, when airborne, a small flask filled with rum. At altitude in winter his moustache would get frozen into a block of ice. 'A nip of alcohol had an immediate and glorious effect.'

Squadron life was a therapy in itself, something which men on 'rest' in England longed to return to, despite the dangers. They missed the camaraderie that is only present in a fighting unit. The flying itself could be enjoyable, and when it was over the freedom itself was intoxicating: one's time was one's own. Trenchard's policy of no empty chairs, old faces dissolving into new, checking any tendency to brood, was brutal but effective, and Mess nights, with uninhibited horseplay and the singing of traditional songs ('The Young Aviator Lay Dying' etc.), were invaluable for *esprit de corps* and for letting off steam.

Everyone was made aware sooner or later, in the loss of close comrades, that it could happen to them. But as in training, so in battle, a man would rather die than drop out. Labels like LMF – lack of moral fibre – were not yet known, and a loss of nerve was not classed as a crime. But the quitter, in addition to loss of self-respect, faced an uncertain future. If he had a regiment he would be returned to it, which was in itself a humiliation. If not, it could mean a transfer to the infantry.

The tradition that 'Flying will continue as usual', established at the outset, was doubtless a wise as well as a cherished one, but when it was applied to individuals there were dissentients. Surgeon Lieutenant H. Graeme Anderson, of the RNAS, learnt to fly himself to test his theories, and they proved contentious. 'If a pupil crashed and was apparently uninjured,' he wrote, 'he was ordered to go up again in another machine almost immediately. This was supposed to prevent loss of nerve, or, if known to be lost by the crash, [help] the immediate recovery of it. The author has seen the results of this method of treatment, and can say emphatically it is a method to be condemned . . .'

Bryan Sharwood-Smith (48 Squadron under Keith Park, and later knighted for his work in the Colonial Service), having narrowly survived a nerve-shattering dog-fight, was sent over the lines again within forty-eight hours. 'Such was the rule and a good one,' he wrote. 'Too much time for reflection was fatal.' But the reaction came a few weeks later, on home leave, when, after a chance remark by his sister, he broke down completely in front of his family. Yet the home leave did the trick: he had recovered by the end of it.

'I suppose most people live in a perpetual state of wind-up during a patrol,' wrote Bernard Oliver; and the actor Mervyn Johns said: 'I don't think there was a single moment when I was not scared to death.' But the impression that most men crossed the lines in a state of blue funk is not borne out by contemporary diaries and letters. The admission that they were often scared was general amongst RFC veterans, but a proper appreciation of mortal danger was essential for any chance of survival. The man who knew no fear was a freak.

According to John Quinnell, pilots sent back to England before they broke down had every chance of recovery, but if they broke down in France through being there too long they were seldom much use abroad. Two known exceptions were Harold Balfour, who was said to have gone 'loony' after a crash in a 1½-strutter but returned to do great things; and Ewart Garland. 'Bad weather meant a holiday,' Garland noted, 'otherwise one kept on flying to the limit of endurance and beyond.' Garland, like a good many others, was tested to destruction: understandably, he had a sudden breakdown at 10,000 feet and was given a staff job at Brigade Headquarters as a rest-cure. This was after he had been in action for eight months.

For Garland, as for many others, the monotony of staff work proved a short cut to rehabilitation. 'I have that deep down feeling that I ought not to have this soft job,' he wrote. 'My conscience pricks me when I am recording pilots' activity in action.' What he missed above all was the comradeship. Fed up with the staff and all its connotations of pomposity and red tape, he added: 'The sooner I fly again the better.' He got his wish, but not in a squadron in France: he was posted to a reserve squadron in England to help work it up to operational pitch.

While there were certainly men, like Cecil Lewis, whose confidence in their own survival was not misplaced, most, like Albert Ball, soon lost any illusions of indestructibility. Others had premonitions, and knew that their time had come. Norman Macmillan, who later gained distinction as an aviation writer, talked to his tent companion one summer evening of joining others in a walk into the local town of Cassel for a meal. 'No thanks, Mac,' was the reply, 'I've got some letters to write.' When Macmillan got back to the tent he was asked: 'If anything happens to me tomorrow, Mac, will you post these letters for me and see that my kit is sent off to these two addresses?' With that he turned in and fell into a deep and untroubled sleep. Next morning the crews of eight 1½-strutters were briefed to get photos of Menin railway station, which they knew would be a tough assignment. 'I'm sorry I couldn't get you an escort,' concluded the squadron commander. They got their photographs but were intercepted on the way back. Many suffered damage, and of the two who were shot down, one was Macmillan's tent companion. Letters and kit were posted as requested.

There was one sure way of escaping with integrity intact, and there were few men who did not know a pang of envy of those who profited from it. Convinced he had been shot through the arm and that he could feel the warm blood flowing, Tommy Traill was already envisaging the hospitalisation and the posting home when, on examination, it was found he had not been shot at all, but merely grazed. 'To go home wounded,' he admitted, 'would have been an honourable way out of immediate danger and a temporary relief from the conflict.' The conflict he was referring to was not so much the war but fear itself, above all the fear of burning, and, almost equally, the fear of human weakness, the fear of failing one's comrades.

Nobody, it seemed, could stand the strain indefinitely. 'Ultimately it reduced you to a dithering state,' wrote Gwilym Lewis, 'near to imbecility. You had to go out and do the job, you could never say frankly: "I am afraid, I can't face it any more." So you continually had to win battles over yourself and your fears.' The result, believed Lewis, was damage to the essential tissue of one's being.

Men blessed with a spiritual faith were the stronger for it, but organised religion gave solace to few. 'You never hear anyone talking religion,' said Lee, 'whether in the Mess or privately. We do have padres, and they occasionally hold services, but mostly they organise cinema shows and bury people. They can't even do much for anyone whose nerve is beginning to crack, the doctors come in on that.' Service padres were hopelessly under strength, few were resident, and Church parades were rare. 'I have been to Church this morning,' wrote Gwilym Lewis in a letter home, 'I attend when I can.' But no one was more fiercely critical of the padres. 'Most of these fellows who stand in pulpits I often feel I would like to get hold of, shake them thoroughly, kick them hard and tell them to go and have a look at the world as it really is, and then start talking about it.' One padre, unable to bear the distressing sequence of casualties and replacements – or perhaps discouraged by rejection – applied for a posting to a regiment in the line.

Innermost thoughts, never revealed, undoubtedly dwelt on more spiritual matters, but outwardly, more attention was paid to superstition. Many carried mascots and were inconsolable if they were lost. Lee touched wood before a scrap. Prayers were a form of insurance, only heartfelt in moments of crisis. 'Why should God grant me any special favour?' asked Lee. 'The Hun I'm fighting may be calling on him too . . . How can anyone who has to fight believe in God, with all the mass killings? How can I call on God to help me shoot a man down in flames?'

Home leave could be confusing as well as therapeutic. There was

[201]

a quiet satisfaction in seeing the crowds of holidaymakers on beaches in midsummer, yet it was a reminder of how remote the civilian was from the war, with no conception of what it meant to the fighting man. The underlying stoicism of the masses, and the pride in bereavement, were not easily divined. More visible were the profiteers, the strikers, the conchies, the people with cushy jobs for whom the war couldn't last long enough, bitterly resented by men for whom there was no escape from a return to danger and probable death. Yet that return could be strangely uplifting. Lee wrote of the sensation of coming home, of welcome and comradeship, of a feeling that this was where one belonged, not amongst the money-making and pleasure-seeking mob that one could not escape from in London. Communication might be limited, the eternal verities were seldom discussed; who they were, where they came from, what made them tick – none of this mattered. All that counted was whether the other chap had what it takes.

20

CLASHES WITH DOWDING AND TRENCHARD: THE DEATH OF BOELCKE: HAWKER'S DUEL WITH VON RICHTHOFEN

ARRIVING in France in October, commanding a new squadron of Sopwith 1½-strutters, No. 45, and impatient for a third crack at the enemy, was Willie Read. But it was not a happy return. At Candas on the Somme, where a second aircraft park had been established the previous year, there was snow on the ground when they landed, and as nothing had apparently been prepared for them, the aspect was bleak. Read had expected to be met by the commander of the wing they would be serving under, 'Stuffy' Dowding, but Stuffy was not in evidence. Candas happened also to be Trenchard's headquarters, and it was 'Boom' himself who came across to welcome him and his twelve machines. 'Boom asked if we were all right,' Read related afterwards, 'and I said we would be later.'

'Rations all right? Where are your tents?'

Trenchard's questions were rhetorical: it was obvious that none of these items had been provided. But he left without further comment. 'I think he twisted Stuffy's tail,' said Read. 'This was rather unfortunate as Stuffy and I were not very fond of each other.' Early in 1914 they had had a row at CFS, owing, according to Read, to Dowding's 'pugnacious temperament'. The self-willed

Read could be pugnacious himself, and they had nearly come to blows.

There were two Bessoneau hangars – canvas-covered, wooden-framed sheds capable of holding four machines each – on the perimeter, not enough to house the twelve Sopwiths, so in the absence of tents Read decided to quarter the men in the hangars and picket the machines outside, the obvious solution to a man accustomed to looking after his men. Then Dowding arrived. 'Turn the men out of the hangars', he ordered, 'and put the machines inside.'

'And where are the men to go?'
'Now you are being insolent.'

Dowding sent him some tents, but the incident rankled. 'Stuffy had his knife into me,' said Read, 'from then on.'

It was normal for a new squadron to be given at least a week in which to get acquainted with conditions before venturing over enemy territory, but 45 was ordered off at once by Dowding. 'On our first patrol of three machines only one came back,' bemoaned Read, 'and I lost my best flight commander, one Porter by name.' Read's anger and distress, at the start of what he had hoped might be a brilliant campaign in the Sopwith, may be imagined. To wing headquarters the missing men might be no more than names on a casualty list, but Read, like any good squadron commander, had made it his business to get to know all his crews. Porter, for instance – Leslie Porter – an Ulsterman, married with three young children, was a distinctive figure at the mature age of thirty-five, a pioneer in the motor industry in Belfast and a prominent figure in motor racing before the war. In Read's view he would certainly have gone on to command a squadron. His death in captivity, within a few hours of the action, was later confirmed. (Twenty-five years later his son David was luckier in surviving being shot down and captured.)

Struggling to launch raw pilots in an imperfect machine, Read suffered such severe losses in that first month that his squadron, as Smith-Barry's had been, was sent away to recoup. To add insult to injury, Dowding blamed their losses on inefficiency. But at least the transfer switched them to a different wing. 'I was glad to get away from Stuffy,' said Read. But he still found the control exercised over him by his new brigade commander, T.I. Webb-Bowen, irksome. Occasionally he led a formation himself, in defiance of the order that squadron commanders must not fly over the lines, and the operation reports reflected this. 'I was continually getting snorters from HQ for disobeying orders.' How was it possible, he argued, to keep in touch and direct and criticise his pilots and observers unless he took part in affairs himself? Pugnacious or not, Read was certainly headstrong, and instead of giving way he dug his toes in. Webb-Bowen used to visit the squadron with the object, Read felt, of finding fault, and he became very unhappy. He stuck it for six months and then applied to go back to his regiment. 'Boom was very annoyed with me for applying, and when he finally agreed he said: "In a few months' time you will ask me to take you back and I shall say no – as I have to everybody else so far."' But Read persisted, and in April 1917 he went back to the King's Dragoon Guards, reverting to captain, after a sad leave-taking from the squadron he himself had formed and led.

'I had another reason for wanting to go back to the regiment,' admitted Read. 'It looked at about this time [just before the Battle of Arras] as if we were going to advance and get the Bosch on the run, and by going back to the regiment I saw the possibility of getting a gallop with them.' But the gallop didn't come off, and for the rest of 1917 he watched with a wistful nostalgia as the corps machines circled overhead. Would Boom, for old times' sake, take him back after all? The time came when he decided to try.

A fresh hazard of air fighting, as formations got bigger and dogfights between opposing groups proliferated, was collision, and it was ironic that the man who had done more than anyone to develop team fighting should be one of its first victims. On 26 October 1916 Oswald Boelcke brought his personal score of victories to 40, but he was already admitting to his closest friend and colleague Erwin Boehme that he was feeling the strain. It was in this state that a moment's inattention or over-confidence could be fatal. Certainly when they took off again two days later, on the 28th, there seemed nothing in the opposition – two DH scouts of Hawker's squadron – to trouble the five Albatros pilots Boelcke was leading. Having recently captured a DH2, the Germans had proved in mock combat what they already knew, that their new machines were far superior. Yet the two DH2 pilots manoeuvred so cleverly that they must be given some credit for what followed: their names were Lieutenant A.G. Knight and Second Lieutenant Alfred McKay.

Six more German fighters arrived as Boelcke started his attack, and this may have led to confusion. Anyway, he and his friend Boehme dived for the same target, and neither saw the other. The horror of the German pilots, as Boehme's undercarriage struck Boelcke's upper wing, was fleetingly relieved as Boelcke dropped away apparently under control, but then they saw the wing break away, and as Boelcke fought in vain for control they knew that his death was certain. Boehme escaped unscathed, while Knight and McKay, who continued their manoeuvring, deserved their luck. In pursuance of the mutual respect and camaraderie that distinguished air combat, the RFC dropped a laurel wreath over the German lines next day, bearing the inscription: 'To the memory of Captain Boelcke, our brave and chivalrous foe.' Sadly, Knight was killed just before Christmas 1916, McKay a year later.

Boelcke had not merely inspired the German Air Force while he was alive, he had left behind an indelible legacy. Meanwhile the leading air tactician on the British side, whose motto of 'Attack EVERYTHING' still graced the notice board of 24 Squadron, remained in command. He still flew regularly if less frequently, and when he did he continued to take a subordinate role in the formation, lest he betray any hint of rustiness. The flight commanders flew almost daily, and he was content to follow them, usually replacing a tired pilot, and usually in a strange machine. It was a difficult time for DH2 pilots, called upon to face superior machines, their weaknesses known and their tactics rumbled. Experienced pilots were thinning out, and there was too little time to train the new ones or break them in properly, while their shooting was often abysmal. Hawker did all he could, but with demands for patrols unceasing he was forced to compromise. He could do little more than keep an eye on the general health of his pilots, and recommend them for leave if he felt they needed it, or to be sent home as instructors if he felt they had done – or had had – enough. He knew from personal experience that lack of leave had an effect on efficiency: reactions became slower, perceptions less acute.

He himself was feeling wartorn before the summer was out, without much hope of a rest. The approach of autumn removed a favourite form of relaxation: it was too dark after tea to play tennis. If at times he felt stale, he gained rejuvenation from the eagerness of his pilots and their high spirits at Mess parties and Mess games. When at last he did go on leave, on 5 November, with the Somme battle foundering in a sea of mud, his betrothal to Beatrice was unofficially confirmed. He expected to serve another two or three months in France and then be promoted to lieutenant-colonel and a staff job, when marriage would follow. Yet he found London depressing. Of The Empire Leicester Square, then a music hall and hitherto a frequent haunt of his wartime colleagues, he wrote: 'I didn't meet a soul I knew.' It brought home to him the shocking carnage of the past two years: either his contemporaries were dead or they had been promoted out of sight. Meanwhile expansion had changed the face of the RFC completely; no longer did everyone know everyone else.

Although by the time he got back to France the ground battle was stagnating, the DH2s were still penetrating enemy territory in support of Trenchard's determination to maintain air superiority over the lines. Hawker was soon back in action, and on 23 November he took off with two of his senior pilots on an offensive patrol. The leader, the tall, dark-haired, pencil-moustached J.O. (Jock) Andrews, a striking figure in his Highland forage cap, had joined the squadron a year earlier at Hounslow and, with Hawker, was the last surviving original. The third member of the patrol, R.H.M.S. 'Bob' (sometimes 'Sandy') Saundby, who would one day be 'Bomber' Harris's deputy at Bomber Command, had been on the squadron four months following distinguished anti-Zeppelin service in England. Quite simply, on patrols of this nature they were looking for trouble.

Over Bapaume at about 9,000 feet they spotted below them what Andrews, caring nothing for the niceties, later described as 'a few fat Huns'. It seems likely that these were a decoy. Above them an umbrella of Albatros scouts, led by Richthofen, was waiting to pounce. (Richthofen by this time was the leading living German ace with ten victories.) Andrews was about to abandon the pursuit of the obese two-seaters when Hawker dived past him, intent as ever on attack. A Hun scout followed, but Andrews drove him off, firing about twenty-five rounds at close range. Soon Andrews too had a Hun on his tail, 'pumping shells into his backside,' as he put it, and his engine (a pusher in the DH2), was hit. He had no option but to try to limp back over the trenches. He saw Hawker hesitate as though to assist him, and then, perhaps satisfied that his leader could look after himself, chase after one of the Hun scouts. The last Andrews saw of him he was scrapping with a hostile, apparently under control.

Soon afterwards Saundby saw Hawker in a circling fight with a German at about 3,000 feet, but by this time his own engine was out of action and he could do nothing to help. Knowing Hawker's skill, however, he wasn't unduly perturbed. He was not to know that his commander was pitted against perhaps the only pilot in the German Air Force with a reasonable chance of shooting him down in a duel.

Hawker's experience, and the manoeuvrability of the DH2, might well compensate for the overall superiority of the Albatros, but he could not manoeuvre indefinitely. Under the prevailing wind, every turn was taking him farther from the lines, and sooner or later shortage of fuel would compel him to run for it. For the moment, though, as he waved spontaneously to his adversary – who reciprocated – he was giving every indication of enjoying himself.

'We circled round and round like madmen,' wrote Richthofen afterwards, 'twenty times to the left, thirty times to the right . . . I had quickly discovered that it was not a novice that I had to deal with . . . it was clear to me that I was being tackled by a flying champion.' A group of German grenadiers were in no doubt that they were watching a duel between 'first-rate champions of the air'. Inevitably the time came when Hawker, despairing of pinning his man down, had to break off, and after a few stunts he began a sudden zig-zagging dash for the lines at low level. Richthofen followed, firing all the time, and victory for him seemed certain until his guns jammed. Hawker was only fifty yards short of the lines when, perversely, a single bullet from that final burst found its mark, and he fell, shot through the head.

Richthofen's pride in downing what he called 'the English Immelmann' was immense, and he concluded his account: 'His machine-gun was dug out of the ground and it adorns the entrance to my room.'

21

TRAINING, AND THE LACK OF IT

'Our so-called instructors were not flying instructors at all.'

AIR MARSHAL SIR HUGH WALMSLEY

T HE men who flew to France in August 1914 had all been trained, at their own expense, by professional flying instructors at one or other of the civilian schools. Having been taught to fly, and having gained their Royal Aero Club certificate, they reported to the Central Flying School to be passed out for their wings. This, according to Jack Slessor, was a perfunctory business, calling for no particular skill. The anxious candidate was asked some rudimentary questions about the theory of flight, the internal combustion engine, and the organisation of the RFC, while dual instruction consisted of a few circuits and landings, in which the instructor flew the aeroplane, with the pupil having his hands and feet on the controls 'to get the feel of them'. An occasional bang on the back to attract the pupil's attention revealed the instructor waving his hands to show that he had relinquished control. Afterwards the pupil was asked whether he felt confident in himself, and if he answered 'Yes' he was sent off solo. 'I do not remember,' recalled Slessor, 'anyone having the moral courage to answer "No" to that stock question, though I personally felt anything but confident in myself.' Yet the pre-war service atmosphere, with pilots allotted their own machine and flying almost where they chose, to visit other squadrons, to attend race meetings and similar events, landing where they could, soon bred skill and confidence.

On the outbreak of war, experienced civilian instructors were

quickly absorbed into the service, but the rapid expansion that followed soon exhausted their capacity. Complaining that the situation
with new pilots was unsatisfactory, Brancker reported that the right
kind of young men were coming forward in gratifying numbers, but
that the shortage of aeroplanes and engines was only equalled by
the paucity of skilled pilots capable of imparting their knowledge
and experience. Long waiting lists accumulated.

There were few branches of service tuition in which errors could
be so catastrophic as in the training of pilots. This was before the
days of flight simulators, and almost from the outset the syllabus
exposed the pupil to the ultimate danger. Crashes could be especially
costly for the pupil, who, in the flimsy machines of the time, occupied
the front seat. Whereas the rear cockpit might remain more or less
intact, the forward cockpit was often demolished.

There was no standard manual for instructors, no aptitude tests,
and no instructors' schools. Most of the men recruited as instructors
were home from the front 'on rest', and if many of them approached
the task with a minimum of enthusiasm it is hardly surprising. They
saw the posting as a come-down; yet it required courage to turn the
controls over to a raw pupil, and it was certainly no rest for the
nerves. They had to be continually on the alert, and they were overworked and over-stressed.

In Jock Andrews's experience, if the instructor wasn't on rest he
was probably waiting impatiently to go overseas. There were even
some who had been categorised as suitable for reserve squadron duties only. Their results were not monitored, they worked
without a proper syllabus, and they looked upon their work as
drudgery.

When Peter Portal went home after Christmas 1915 to learn to
fly at Castle Bromwich, after his stint of observing, he was astonished
at the ignorance of the majority of his instructors. Some were good,
but some he thought disgracefully bad, and all were idiosyncratic,
teaching in their own way. Most were competent pilots, but few had
the technical knowledge or the qualities of character and temperament likely to inspire confidence in others. Morale amongst the pupils
was correspondingly low, and when Portal graduated to CFS he

[211]

found the ambience even worse, the rot starting at the top. 'Certain senior officers refused to fly certain types of aeroplane.'

The best instructors, not surprisingly, were those who had graduated pre-war and had war experience as well. Tom Mulcahy-Morgan, before his return to the front for a spy-dropping role, soon forgot the fatigue of the retreat and actually enjoyed instructing, finding his keenness revived by it. 'There are great compensations in instructing,' he wrote. 'One sees progress daily and feels there is a visible result for work done.' Channel-Islander Henry Brock found the much maligned BE8 Bloater 'a good school machine', but he was critical of the lack of efficient control from the front seat, which, as Smith-Barry objected, left the pupil to attempt his first solo from an unaccustomed position.

Perhaps not surprisingly, in view of his humanity, Willie Read made an ideal instructor. 'From the start Read treated his pupils,' wrote one of them, 'with a degree of friendliness that was altogether charming. He let his pupils do all the work, making corrections only when necessary.' The result was 'nerves nil, confidence max'. In the paternal care of this notable live-wire, pupils progressed in an atmosphere of serenity.

Unfortunately, natural tutors like Mulcahy-Morgan, Brock and Read were rare. Not every seasoned flyer was correspondingly gifted. 'Our so-called instructors were not flying instructors at all,' wrote Hugh Walmsley (a future air marshal). 'They were chaps who'd survived a tour in France and come home for a rest. The only rest they could be given, because there was such a shortage of pilots, was to go to a reserve squadron as a flying instructor.' Many of these men found the exhaustion of a day's instructing more than a night's rest could restore.

A compensation was the preservation at home stations of the peacetime attitude to 'social' flying: borrowing a machine to fulfil some social engagement. Ewart Garland's instructor, having promised that he would send him off solo that day, announced that he would start by fulfilling an assignation. 'First of all the instructor went with me and did a few stunts over Worthing and landed on the wet sand. We stayed there for twenty minutes while he talked to his girl and while the crowd gazed on the machine and us with awe. Then we went back to the aerodrome and landed and he got out and after a few advices I started alone.' This liberal attitude was extended to 'Huns', an appellation for pupils born of the Teutonic-like protective helmets they were ordered to wear.

Some instructors, because of the strain they were under, only aggravated the fears of their pupils. Such reported invocations as 'Shove her nose down, you bloody fool, do you want to kill us both?' were hardly calculated to inspire confidence. Vernon Brown, later to become a leading test pilot and accident investigator, learnt to fly on a Vickers Gunbus at Joyce Green: the machine had no dual control, so the instructor sat on the fuel tank behind Brown with his hand on Brown's shoulder, though it was Brown's hand on the joystick. 'Right rudder, you fool!' Brown would hear him shouting. 'Now pull her up!' And then: 'Look out! You'll go through the floor if you do that!' Such irascibility hardly made for relaxed flying. But Brown passed his test. 'You appear to be a perfectly good pilot,' he was told at CFS. 'You can be an assistant instructor here.' With fifteen hours solo on various types he started teaching others to fly.

Brown's experience typified a tendency to keep back the bright boys from one class to teach the next. Some doubted if this was sound in principle: the last men you wanted as instructors, it was said, were those to whom flying had come easily.

Instructors found it difficult to gauge whether a man had the essence of it in him or not. Even on a reserve squadron there was a unit as well as a personal pride, which drove men on. Some of those who took longest to go solo made the best pilots. But the reverse was also true. Robert Money's ambition was to be the first on his course to go solo, and he achieved it. Of the last one to go solo he wrote: 'I don't think even then he thought he was fully competent, but he hated the idea of being left behind.' Three days later he was killed.

What were the ideal characteristics of a wartime pilot? The high spirits and resilience of youth came high on Trenchard's list. They could not all be eighteen or nineteen, that would be too restrictive,

[213]

but they should be under twenty-five, and unmarried. There were exceptions, but marriage was reckoned to have an inhibiting effect. Athletic, alert, cheerful, even happy-go-lucky, the paragon would also reveal initiative and a sense of humour. A desirable weakness might be a lack of imagination. The greatest strength was an incurable optimism. 'It's the other chap who gets the chop,' said trainee Gerald Dixon. 'It never entered my head that I was going to get killed.'

However desirable extreme youth might be, it posed accompanying disciplinary problems, though these were generally viewed with indulgence. 'They treated us like schoolboys,' said John Chrispin, a pupil at Old Sarum, 'which we virtually were.' Sent to Hendon to collect a new machine, Chrispin conceived the notion of deliberately mistaking the GWR line out of London, which would take him past a small field next to his uncle's house at Wantage, for the LSW line to Salisbury. After 'force-landing' in the field he reported his whereabouts by telephone, promising to fly off next morning. But overnight the wind changed, and he nearly killed himself on take-off, just squeezing between two trees. Back at Old Sarum, his CO, Major E.J. Fuller, one of the 3 Squadron originals as a second lieutenant, came out to meet him. 'Glad to see you back. What happened?' As Chrispin told his story, Fuller had to turn away to hide his amusement. All he said was: 'Be more exact with your map-reading.' On another occasion Chrispin, on a cross-country training flight, decided to fly to Huddersfield and land in one of his mother's meadows on a farm on the edge of the town, which delayed his return. He later learned that Fuller and the chief instructor, a man named Ruxton, had been pacing anxiously up and down, fearing for his safety. 'Shall I go and play hell with him, sir?' Ruxton asked Fuller when Chrispin eventually arrived. 'No,' answered Fuller resignedly, 'as long as he's safe it doesn't matter.'

Maurice Kay, sent from CFS to pick up a new Sopwith scout at Coventry, got fed up with waiting for better weather as advised and set out of his own volition. Caught in a mist as he crossed the hills between Cheltenham and Cirencester, he flew through the branches of a tree at 80 m.p.h. 'My machine lurched and I thought I was going to nose-dive to earth.' He didn't, but his left lower wing was badly damaged and half his undercarriage was gone. The engine was vibrating alarmingly, but somehow the Sopwith kept flying. He made a perfect landing back at Netheravon, despite a missing wheel, a cracked wing, three cylinders out of action, and a badly chipped propeller. Everyone was amazed that the machine had held together, the old hands hardly crediting that it could have flown at all. 'The commandant was awfully pleased', boasted Kay, 'and told me to write an account, that he thought it was a very fine effort, and that he would forward the account to higher authority as a record.' Nothing was said about his decision to fly south against expert advice. Much was forgiven of a press-on type, and of extreme youth. The same indulgent attitude was prevalent in France. 'I should always like to be eighteen,' wrote Gwilym Lewis. 'You can do just what you like and no one considers you responsible for your actions.' Perhaps this was fair. Manhood was not reckoned to be reached until twenty-one.

Pupils went through fevers of self-doubt in the course of their instruction, many having to summon up reserves of courage to continue. One sensitive young pilot, barely free of his mother's apron strings, kept a diary – anonymously – in which he noted when he was booked for flying. One such entry carried the comment: 'I got one of those spasms of wind-up and dodged it. I do not think I shall ever make an airman. I'm on tenterhooks all the time I'm up – and I shall be in France next month so God help me.' He was thinking of going to the adjutant and asking for a transfer to observer.

Over the next eight days the saga moved to a climax. On the Saturday he knew he was down to fly, but when he got to the hangars someone had rubbed his name off the board, and he kept out of the way. 'Then began a day's torture, my mind being in a ferment all the time. The struggle was on as to whether or not I should chuck up flying and apply to be transferred as an observer.' At last he decided to go and ask his instructor, a man named Stewart, to wash

him out, but Stewart wasn't in his office, and in a trauma of inde-
cision he 'wobbled away'. It did not help that 'Poor old Barradale
has been killed in an RE8 this afternoon.'

The weather clamped next day and he played solo-whist, but it
cleared up later. 'About 6.30 they started to fly, and I was down at
the hangars three times looking for my instructor, and feeling wind-
up for fear that I should find him. But I didn't.' That night he played
solo again. Next day Captain Stewart sent for him, and when he
told of his lack of confidence, Stewart promised to have a word
with the CO, and added something about getting him transferred to
scouts.

Two days later: 'Captain Stewart saw me after tea and said that
he had seen the CO (which I doubt, as the latter would have sent
for me), and that he had said I could either carry on or go back to
my regiment. This was a bit of sarcasm, because Stewart knows jolly
well I haven't got a regiment. I knew he was determined to stop me
when he mentioned scouts.' He was damned if he wanted to be an
observer, 'only I shall probably kill myself on these RE8s.' Yet he
felt he had far better kill himself than resign his commission. That
would mean total humiliation.

An unnerving experience with Stewart at the controls with a dud
engine 'put the wind up Stewart as well'. In the next two days Stewart
took him up to 5,000 feet, the highest he'd been, and then to 10,000
and 12,000, but 'height jiggers me ... If I had been solo I should
have crashed as sure as eggs are eggs.' He told Stewart this, and
asked him to take him up high regularly. 'I finished up the night in
the ante-room, writing up this diary, and reading. I also refused to
play solo as the mater doesn't wish me to gamble.' Here was another
young man of eighteen still answerable to mother.

As the war progressed and manpower became stretched, suitable
candidates for training became rarer, and almost anyone medically
fit was considered. It became not unusual for gun-shy trainees, especially once they had been commissioned, to employ all manner of ruses
to delay posting to France, knowing how difficult it was to get them
reduced in rank and sent to the trenches. Stewart would have met
some of these, which would explain his cussedness. But eventually

he accepted that this particular (anonymous) pupil was genuine and let him go.

The need for pilots became so urgent that below average pupils might be given the benefit of the doubt, often with tragic results. Instructional hours were reduced, and trainees might be required to go solo before they had attained a proper proficiency. This resulted in so many accidents that Australian Francis Penney, after a spell as an observer on 12 Squadron, was required, on starting his pilot's course, to contribute a lump·sum for the purchase of wreaths for those killed, on a *pro rata* basis: trainees two shillings and sixpence, administrative officers five shillings, instructors seven-and-six. The weighting against instructors was logical – if they did their job properly they wouldn't have to pay up. Those not on the flying roster were liable for duty as pall-bearers.

Trainee pilots awaiting advanced instruction in combat tactics, air firing and formation flying were liable to be diverted overseas to fill empty cockpits, the intention being that the squadron should train them. But preoccupation with urgent tasks generally meant that training, where it existed at all, was sketchy. 'Many went out with as little as five hours on their service machines,' wrote Second Lieutenant Harold Seymour. 'The two lads I crossed the Channel with and talked to on the boat were both shot down before I had been over the lines.' Seymour was lucky in that his CO made newcomers fly behind the lines for a fortnight before sending them on patrol.

The demand for replacements at the front remained insatiable, and although senior instructing staff were not unconscientious, and many did what they could for their charges, decisions on postings were outside their control. Some made a strict rule that, irrespective of personalities, if a pupil had not gone solo after a fixed period he was automatically turned down. Undoubtedly this saved many lives. Pupils aiming to be scout pilots were transferred to heavier types if they didn't adapt quickly.

Arthur Gould Lee was another of the lucky ones. A major crash in training so lengthened his learning period that he accumulated many more solo hours than the average. He had been kept in England long enough to learn properly, and he believed it was no accident that, where so many fell in their first few weeks, he survived.

Gerald Dixon, on his first solo at Catterick, 'had absolutely no idea what to do. Only a natural aptitude saved one from catastrophe.' He insisted that, although he *learned* to fly, he was never *taught* to fly. Under the pressures of the time, perhaps this was inevitable. Yet even on his first solo he felt no fear: he was far too busy keeping the machine in the air. Many others remember their first solo as among the most exciting moments of their lives, anyway in retrospect.

Perhaps the casual approach taken by many instructors was relaxing for the pupil. 'Off you go,' F.C. Ransley was told, 'tootle around the perimeter of the aerodrome two or three times and try some landings. An ambulance is handy if you crash.' The tradition that 'flying will continue as usual' applied equally to pupils. Provided they were uninjured, it was still thought good psychology to send them up again straight away after a crash.

On-the-squadron training varied, but, as already indicated, was frequently minimal. Eighteen-year-old Harold Tambling, with thirty-one hours solo, felt his training at home had been sound. He had progressed to the F2b Bristol Fighter, and he found it a revelation. But on joining 22 Squadron, which had just been re-equipped with the type, he had what he called 'a very cursory interview' with his commanding officer, Major L.W. Learmont. Leonard Learmont had a distinguished career ahead of him, but at that stage he seems to have been overwhelmed by his problems. 'You'd better take a plane up and see how you feel,' he told Tambling. Next day Tambling was allotted an observer – Flight Sergeant W. Organ – and didn't realise at first how favoured he was, since Organ was an experienced man and therefore in great demand. Two days out of three they were over the lines on various tasks, generally with four or five others. Tambling had had some formation flying practice in England, but none on the squadron, and they flew in a sort of gaggle, never very close: this allowed them to weave about when they were Archied. There was no particular briefing beforehand, and no tactical discussions;

they were just given a line to patrol. In a scrap it was every man for himself.

Tambling developed no particular friendships – the turnover inhibited this. 'We hardly knew each other, there was a completely new squadron every few weeks.' There were no high jinks, everyone was too preoccupied, and they weren't encouraged to get together. He didn't drink, nobody did, so far as he knew, and he didn't even feel the baby of the squadron – there were others of a similar age, with a similar lack of experience. The one fellow he thought might become a friend was killed while practising air-to-ground firing. It was accidents like this, and the frequency of patrols, which inhibited a full training programme. But he had great confidence in the Brisfit, and the actual flying he thoroughly enjoyed.

Despite occasional victory claims their casualties mounted. Tambling recorded in his log book, in a period of under three weeks, five crews either prisoners or dead, one pilot killed on the aerodrome, and five wounded, one of whom died. The squadron ambulance juddering across the grass to collect casualties from crippled machines became a familiar sight. Consistent with the average, Tambling was shot down himself within a month of arrival, on a dawn patrol which started badly. Of six machines detailed, the leader had engine trouble and had to abort, and the deputy leader had to turn back half-way to the line. The remaining four pressed on and had just about reached the limit of their patrol when Tambling saw the machine on his right stagger and burst into flames.

He heard Organ firing the Lewis behind him, and he tried a few speculative bursts from the front Vickers at the scarlet, wasp-like machines that buzzed around him, but then he felt the Bristol shudder as it was hit and they started to slew round in circles. He couldn't correct the slide, and as they descended he knew he was being fired at continually as fuselage and wings took a peppering. He was thankful now for the experience of Organ, whose accurate return fire was keeping their assailants off their tail. Organ's coolness protected them from total destruction until they struck a tree as they neared the ground and the machine was thrown on to its starboard wing-tips, cushioning their fall.

[219]

Miraculously, neither man had been hit or badly hurt, and soon a party of Germans, who had been following their descent, arrived in a truck and took them prisoner. Separated from his NCO observer, as was the custom, Tambling never saw him again. He was taken to the Officers' Mess for a meal and interrogation: he couldn't tell them much because he knew so little.

More rewarding, perhaps, was his own self-examination. It had been his first real scrap, and he had been totally green. He had arrived on the squadron simultaneously with a change of aeroplane, from FE2b's to Bristol Fighters, which reversed the positions of pilot and observer, and of the engine in relation to both, calling for major adjustments in outlook and tactics. Yet he knew of no attempt to develop their confidence and skill. They had simply flown north until they could see the coast, then flown back again, that was their patrol. Later Tambling concluded: 'We were simply looking for trouble, and this time we got it.'

The experience of C.B. 'Ben' Lefroy, a test pilot at St Omer, was that 'there were a lot of boys who shouldn't have been out there at all – they just didn't know how to fly'. He blamed this on the corners that were being cut for the sake of expansion. Lee deplored 'sending fellows out to fight when they haven't even learned to fly . . . newcomers had to be pushed out on patrol before they'd found their feet'.

The failure to impose strict training programmes on new squadrons as they arrived, and to organise routine training programmes on all squadrons in France, surely amounted to culpable if not criminal negligence. Certainly Harold Tambling, like Oscar Greig before him, blamed his downfall on the lack of squadron training. Squadron and flight commanders, although under pressure to fulfil commitments, cannot be held blameless; but the pressure came from the top. As always, whatever the army demanded, Trenchard felt duty bound to provide. Whether such a degree of compliance was always essential remains controversial.

In the army or fighting units, squadron and flight commanders had little option but to take the men sent to them on trust. They may well have felt it was too late for more than local familiarisation, backed up by experienced leadership. In any case, they may have argued, by far the best training was battle. 'New pilots arrived untrained in formation flying and had to be initiated in action,' recalled Lee. 'Of four new pilots who arrived in mid-June 1917, none had been given proper training in formation flying.' For a long time there was no school anywhere for scout pilots – they arrived at squadrons raw.

There was more chance for the preparation and training of crews in the corps squadrons, where instruction was given in camera work, gunnery, and liaison with batteries. Challenging as the work was, it was more a matter of routine. By giving a raw pilot an experienced observer, and vice-versa, new men could be introduced to the job without any great loss of efficiency.

22

WATERSHED

I F the year 1916 disappointed as a turning point, stimulating a scepticism, cynically voiced in the trenches, that the war would last for ever, it nevertheless qualified as a watershed. The year had begun with the Fokker scourge, forcing the RFC to resort to measures to reduce casualties that brought a shrinkage in operational capacity instead of the planned expansion. Yet, as recorded earlier, the Fokkers had never mustered more than fifty machines in front-line service at any one time, their period of ascendancy had not contributed decisively to any ground campaign, and it had been ended by the advent in the spring of the DH2, the FE2b, and the Nieuport. The RFC then became an expanding force again, with a brigade attached to each of the five British armies in the field.

Partly because of unseasonable weather, the Somme battle had ended in stalemate. It had virtually destroyed Kitchener's volunteer army; yet the loss of life had not been totally futile. So far as such slaughter is susceptible to sober analysis, certain minimum objectives had been achieved. First, the critical situation at Verdun had been relieved. Secondly, the enemy had been kept fully occupied at a time when the French were on the verge of collapse. Thirdly, in the retrospective view of the official RFC history, the campaign had 'dealt a blow at the morale of the enemy troops from which they never recovered'.[1]

The Allies had shown their preparedness to continue a war of attrition to the point of exhaustion. For the enemy, this dictated policy revisions which, unless they proved outstandingly successful, doomed them to eventual defeat.

By the beginning of the Somme battle, the air situation had been transformed. Corps machines photographed the German trenches 'without once being attacked by the Fokkers', noted General Rawlinson. Artillery co-operation had become an essential part of the battle scene, aided by the Sterling wireless transmitter, weighing less than 20 lb and now in general use. Bombing was more concentrated and had been extended to the hours of darkness. Contact patrols fed an up-to-date picture to army commanders. And Trenchard's doctrine of unceasing and relentless offensive had driven the German air force back to its own side of the lines. This was the positive side. Against it had to be set the heavy and often disproportionate losses that resulted for the RFC, in the ratio of four to one against those of the enemy.

Between July and December 1916 Trenchard lost 499 pilots and observers killed or missing and another 250 wounded or injured and put out of action. A further 250, for various reasons – unsuitability, physical or nervous debility – had been removed from strength. Meanwhile, by September, Germany was fast bridging the numbers gap and producing superior machines with better trained pilots. Prospects for the early delivery of the new British scout machines on order – the Bristol two-seater and the SE5 and Camel single-seaters – were scant, as Trenchard well knew, hence his pleadings for acceleration. As for his complaints about the quality of his reinforcement pilots, Brancker, in his reply, did not spare him. They were paying the price for too-rapid growth and for rushing new squadrons into the line prematurely. Trenchard was unabashed. ('We are fighting a very big battle.') There was no escape from casualties.

Trenchard's warnings, amounting to forecasts of impending

1. Jones, H.A., *The War in the Air* (The Clarendon Press, Oxford 1928–1937).

catastrophe failing the reinforcements he sought, reached a new fervour that winter. Germany too was beginning to realise the importance of taking the offensive in the air, and the DH2 and the FE2b were outclassed in their turn by the new Albatros and Halberstadt scouts. More and more Jastas were forming – twenty-five in all by the end of the year. On 16 November, in a further appeal to the War Office, Trenchard asked for another twenty of the new scout squadrons to protect his corps machines, in addition to those already agreed, making a ratio of two scouts for every corps machine at the front.

Production capacity at home was slowly improving to cope with these demands, and by late summer a rapidly expanding labour force had already reached 60,000 engaged in the manufacture of aeroplanes and another 20,000 in building aircraft engines. Yet British production, in quantity and quality, still lagged behind the German and the French. The combined Allied total, however, outnumbered the German. This accounted for the latter's policy of husbanding their resources and concentrating them where and when local superiority was needed. 'Our fighter squadrons,' ordered Hindenburg, 'which are far from numerous must not be equally distributed over the whole front ... They must be grouped sometimes here, sometimes there, so as to prevent the enemy's observation for a few hours at least, and make our own observation possible.'

Political changes that autumn promised a greater energy in the prosecution of the war. In Germany, Ludendorff's position was strengthened. In Britain, Lloyd George succeeded Asquith as prime minister. One of his first appointments was that of industrialist William Weir, formerly director of munitions in Scotland, to the crucial post of controller of aeronautical supplies in the Ministry of Munitions. He also appointed Weir to a seat on the Air Board. Henderson, for his part, recognising that the Royal Aircraft Factory had failed to keep pace with design progress and had become a political and industrial liability, terminated O'Gorman's contract as superintendent and appointed one of Weir's men in his place.

Criticism of Trenchard's doctrine of the offensive continued, but he remained unmoved. The aeroplane was basically an offensive weapon, not a defensive one, even against other aeroplanes: he did not see this doctrine as being impaired in any way by his losses. It was a doctrine not perhaps seriously challenged until the advent of radar.

Since taking over command of the RFC in the field in August 1915 Trenchard had pursued his policies unimpeded except by material and personnel defects and shortages, winning Haig and the army over to a belief in and indeed an implicit reliance on air support. Above all was the success of the corps squadrons, of whom Rawlinson wrote that 'his experiences in the battle had brought home to him the enormous importance of aeroplane and artillery cooperation.' He went on to emphasise the necessity for maximum development of this branch of aerial warfare.

From the tentative and underrated probings of August 1914, air power had become a factor in all military engagements. As industry on both sides responded rapidly to the need, aeroplanes became more numerous, more reliable, and flew faster and higher. Advances in technology, in weaponry and fire-power, and in communications and surveillance, threw mounting strains on individual airmen. In the RFC, the human element, far from being eliminated, remained paramount. This found its expression in the emergence of public heroes, but it was equally true of the daily round. And in the campaigns to come it was the RFC, and on the ground the BEF, who were to bear the brunt of the fighting.

Of Trenchard, Professor Trevor Wilson, in his book *The Myriad Faces of War*, has written: 'He gave the RFC determined leadership and a clear sense of direction. He won for it the admiration and devoted support of the army command . . .'[1]

If the second panegyric had been truly won in the skies, it could not have been achieved without Trenchard's dynamism.

1. Polity Press, Cambridge, in association with Basil Blackwell, Oxford, 1986.

[225]

PUBLISHED SOURCES

A.G.D. ALDERSON, *The First War in the Air* (Privately published 1990)

RICHARD TOWNSHEND BICKERS, *The First Great Air War* (Hodder 1988)

EZRA BOWEN, *Knights of the Air* (Time-Life 1980)

CHAZ BOWYER, *The Air VCs* (Kimber 1978, and Grub Street 1993)

— *History of the RAF* (Hamlyn 1977)

— *The Flying Elephants* (Macdonald 1972).

ANDREW BOYLE, *Trenchard* (Collins 1962)

ANTHONY BRUCE, *An Illustrated Companion to the First World War* (M. Joseph 1989)

JOHN BUCHAN, *A History of the First World War* (Lochar 1991)

J.A. CHAMIER, *The Birth of the Royal Air Force* (Pitman 1943)

LIONEL CHARLTON, *Charlton, an autobiography* (Faber 1931)

ALAN CLARK, *Aces High* (Fontana/Collins 1973)

CHRISTOPHER COLE, *McCudden VC* (Kimber 1967)

— *RFC Communiqués 1915–16* (Kimber 1969)

BASIL COLLIER, *Leader of the Few* (Jarrolds)

BRYAN COOPER, *The Story of the Bombers 1914–1945* (Octopus 1974)

A. CORBETT-SMITH, *The Retreat from Mons* (Cassell 1916)

LORD DOUGLAS OF KIRTLESIDE, *Years of Combat* (Collins 1963)

MARTIN GILBERT, *First World War Atlas* (Weidenfeld and Nicolson 1970)

DUNCAN GRINNELL-MILNE. *Wind in the Wires* (Aviation Book Club 1933)

JOHN HAMMERTON (EDITOR), *War in the Air, Aerial Wonders of Our Time* (Amalgated Press c.1936)

HAROLD E. HARTNEY, *Up and At 'Em* (Bailey and Swinfen 1974)

TYRREL M. HAWKER, *Hawker VC* (Mitre Press 1965)

PRUDENCE HILL, *To Know the Sky* (Kimber 1962)

GODERIC HODGES, *Memoirs of an Old Balloonatic* (Kimber 1972)

ROBERT JACKSON, *Fighter Pilots of World War I* (Barker 1977)

WALTER RALEIGH AND H.A. JONES, *The War in the Air, Vols. I to III* (The Clarendon Press, Oxford 1923–31)

J.E. JOHNSON, *Full Circle* (Chatto 1964)

PHILIP JOUBERT, *The Third Service* (Thames and Hudson 1955)

ARTHUR GOULD LEE, *No Parachute* (Jarrolds 1968)

CECIL LEWIS, *Sagittarius Rising* (Peter Davies 1936 and Greenhill 1993)

GWILYM H. LEWIS, *Wings Over the Somme* (Kimber 1976 and – a new edition – Bridge Books 1994)

PETER LIDDLE, *The Airman's War* (Blandford Press 1989)

WINIFRED LORAINE, *Robert Loraine* (Collins 1938)

JAMES MCCUDDEN, *Five Years in the RFC* (Aeroplane and General 1918)

ALEXANDER MCKEE, *The Friendless Sky* (Souvenir Press 1962)

NORMAN MACMILLAN, *Sir Sefton Brancker* (Heinemann 1935)

– *Into the Blue* (Jarrolds 1929)

R.R. MONEY, *Flying and Soldiering* (Nicolson and Watson 1936)

ALAN MORRIS, *The Balloonatics* (Jarrolds 1970)

JOHN H. MORROW JR., *The Great War in the Air* (Airlife 1993)

JACQUES MORTANE, *Special Missions* (Aeroplane and General 1919)

ALEX REVELL, *British Fighter Units on the Western Front, 1914–1916* (Osprey 1978)

LINDA RHODES-MOORHOUSE, *Kaleidoscope* (Barker 1960)

MANFRED VON RICHTHOFEN, *The Red Air Fighter* (Aeroplane and General 1918)

D.H. ROBINSON, *The Dangerous Sky: A History of Aviation Medicine* (Foulis 1973)

ROBERT SAUNDBY, *Air Bombardment: The Story of Its Development* (Chatto 1961)

HILARY ST G. SAUNDERS, *Per Ardua* (OUP 1944)

MICHAEL SHAW, *Twice Vertical, the History of No. 1 Squadron* (Macdonald 1971 and Ian Allen 1986).

GORDON S. SHEPHARD, *Memoirs* (Privately printed 1924)

CHRISTOPHER SHORES, NORMAN FRANKS, AND RUSSELL GUEST, *Above The Trenches* (Grub Street 1990)

JOHN SLESSOR, *The Central Blue* (Cassell 1968)

GUY SLATER (EDITOR), *My Warrior Sons: the Borton Family Diaries* (Peter Davies 1973)

HORACE SMITH-DORRIEN, *Memoirs of 48 Years Service* (Murray 1925)

OLIVER STEWART, *Words and Music for a Mechanical Man* (Faber 1967)

LOUIS STRANGE, *Recollections of an Airman* (John Hamilton 1933)

A.J.P. TAYLOR, *The First World War* (Hamish Hamilton 1963)

J.W.R. TAYLOR, *CFS – Birthplace of Air Power* (Putnam 1953)

ROBERT THOMPSON, *The Royal Flying Corps* (Hamish Hamilton 1968)

FRANK D. TREDREY, *Pioneer Pilot – The Great Smith-Barry* (Peter Davies 1976)

S.F. VINCENT, *Flying Fever* (Jarrolds 1972)

HERBERT S. WARD, *An Erratic Odyssey* (Odyssey Books 1988)

W. ALISTER WILLIAMS, *Against the Odds: The Life of Group Captain Lionel Rees* (Bridge Books 1989)

H.J. WILLIAMSON, *The Roll of Honour RFC and RAF for the Great War 1914–1918* (Naval and Military Press 1972)

DENIS WINTER, *The First of the Few* (Allen Lane 1982)

FRED WINTERBOTHAM, *The Ultra Spy* (Macmillan 1989)

ENCYCLOPAEDIAS: *Encyclopaedia of Air Warfare* (Spring Books 1975)

MAGAZINES: *Aeronautics, Aeroplane, Aerospace, Flight, Cross and Cockade* (GB). *Society Journal, Journal of the RAF Historical Society, Air Mail (Journal of the RAF Association)*.

INDEX

(Ranks in most cases are omitted)